New Riders' Guide to
Modems

Esther Schindler
Steven Vaughan-Nichols

NRP
NEW RIDERS
PUBLISHING

New Riders Publishing, Indianapolis, Indiana

New Riders' Guide to Modems

By Esther Schindler, Steven Vaughan-Nichols

Published by:
New Riders Publishing
201 West 103rd St.
Indianapolis, IN 46290 USA

Printed in the United States of America 1 2 3 4 5 6 7 8 9 0

Library of Congress Cataloging-in-Publication Data

```
Schindler, Esther, 1958-
  New Riders' guide to modems / Esther Schindler, Steven J.
Vaughan-Nichols.
     p.   cm.
  Includes index.
  ISBN 1-56205-302-7 : $24.95
  1. modems.   I. Vaughan-Nichols, Steven J., 1956-   II. New Riders
Publishing.   III. Title
TK7887.8.M63S35 1994
004.6'165--dc20                                    94-7720
                                                      CIP
```

Publisher	Lloyd J. Short
Associate Publisher	Tim Huddleston
Acquisitions Manager	Cheri Robinson
Managing Editor	Matthew Morrill
Product Development Manager	Rob Tidrow
Acquisitions Editor	Alicia Krakovitz
Marketing Manager	Ray Robinson
Senior Editor	Tad Ringo
Production Editor	Patrice Hartmann
Editors	Kelly Currie
	Cliff Shubs
	Phil Worthington
	John Kane
	Lisa Wilson
	Peter Kuhns
Technical Editor	Robert Waring
Acquisitions Coordinator	Stacey Beheler
Editorial Assistant	Karen Opal
Publishing Assistant	Melissa Lynch
Production Manager	Juli Cook
Book Design	Roger Morgan
Production Analysts	Dennis Clay Hager
	Mary Beth Wakefield

Production Team

Lisa Daugherty	Terri L. Edwards
Rich Evers	Angela P. Judy
Chad Poore	Casey Price
Bobbi Satterfield	Kim Scott
Tonya R. Simpson	SA Springer
Michael Thomas	Scott Tullis
Elaine Webb	

Indexed By	John Sleeva

About the Authors

Esther Schindler is an online modem junkie who has served as a CompuServe Sysop for several years. Esther is a computer consultant who writes and teaches about computers. She is vice-president of the Phoenix PC User's Group and coordinator of the OS/2 Special Interest Group. Esther is primary Sysop of the ZiffNet Executives OnLine forum and an outspoken user advocate. She is co-author of *Inside OS/2 2.1*, published by New Riders Publishing.

Steven Vaughan-Nichols, a mild-mannered historian by training, earns his daily bread as a full-time freelance writer. He is the online services columnist for Computer Shopper and has also written for *PC Magazine*, *Byte*, *PC Week*, *PC Computing*, *SunWorld*, *Compute*, and *Government Computer News*. When he is not plying his trade, Mr. Vaughan-Nichols goes to the theater, listens to music, reads science fiction and mysteries, and pretends—in the Society for Creative Anachronism—that the 11th century isn't over yet.

Dedication:

From Esther Schindler:

To my beloved husband Bill, who has always believed in me.

Special thanks to the people who have helped to transform me into a modem weenie. Thanks to Dennis Fowler and Steven Vaughan-Nichols, for helping me with this book more than they realized. Thanks to the denizens of the Dungeon, who are proof that absurdity exists everywhere—even in universes that don't exist. Thanks also go to Cheri Robinson, Rob Tidrow, and Patrice Hartmann at New Riders, who somehow managed to survive me.

Trademark Acknowledgments

New Riders Publishing has made every attempt to supply trademark information about company names, products, and services mentioned in this book. Trademarks indicated below were derived from various sources. New Riders Publishing cannot attest to the accuracy of this information.

America Online is a registered service mark of America Online Inc.

AT&T and AT&T Mail are registered trademarks of the American Telephone and Telegraph Company.

CompuServe is a registered trademark of CompuServe, Inc.

Dow Jones News/Retrieval is a registered trademark of International Business Machines Corporation.

GEnie is a service mark of General Electric Corporation.

MCI and MCI Mail are registered service marks of MCI Communications Corporation.

Microsoft, Microsoft Word, and Microsoft Windows 3.1 are registered trademarks of Microsoft Corporation.

pcANYWHERE is a registered trademark of Symantec Corporation.

Prodigy is a registered trademark of Prodigy Services Corporation.

SprintNet, SprintMail, and SprintNet's PC Pursuit are registered trademarks of US Sprint.

Trademarks of other products mentioned in this book are held by the companies producing them.

Warning and Disclaimer

This book is designed to provide information about modems and modem software. Every effort has been made to make this book as complete and as accurate as possible, but no warranty or fitness is implied.

The information is provided on an "as is" basis. The author and New Riders Publishing shall have neither liability nor responsibility to any person or entity with respect to any loss or damages arising from the information contained in this book or from the use of the disks or programs that may accompany it.

Contents at a Glance

Table of Contents

Part Three: What You Can Do with a Modem   155

Part Four: The Online Toolbox   273

Introduction

I never really wanted a modem in the first place.

Several years ago, my husband decided that we needed a home computer. Bill wanted to get a modem as part of the purchase, which I thought was a darn-fool idea. Sure, I wanted a PC, but a *modem*? Who did I need to talk with, after all? I had plenty of friends, plenty of people to talk to at work, and many resources to get technical questions answered.

Then, one day, I found myself home alone with the PC and modem. I figured I'd just try out this online service for a few minutes. And then I was hooked. Since that day more than ten years ago, I've become an online junkie. I am now a Sysop (forum manager) on CompuServe, the world's biggest online service, and I go into withdrawal if I don't hear a modem squeal at least once a day. On the other hand, I've become close friends with people I've never met; I've done business with people on the other side of the planet; and I've found a never-ending source of sick jokes.

So, maybe it wasn't such a bad idea after all.

In this book, I'll share my enthusiasm for modems and telecommunications with you. I'll give you enough information to help you get started, but hopefully not so much that you get intimidated.

Modem hardware is dull. In my opinion, a book about modem hardware is as exciting as a manual about how to use the telephone. You don't care how your telephone works; you just want to talk with people. With modems, too, what's exciting is not the hardware, but what you can *do* with it.

This book is intended for the confidence-impaired new user. It focuses on what you can *do* with your modem. The first section helps you to get your modem hardware working, and the second section shows you how to use the modem to connect with the outside world. However, the true joy in modems is using them to communicate with the outside world, and that's what most of this book addresses.

Learning What You Need To Know

This book provides you with the most up-to-date information on using and getting the most out of your modem. Modems are just one of many computing areas in which technology changes rapidly. The minute you begin to feel comfortable with what you have already learned about modems, a new model with enhanced capabilities becomes available, or rules or other information about using modems is updated. This book keeps you in-the-know about the latest technologies.

If you're like many computer users today, you probably have an extremely limited amount of time in which to learn to use new hardware or software programs. After you buy your new modem (or upgrade your existing one), you want to start using it as soon as possible. *New Riders' Guide to Modems* helps you learn the basics about modems in a short amount of time by giving you simple explanations and examples that reinforce the concepts you learn.

This book explains the hows and whys of modems from a general perspective. *New Riders' Guide to Modems* won't teach you everything there is to know about modems; it just teaches you what you *need* to know so that you can use—and make decisions about using—modems.

Who Should Use This Book?

New Riders' Guide to Modems is for the new user as well as the experienced one. You might be thinking about buying a modem, for instance, but you want to know more about them before handing over your hard-earned dollars. This book gives you that information.

Or maybe you already have a modem, and you just want to take advantage of certain services modems offer—such as the capability to send messages over electronic mail to your brother who lives in Providence,

Rhode Island. Maybe you want to access the latest stock market tips or gain instant access to travel information. This book gives you all the inside information on those services.

Why Use a Modem?

Gone are the days when computers were just for computing or word processing. Today, computer users can access various realms of information or talk to other users across the country or world. For those PC junkies who want the capability to do more than just crunch numbers or type up long tedious reports, a modem (along with this book) can help.

In a world of rapidly changing technology and communication, modems can give you an edge—and an advantage. Before you know it, you will be uploading and downloading files like a pro, taking part in conversations with users who used to be strangers (but now are friends), and maybe even becoming a Sysop of your own bulletin board system one day.

Understanding the Conventions

Throughout this book, conventions are used to help you distinguish various elements of DOS, OS/2, Windows, their system files, and sample data. These conventions include the following:

- Shortcut keys are normally placed in the text where appropriate; for example, Ctrl+N is the shortcut key for **N**ew file.

- Key combinations appear in the following formats:

   Key1+Key2. When you see a plus sign (+) between key names, hold down the first key while you press the second key, then release both. If, for example, you see "Press Ctrl+F2," hold down the Ctrl key and press the F2 function key, then release both keys.

   Key1,Key2. When a comma (,) appears between key names, press and release the first key, then press and release the second key. "Alt,S" means, for example, press the Alt key and release, and then press the S key and release.

Hot Keys. On-screen, Windows underlines the letters on some menu names, file names, and option names. The File menu name, for example, is displayed on-screen as <u>F</u>ile. This underlined letter is the letter you type to choose that menu, command, or option. In this book, such letters are displayed in bold, underlined type: **<u>F</u>ile**.

© Information you type is in **boldface**. This rule applies to individual letters, numbers, and text strings. The convention, however, does not applys to special keys, such as Enter, Tab, Esc, or Ctrl.

© New terms appear in *italic*.

© Text that is displayed on-screen but is not part of Windows or a Windows application—such as DOS prompts and messages—appears in a `special monospace typeface`.

© In the text, function keys are identified as F1, F2, F3, and so on.

Mouse Notes

This book repeatedly uses terms that refer to mouse techniques: *click, double-click, Shift-click,* and *drag-and-drop. Clicking* on an object or menu item selects the object or item. *Double-clicking* usually performs a function, without the need to click an OK button in a dialog box. You use *Shift-clicking* to select more than one object. By holding down Shift, you add objects to the already selected objects. *Dragging* means to hold the mouse button and move the mouse and on-screen pointer to a new location, usually taking the selected object to the new position.

Reader Icon Aides

This book also has margin icons that provide added information, including tips, notes, stops, and shortcuts that help you use the book and the program. You can find these margin icons easily and refer to them in the future. Examples of each are included on this page.

A Note includes "extra" information that you should find useful but that complements the discussion at hand instead of being a direct part of it.

A *Tip* provides quick instructions for getting the most from your modem. A tip might show you ways to conserve memory or speed up a procedure, or provide ideas for creating specific types of artwork.

A *Warning* is a signpost that tells you to proceed with caution before executing an upcoming step. No one likes to make a mistake that costs time, particularly when it's over a paying assignment, so the text points out potential areas to watch out for when working with your modem.

Understanding What the Book Includes

New Riders' Guide to Modems is divided into six parts, which present the features of modems in a logical, step-by-step method for use by inexperienced users as well as proficient modem users. Each chapter builds on the previously covered topics. The following paragraphs provide a brief summary of the topics covered in each part of this book.

Part 1: Using Your Modem for the First Time

In Part 1, you learn the basics of modems: how they work, how to buy one, and how to install one.

Chapter 1, "What Is a Modem?" tells you all about the nifty things modems can do. You learn about how modems can make your work easier and a bit about modem hardware and software, and you receive a brief description of internal and external modems.

Chapter 2, "Choosing a Modem," helps you determine what kind of modem will best meet your needs. Should you buy an internal modem, for instance, when an external one would meet your needs just as well? Should you go the "conservative" route and purchase a 2400 bps modem, or should you break open your piggy bank and buy that hot little 9600 number? This chapter helps you answer these questions and much more.

Chapter 3, "Installing an External Modem," explains how to do exactly that: hook the darned thing up to your computer. You learn the different tools that you should have on hand; you receive expert tips on avoiding installation problems; and you learn what all the different cords and cables are for—among other things.

Chapter 4, "Installing an Internal Modem," takes you through the steps of installing an internal modem. This chapter practically holds your hand as you learn to open up the computer and find a place to put the modem card. You also learn to connect the modem to the phone line, using the phone cable supplied by the modem vendor.

Chapter 5, "Modem Guts," gives you all the inside information that you'll need to know about the parts of your modem. You learn, for instance, what all those blinking lights on an external modem are for. This chapter also helps you understand how your modem actually communicates with another modem.

Part 2: Learning about Modem Software

Part 2 helps you get started using your modem by showing you how to install and use the communications software. You then make your first call.

Chapter 6, "Installing and Using the Modem Software," explains about the software (Hilgraeve's HyperACCESS/5) included on the disk with this book. With Hilgraeve's HyperACCESS/5, a popular communications program, you can call other systems, answer calls, transfer files, and automate many everyday communication tasks. This chapter helps you understand and get the most from that software.

Chapter 7, "Making a Call (A Quick Tour)" covers everything you need to know to make that first call to a BBS or online service. You learn the commands to type in so that your modem knows who to call. You also learn a little about what to do when you need help, and you learn about BBS etiquette—such as using your real name when identifying yourself.

Chapter 8, "Learning More About Communications Software," explains the fundamentals of modem software, including the terms that "everyone" seems to know. After you understand what's going on, your online sessions will be much more meaningful to you.

Part 3: What You Can Do with a Modem

Part 3 includes information about the information superhighway: online services, bulletin board systems (BBSs), and the Internet.

Chapter 9, "What Do Online Services Provide?," tells you how you can get the most from online services. Several different kinds of online services are available, including electronic mail services, information banks, and more. In this chapter, you learn the ins-and-outs of using these services.

Chapter 10, "Bulletin Board Systems (BBSs)," takes you on a tour of electronic bulletin boards. Bulletin boards, or BBSs, give you access to thousands of files, enable you to exchange messages with other people, and provide an electronic community. This chapter looks at BBSs in detail—how they work, how to use them, and the tacit rules of behavior followed on BBSs and other online services.

Chapter 11, "Cutting Costs with Your Modem," gives you information about such things as file transfer protocols, file compression, and other features that help you take up less time online—thus saving you money on your phone bill.

Chapter 12, "Beyond BBSs and Online Services," discusses other types of communicating you can do with your modem. The most well-known uses for modems are to access online services, databases, and BBSs. There also are some comparatively unusual uses for modems that are really cool, however. This chapter will give a brief overview of what else you can do.

Chapter 13, "Journey to the Internet," helps you navigate that vast information superhighway known as the Internet. Imagine a sophisticated office local area network (LAN) that connects PCs, Macintoshes, and workstations into a harmonious whole. Now imagine a LAN that spans the globe rather than just an office, and you have the Internet. This chapter explains how to access the Internet and what you can do while there.

Part 4: The Online Toolbox

Part 4 gives you practical advice about how to protect your software and hardware from corrupted software and tells you about cool peripherals that you might want to invest in—such as fax/modems.

Chapter 14, "Virus Protection," tells you how to keep your computer virus-free. A common fear that prevents many people from going online is that, somehow, their computer will become infected with a computer virus. What are viruses, and what can you do to prevent getting one in the first place or to cure one if you do? This chapter answers those questions and more.

Chapter 15, "Fax/Modems," discusses fax/modem capability. Computer faxing gives you the option to print only the pages you need and eliminates wasteful printing of junk faxes. Computer faxes are much clearer and crisper looking than even the plain-paper, stand-alone fax output.

Part 5: When Things Go Wrong

Part 5 is a short but important section of this book. You learn what to do when your modem acts up or when your communications program goes belly up.

Chapter 16, "Troubleshooting Telecommunications," does exactly what its name implies. This chapter discusses the kinds of problems you might encounter with modems and with telecommunications software. You receive advice about how to solve those problems. Finally, you learn some suggestions about where to turn if the advice fails.

Part 6: Appendixes

Part 6 includes appendixes A through C, offering additional information you might need when using your modem.

Appendix A, "BBS Listings and Online Services," gets you started on your modem adventure by providing a listing of various BBSs and online services.

Appendix B, "Contact Information for Companies Mentioned," gives you the addresses and phone numbers of some of the companies mentioned throughout this book.

Appendix C, "Important AT Commands," gives you a list of AT commands that you can refer to when using your modem and modem software.

The Glossary provides a listing of telecommunications terms that you might want to refer to after you finish reading this book.

Publisher's Note

The staff of New Riders Publishing is committed to bringing you the very best in computer reference material. Each New Riders book is the result of months of work by authors and staff, who research and refine the information contained within its covers.

As part of this commitment to you, the NRP reader, New Riders invites your input. Please let us know if you enjoy this book, if you have trouble with the information and examples presented, or if you have a suggestion for the next edition.

Please note, however, that the New Riders staff cannot serve as a technical resource for modems or modem-related problems. Refer to the documentation that accompanies your modem or communications software package for help with specific problems.

If you have a question or comment about any New Riders book, please write to NRP at the following address. We will respond to as many readers as we can. Your name, address, or phone number will never become part of a mailing list or be used for any other purpose than to help us continue to bring you the best books possible.

New Riders Publishing
Macmillan Computer Publishing
Attn: Associate Publisher
201 W. 103rd Street
Indianapolis, IN 46290

If you prefer, you can FAX New Riders Publishing at the following number:

(317) 581-4670

We welcome your electronic mail to our CompuServe ID:

75250,1433

Thank you for selecting *New Riders' Guide to Modems*.

Part 1:

Using Your Modem for the First Time

Chapter 1

What Is a Modem?

Do you feel like roadkill on the information superhighway? Do you even know what the information superhighway is?

If you feel like you might have some catching up to do, read on:

- ℂ Do your friends and co-workers mumble about "throughput" and "emoticons" and "V.FAST" as if they know what they're talking about?

- ℂ Do they talk about uploading files to Melbourne or "logging-in" or "MNP"?

- ℂ Do you stare at them as if they have just arrived from outer space, and they haven't turned on the Universal Translator yet?

- ℂ When you ask them to explain what they really do with their modems, do they give you a perfectly clear, lucid answer, which just happens to make no sense at all?

If you answered yes to any of the preceding questions, you have picked up the right book. This book explains what a modem is and what you can do with it. Frankly, modems themselves (like most computer hardware) are about as exciting as a lecture about grass clippings. It's what you can do with a modem that's fun, exciting, and, yes, actually useful!

Why Use A Modem?

Perhaps you received a modem as a gift. Maybe your boss suggested that telecommuting would save time and money, so he gave you a computer and modem to use at home. Or your computer purchase might have included a free modem. At any rate, you have a modem—or you're considering getting one. What possible use can this thing be? What benefits can you get from owning a modem that can convince you that you should keep it, instead of swapping it for a collection of classic Batman comics and an air compressor?

Here are just a few scenarios where owning a modem can save time or money—or get you a hot date:

- ☾ You get to work and realize that the document you took home last night—and worked on until 1 a.m.—is still on the hard disk of your home computer.

- ☾ You need to work on a report with a co-worker, but he's in Los Angeles—and you're in Atlanta.

- ☾ You're certain that you saw an article written about puns in the Middle Ages, but you can't remember where you saw the article. And you absolutely must have that information now!

- ☾ You want to find out why your report won't print from your favorite word processor, and it's 7 o'clock on a Saturday night. The company's technical support department won't open until 9 a.m. on Monday, and that's when the report is due!

- ☾ You want someone to play contract bridge with.

In every one of the preceding cases, a modem can help. You can use a modem (and the software that works with it) to connect your computer with the one at home, or with a co-worker's machine. You can use your modem to dial into databases that cover just about any subject. (Migratory habits of Canadian geese? The legal status of disadvantaged children? Science fiction written by women in the last twenty years? Sure thing!) You can get technical support, both from company representatives and from other users who have faced similar problems. And, best of all, you can talk to, work with, and become friends with people all over the world.

Modems make the world a better place. C'mon in, and learn more about them.

So, Like, What's a Modem?

The word modem stands for modulator-demodulator. Isn't that cool? Doesn't that tell you everything you wanted to know?

No, huh?

A modem is the equipment that lets your computer communicate with other computers across a telephone line. That's all the definition you need to get started; we'll go into detail about how a modem works soon enough. Modems can be external (a box separate from your computer, and another thing to dust) or internal (hidden inside the computer itself).

Avoiding Hardware Intimidation

The computer industry has made a distinct effort to make PCs easy to use. In many ways, the industry has succeeded; installing a word processor, for instance, is no more difficult than learning how to program a VCR (although that doesn't really say a whole lot). Modems are another story, however. When it comes to modems, you soon find out that there is no such thing as absolute simplicity.

A good example of how modems are a little more complicated than PCs is when it comes to troubleshooting. With most PC hardware, you easily can see if everything's going okay: you just look at the printer. If your computer is communicating correctly with the printer, you can tell by looking at what the printer prints. Even if you run into a problem, the symptoms are straightforward, and you can see what is wrong. With modems, however, it's a little harder to tell what's happening—at least at first. Because you're communicating with a computer that's remote from you, you can't see what's happening at the other end.

Nobody likes to be intimidated by a dumb piece of hardware. In the case of modems, the best way to avoid intimidation is to learn about them. That's what this book is for. It will help you discern the distinction between the hardware (the modem) and the software (the communications program).

Don't let the hardware intimidate you. Modems can be intimidating because they are boxes with the intelligence of a small computer and technical languages of their own. If you find yourself around a bunch of modem geeks, you might hear them use terms such as AT commands, S registers, CCITT V standards, parity, and flow control. At this point, turn up your nose and ignore the geeks (unless, of course, they offer you some chocolate). You will learn what they're talking about soon enough. But you'll never become a geek. No way. No how.

So, don't worry about feeling a little dismayed at first. This book takes things one step at a time and points out what you need to know, as compared to what's neat to know.

Understanding How a Modem Works

The most common confusion, for telecommunication beginners, is the distinction between the modem hardware and the modem software. Modem software is also called communications software, or telecommunications software.

"Tele-" means "over distance." For example, television is vision over distance. So, telecommunications is communications over distance; the subject incorporates regular telephones, satellite transmissions, and cable TV as well as modems. In this book, however, telecommunications usually means modem-based communication.

Modem hardware is easy to define: it's the part that you can bang your knuckles on (or, the part you can kick). What a modem does is translate information from the binary format stored on your computer into a format that can travel across a phone line. (Look at table 1.1 for a comparison.) The modem turns the bits and bytes into tones. The modem at the other end of the telephone line turns the tones back into bits. The process of turning binary data into tones is called *modulation*; converting from tones into bits again is called *demodulation*. (That's the MOdulation-DEModulation from which the term modem originates.)

Table 1.1
People Speak versus Binary Speak

Binary format: how your computer sees information.

This is what you see:	This is what the computer sees:			
I want to have your love child.	01001001	00100000	01110111	01100001
	01101110	01110100	00100000	01110100
	01101111	00100000	01101000	01100001
	01110110	01100101	00100000	01111001
	01101111	01110101	01110010	00100000
	01101100	01101111	01110110	01100101
	00100000	01100011	01101000	01101001
	01101100	01100100	00101110	

Communications software drives, or *controls*, the modem, sending commands and data to the hardware. It's easiest to understand how communications software works if you think about something familiar, such as a printer. Consider this scenario, for example: a word processor sends commands to the printer, telling it to use Helvetica or to print in a bold typeface. The word processor also sends data, that is, the text you want printed (such as, "Meet me at Graceland. —Elvis"). A different applications program (say, a time-management system) communicates to your printer in the same general manner, but your interaction with that program itself is quite different.

Similarly, the communications software instructs the modem, sending both commands ("dial this number") and data (transmitting your database of emu farms to your brother in Cheyenne). Communications programs also help you in other ways by doing the following:

- ℭ Managing your online sessions
- ℭ Keeping a directory of phone numbers
- ℭ Helping you automate frequent tasks

As with any other type of software, you have plenty of choices. You can opt for a simple, inexpensive communications program, or go for a more expensive, powerful one. This book will describe different kinds of communications programs, and how they work. It will show you how to use them to reach the various services in the online universe, and what you will find when you get there.

You also can choose from dozens of special-purpose communications programs, such as those used to access just one online service (for instance, Golden CommPass for CompuServe, or WinSock for Internet), or to access a computer at the other end of town (for example, pcANYWHERE). In Chapter 12, "Beyond BBSs and Online Services," you will learn how to use special purpose programs like these.

The programs you use to access the various services vary in ease-of-use and user-friendliness. Some of them, such as the graphical Windows CompuServe Information Manager, put a pretty face on a service that is, on its own, awkward and rather ugly. These programs can make it much easier to access the services that your modem makes available to you, and they decrease the intimidation factor. They're good to begin with.

Good looks aren't everything, as you already know if you ever went on a blind date. Other software is less attractive, perhaps, but more efficient and cheaper to use.

Comparing Internal and External Modems

Your modem might be external, with its own case and power supply. Or you might have an internal modem. Internal modems are cards that fit inside your computer, with a metal plate that provides connections to the outside world (such as the actual phone line). External modems almost always have visible lights which, depending on their status, indicate what the modem is doing. For instance, when the OH (Off-Hook) light is lit, that's the modem's way of saying that it has "picked up the phone," so to speak.

Chapter 2 covers the advantages and disadvantages of both internal and external modems. Figures 1.1 through 1.3 show you what each looks like.

Figure 1.1
The guts of an internal modem.

Figure 1.2
What an internal modem looks like from the outside.

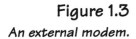

Figure 1.3

An external modem.

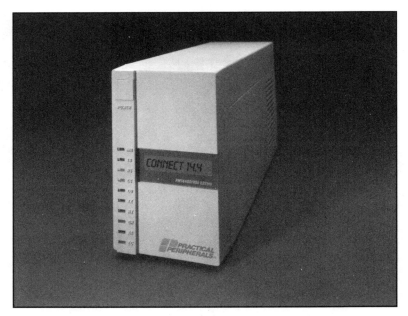

An internal modem is a card—containing a lot of electronics—that plugs into the motherboard inside your computer. Internal modems look complicated, as there are lots of switches and electronic doo-dads on them. Don't worry about it. After an internal modem is installed, you don't have to care what it looks like. Chapter 4, "Installing an Internal Modem," will discuss how to install an internal modem.

External modems need to be plugged into an electric wall outlet. An internal modem gets its power from your PC, so you don't need to plug in anything other than the phone line.

For both internal and external modems, you attach the modem to the telephone line with an ordinary telephone cable, like the one your phone uses. Almost every modem has two phone jacks, allowing you to plug in a regular phone, as well as connect the modem to the wall jack. After all, you probably will want to be able to talk on the phone, too.

An external modem sits on your desk and is connected to your PC with a serial cable. Other than that, it connects to the phone line and to your desk phone just as an internal modem does. In fact, an external modem is almost identical to an internal modem with a small box built around it.

Satisfying A Need for Speed

When speaking or writing, some people can get their message across in a few sentences. Other people deliver the same information, but take fifteen minutes to do so. Same data, different amount of time.

Modems are rated at different speed, based on the number of bits (individual units of binary data) that can be sent per second. The more bits-per-second (bps) that a modem can send, the faster the modem can transfer that all-important spreadsheet—and, since time is money, the lower your telephone bill will be.

We'll discuss how to measure modem speed in the next chapter, but for now, you can think of modems as being available in three speeds:

℗   Slow (300-2400 bits per second)

℗   Fast (9600)

℗   Ridiculously Fast (14,400 and up)

 *Naturally, even as a beginner, you will want the ridiculously fast modem—even if you don't need it. When you first got your driver's license, you wanted a Ferrari, right? Not surprisingly, you'll find that the faster modems will cost you more than the slower ones.*

If you're a home user, or someone who imagines that your modem use will be only occasional (Ha! That's how I started out!), you might imagine that a cheaper, slower modem will be fine for you. I'll tell you the reasons to re-think that viewpoint when we discuss choosing a modem, in the next chapter.

Understanding Fax/Modems

Some modems include hardware that lets the equipment act as a fax machine as well as a modem. Faxing is getting more and more popular—even for home use—so pay attention to this feature.

Realize, though, that the fax and modem pieces are separate circuitry. Your electric can-opener might include a knife-sharpener, but you don't use the can-opener to sharpen your knives; it's just that a knife-sharpener is built-in to the appliance, too. A frequent question is, "Can I use my modem to send faxes?" and the answer is always no. When you have a fax modem, you're using the fax part of the equipment (the knife sharpener), while the modem circuitry twiddles its electronic thumbs.

Fax software, like communications software, manages and drives the fax hardware. These are almost always two separate programs. Look at Chapter 15, "Using Fax/Modems," later in the book, for more detail on this subject.

Chapter 2

Choosing a Modem

So, you've decided to go out and purchase a modem. Cool. Now, imagine that you just finished Driver's Ed in high school, and you are ready to go out and buy your first car. The only problem is that you don't know very much about cars, such as how fast the different models can go. What kind of "smart shopper" do you think you'll be when you reach the used car lot?

The same concepts apply to buying a modem. Modems are available in different speeds, internal or external, and they have prices that range from $39 to $1,200. How can you tell which modem is worth the investment of your hard-earned bucks?

This chapter fills you in on the important criteria in buying a modem. It also discusses what's not important.

Determining Your Needs

When it comes to buying a modem, you are doubtless tempted to get the least expensive modem that meets your minimum requirements. The problem, however, is figuring out what your minimum requirements are, and how long they will remain at that minimum. What suits you now might not be the best choice for the future.

Some half-fast contemplations:

Remember the old saying, "You can't be too rich or too thin"? In computer terms, you can't be too fast.

You'll see this attitude again and again in the computer industry. Equipment that is considered out-of-date and terribly ancient, in microcomputer terms, is still nearly-new by any other standards—especially the standards which the IRS uses for equipment depreciation. You expect to use a washing machine for at least five or ten years, right? So a piece of computer equipment should last about that long too, right? HA HA HA HA HA!

Internal versus External

The debate over which is "better," internal or external, is a passionate one, exceeded only by discussions among chocoholics about whether white chocolate is really chocolate. (It isn't.)

I personally prefer external modems and will recommend an internal modem only under duress (such as being deprived of chocolate). But I'll do my best to be fair. That said, here are the advantages and disadvantages of each:

Because an internal modem is inside the computer, you don't have to give up any of your valuable desk space. It's out of your way, so, most of the time, you don't have to give it any thought.

Also, if you use an internal modem, you don't lose the use of your external serial port. Some systems only have one external serial port, and it's often in use by the mouse. So, if you did want to add an external modem, you would have to add another card to your PC anyway—making the advantage of "you don't have to open up your computer" a moot point.

Internal modems are cheaper than external modems. After all, you don't have to pay for the case and the blinking lights.

Internal modems, especially the faster ones, probably include a 16550 chip, which can be important if you're running a multitasking or pseudo-multitasking operating system. (You will read about the 16550 in a few pages.)

Because an internal modem has no visible lights, however, you can't get a detailed picture of what the modem is up to. If you run into a weird phone connection, and you're not sure if your modem is connected to the system at the other end, an internal modem will give you very little feedback on your status. That is the major reason I personally prefer external modems.

Some communications programs display a visual equivalent of the modem lights on-screen. ProComm Plus for Windows and the Windows version of the CompuServe Information Manager (WinCIM) are two programs that display such lights. So, if you choose a communications program with this feature, the modem lights issue is less of a big deal (see fig. 2.1).

Even so, the communications program sometimes loses track of what the modem is doing, so those blinking on-screen lights may only be interesting to lightening bugs.

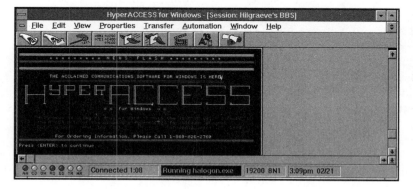

Figure 2.1
The screen of a communications program.

An internal modem can be more convenient if you intend to use your modem only with a laptop computer. (When you're traveling, every ounce counts.) But examine the laptop's modem requirements carefully! Some laptop computers can require internal modems that use the manufacturer's proprietary technology. Proprietary modems are usually more expensive than similar generic external modems, and they might not be reusable in another laptop. That will be important later on, if you decide to upgrade.

If your modem is for laptop-only use, you also should find out if your laptop computer will support the new PCMCIA standard internal modem. PCMCIA is a standard for the new credit-card sized peripherals which are becoming more popular in laptops. Some manufacturers make PCMCIA modems, and they're worth a look.

Despite what you might have heard elsewhere, PCMCIA is not an abbreviation for "People Can't Memorize Computer Industry Acronyms." I can't imagine who would tell you that—unless it was me.

Okay, it really stands for Personal Computer Memory Card International Association. But I like my translation better.

The advantage to PCMCIA peripherals ("peripherals" is just a techie word for "add-on equipment" such as printers, modems, or anything else you'd spend extra for) is that they're tiny and they weigh almost nothing. Also, because PCMCIA is a standard, you can use a PCMCIA modem in any laptop computer that supports that standard—which means most of the new ones. That's a lot different from trying to figure out what to do with a Toshiba T1000 laptop modem (which worked only in that one model of that one brand of computer) when you buy a new ALR laptop system. Figure 2.2 shows you an example of a PCMCIA modem.

If you live in an area that has frequent electrical storms, you might want to rethink any decision to buy an internal modem. Why? Because you want to save your computer from being "fried" by an electrical current (not a pretty sight).

You probably know, for example, that your modem is plugged into an electrical outlet, directly or indirectly—whether your modem is internal or external. But the phone line has a separate electrical current, too; that's why the phone service works even when the lights go out.

What can happen during an electrical storm, then, is this: because an internal modem is plugged into the motherboard, your entire computer is at risk if the phone line is hit by lightening. With an external modem, you might lose the modem, but the computer would be fine.

Figure 2.2
PCMCIA modems fit in a credit-card slot in laptop computers.

A Powerful Message:

Here's an aside about power protection and modems. I recommend using strong power protection for PCs under any circumstances. You probably put a few thousand dollars into your computer, so it only makes sense to give it decent protection.

At the least, get a power strip which isn't just a fancy extension cord in disguise. Go ahead and buy a surge suppresser. You can buy surge suppressers for telephone lines, too. If you live in an area with less-than-perfect power, it's worth the extra pennies to protect your data.

A surge suppresser, as its name implies, suppresses surges (or high voltage peaks) in the power line. Most of them won't protect you during a lightening storm, but they might be worthwhile if a car hits a power pole down the

continues

street. A line conditioner is one step up from a surge suppresser and protects you from brown-outs (low voltage) as well as surges. Statistically, and by my own experience, there are more brown-outs than there are surges (especially on a hot summer day when everyone in town turns on the air-conditioning), so buying a line conditioner is a wise move.

An uninterruptible power supply may or may not provide surge or brown-out protection, but it has batteries that can keep your computer going when the power goes out.

External versus Internal

As mentioned earlier, external modems have several status lights that report what the modem is doing. After you learn what the lights mean (which we'll cover in a later chapter), the lights help you understand exactly what is happening on the phone line, as well as the connection between the computer and the modem.

Some models of external modems provide feedback beyond blinking lights. A few provide an LCD status line that reports, in English (or something very much like it), what the modem is up to (see fig. 2.3). That can be extremely helpful.

Figure 2.3

A modem with an LCD status line.

External modems are easier to set up than internal modems. Because an external modem is simply a box that uses your existing serial port, you can attach or detach an external modem in less than a minute. Well, with just a little practice; it might take you a full five minutes the first time.

Because external modems are easier to set up, they can be better for travel than an internal modem—despite the extra weight. You can grab the modem from your desktop and take it along on a business trip, to use with your laptop or remote site.

If you're willing to pay just a little bit more, you can buy an external modem that's smaller than a pack of cigarettes. You can use the modem shown in figure 2.4 for desktop use, and also take it with you when you travel. In fact, that's what I do with this exact model.

Figure 2.4

A laptop-sized portable modem.

An external modem connects to your computer using a *serial cable*, a special cable that attaches to your computer's serial port. Almost every PC, even one of the oldest ones, has at least one serial port. A primary use of serial ports is modems (which is why you'll also hear it referred to as a *com port* or *communications port*—its full name is an RS-232 serial port). Another common use of serial ports is for hooking up your mouse. Serial ports are also used for special-purpose equipment, such as plotters and some printers.

Before you purchase an external modem, find out if all of your serial ports are in use. You can always buy another serial port (they are inexpensive), but you will want to make the decision ahead of time—not when you're sitting on the floor, surrounded by birthday paper, ready to install your new gift. That's as bad as discovering that a new toy needs the one size of battery that you don't have.

Installing a serial port usually isn't difficult, but it does require that you open up your computer and mess around inside. In fact, you have to go through much of the same process as you would if you were installing an internal modem,

Modems don't come packaged with serial cables, just as printers don't include printer cables. If you don't already own a serial cable and you choose an external modem, make sure that you remember to buy a cable too. Serial cables are available in different sizes, so read about them in Chapter 3, "Installing an External Modem," before you make the purchase.

External modems use an electrical power outlet; internal modems use the PC's internal power supply. If your desk looks anything like mine (I pity you if it does), then there's already a tangle of wires behind the desk that looks like Gordion's knot. With a PC, monitor, printer, lamp, answering machine, and external tape backup all plugged into the same outlet, you might want to consider where you will plug in an external modem.

Understanding Modem Speed

Chapter 1 touched briefly on modem speed. This chapter discusses the subject in detail, because modem speed is probably the most significant feature of any modem.

Time to scurry over to the Novice Corner. The smallest item of computer data is a bit, an electronic on/off switch. Think of a light switch—it has two positions: on & off, zero & one, or true & false. You can store some information very well with two values (True/False: Chocolate is better than peanut butter) but not everything.

By coding bits into bytes—a collection of 7 or 8 bits—a lot more information can be stored. A byte is considered to be one character, because the standard character set (that is, the alphabet, numerals, and the rest of the keyboard characters) can be represented by one byte.

You have probably heard people talk about how many megabytes (millions of bytes) of memory or hard disk space their computers have. Modems, unlike most other hardware in the computer industry, are still measured in the number of bits they transmit.

Modem speed is most properly measured in *bits per second* or *bps*. A modem that transmits at 1200 bps is slower than a modem that transmits at 9600 bps.

When you choose a modem, think about the speed of the modems with which you'll be connecting. Modems can only communicate at the speed of the slower modem. If you have a 9600 bps modem, but you're connected to a 2400 bps modem, the fastest speed at which you can communicate is 2400 bps. This is just like talking with your brother—it doesn't matter how smart *you* are, it only matters how dumb *he* is.

If I told you that I liked your baud, would you hold it against me?

Many modem users use the word baud interchangeably with bps, even though the two terms are not really the same. You will find highly-educated computer professionals who blithely refer to 9600 baud modems. Don't be fooled. The reason for the confusion is that, when popular modem speeds were 300 and 1200 bps, the baud rate was also 300 and 1200, respectively. But, once modems exceeded 2400 bps/baud, the baud and bps rates diverged.

Imagine that you're watching the traffic on an (electronic) highway. BPS is the number of people passing by on the highway, while baud is the number of vehicles.

BPS is a measure of the number of bits of data delivered per second. Baud is the number of changes in the carrier

continues

signal per second. A strict definition of baud is "a variable unit of data transmission speed determined by the rate of change of a modulated signal." Aren't you glad that you don't have to really understand that?

All that matters is that baud and bps are not inter-changeable terms, and that you should talk about bps, especially at higher speeds.

If you're a home user, or if you expect to be an infrequent modem user, an inexpensive 2400 bps modem might look attractive. I can hear that tiny voice inside of you now: "I'm not in a big hurry. So it'll take a little longer to send my files, so what?"

Tell that little voice to shut up.

When people measure how long it'll take to do something, they tend to think in small increments. Getting a lower-wattage microwave or a sewing machine with only 3 stitches, because they're cheaper, can sound like a good idea. But if you use the microwave or sewing machine seriously, you quickly discover the difference between the "save money" model and the "serious" model. Plus, the limitations of the cheaper model may be so annoying that it gets in your way, and you never do get to use it more seriously—just *because* it's a pain to use.

Computer applications grew larger and more complex as microcomputer affordability and power increased. As the applications became bigger, the related files grew, too. Unless you're sending nothing but small data files (such as this book chapter), you will find that a 2400 bps modem *will* make you wait. And wait. And wait.

You'll find that, when it comes to downloading really cool things such as those shareware computer games, you really do need a fast modem. One popular game, Doom, is over two megabytes. It's available on BBSs on a try-before-you-buy basis. At 2400 baud, retrieving that file will take close to three hours. It's still hefty at 9600 baud (it took 40 minutes, which is longer than it took me to lose my first round in the game) but tying up your phone for three hours is much worse than 40 minutes. Especially if you have teenagers in the house.

Time to get specific about the cost of and time savings with a faster modem. What if, for instance, you need to send a one megabyte (1M) file to another computer user. Table 2.1 shows how long it will take to transmit that file at the different bps and compression rates. Compression rates will be discussed in a little while.

Table 2.1
Transmission Times

BPS	Compression Used	Minutes
2400		72.82
2400	MNP5	36.41
2400	V.42bis	18.20
9600		18.20
9600	MNP5	9.10
9600	V.42bis	4.55
14400	V.42bis	3.05

Check out the first and last lines of the preceding table. There's a big difference in time! Now, add to the equation long-distance telephone charges or hourly connect fees on the popular information services. How many 1M files will you need to send cross-country before owning a faster modem actually *saves* you money?

Even if the online services you access (including local electronic bulletin boards and consumer services) support only 2400 bps, get a faster modem. Those services will probably get faster modems soon, so it makes sense to be ready.

If you already own a 2400 baud modem, or someone you love gave it to you as a cherished gift (and tears are welling in your eyes), ignore anything I said above. 2400 is great. It's wonderful. Just start saving your pennies for a new, faster one; you'll want one before long.

Using Slow Modems

Anything that communicates at or below 2400 bps is a slow modem. You can still find some 300 and 1200 bps modems around, mostly at computer flea markets, but they aren't being made anymore.

It's disheartening to consider a 2400 bps modem a slow modem; five years ago, giving someone a 2400 bps modem was a heck of a Christmas present. But if someone gives you one of these today, she's a cheapskate.

You can still get work done with a 2400 bps modem. You just won't get it done *quickly*.

Because they're far from state-of-the-art, 2400 bps modems are very inexpensive. Because the technology has been around for a long time (well, a long time for the computer industry), 2400 bps modems are also physically small. So your new laptop computer might include an internal 2400 bps modem (don't be impressed). Some computers that were sold as home systems also include a modem; in fact, there's a good chance that you bought this book because you discovered, after a year or two, that you have owned a modem all along.

If you already own a 2400 bps modem, go ahead and use it. But I don't recommend that you actually purchase a new one.

Using Fast Modems

A fast modem is a 9600 bps modem. You can transfer files quickly; most online services commonly support 9600, and, under most circumstances, operating at 9600 bps feels comfortable. The response time is acceptable. *Response time* is the measurement of time between the time you do something (such as press a key) and the computer's response (such as display a message that says, "Yes, Master?").

Using Really Fast Modems

A *really* fast modem is one that operates faster than 9600 bps. Modems that operate at 14,400 bps (usually called 14.4 kbps, because nobody likes to type) are quite common and are quickly becoming the norm. 9600 bps modems are readily available, at a reasonable price. However, the price difference between 9600 and 14,400 bps modems is very small, and getting smaller.

Modems that operate at 28,800 bps (or 28.8 kbps) are just coming on the market. They're still on the expensive side, and there aren't many services that support the speed yet. But you might want to consider getting one of these if you will be calling another modem (say, a client at a remote site) who will have the identical modem. Besides, they're really fun—at least if you start giggling when you see big numbers fly across your screen.

Understanding Protocol Basics

The process of translating the data on your computer into electronic sine waves (signals) has become more complex than "how fast can we do it?" The technology of moving the data across the phone line began to interfere with the limitations of the telephone connection. The faster the data needed to move, the more error-prone it became. Thus, error-correcting modems and modem compression technology were born. We'll define these a bit more, later on; you don't need to know everything about them right now, just what to look for on the modem box.

Nearly every modem you buy today will be an error-correcting modem. Such a modem corrects errors that occur during transmission. They have become standard, so you don't even need to check for it on the box. (The $39 Special that you find at Joe's Computer Store and Bait Shop might be an exception.)

Modem manufacturers have had to work together to create standards for both error-correction and for data compression. Those standards have evolved over time, from the Bell 103 "modulation" standard for 0-300 bps North American connection, to the newest term being bandied about, V.FAST. Don't worry what these mean, at least not at this point. If you try to understand the V.whatever standards now, you'll get lost in technical complexities and never hear the modem squeal.

A matter of protocol.

Just to make the subject more complex, the telecommunications standards are also called protocols. You'll run into the word "protocol" again—used in a very different context—when you read about file transfers.

Almost any modem sold that is 9600 bps or above will be V.42bis. The new V.Fast standard is supposed to connect at 28.8 kbps (that's 28,800 bits per second), but the standard isn't scheduled to be agreed upon until mid-1994. Some 28.8 kbps modems are being sold as of this writing, but there are few BBSs for those modems to talk with. I'm using one, of course, but then again, I get all aquiver when I see new technology. By the time you read this, the standards may have been straightened out; be sure to ask your modem salesperson!

There's also an HST protocol, which is proprietary to the modem manufacturer US Robotics. The HST standard has its advantages and disadvantages, but you will only care about them if you happen to dial a BBS that uses an HST modem. Because HST was a protocol that didn't catch on (at least, not as much as US Robotics had hoped for) you may also see modems rated as *Dual Standard*, supporting both HST and V.32. These are quite popular on some BBSs.

When you are ready to put together your modem shopping list, here's what should be on it, with your preferences noted:

- ☎   Internal or external? PCMCIA? Portable?

- ☎   Modem speed (2400, 9600, 14.4, 28.8)

- ☎   V.32 bis

- ☎   Fax capabilities? (What speed?)

Do You Need a Fax/Modem?

Modems aren't the only way to send information across a telephone line. As the prices have dropped, fax machines have become common in even the smallest offices.

Faxes work very differently than modems; they use completely different protocols and "look at" data differently. So it isn't possible to use a modem, per se, to send a fax.

Many modems sold nowadays, however, include fax capabilities. Fax support is separate electronics that are built into the box or on the modem card.

Just as you need telecommunications software to drive your modem, you need fax software to control the fax card. Chapter 15 is devoted to fax hardware and software, but here are a few items to keep in mind as you make your initial modem purchase.

Some older fax/modems advertised themselves as 2400/9600. Without looking at the fine print, it was hard to tell that the modem was a 2400 bps modem, but the fax transmitted at 9600 bps. There are also fax cards and fax machines that transmit at 4800 bps, but they are no longer common.

Plus, there are a few send-only fax cards (you could send a fax but not receive one). You might find these at a computer flea market, but that's about it.

You might not think you need a fax—especially if the modem is for home use—but think again. Faxes are like microwave ovens; you don't realize how useful they are until you own one. Because most high-speed modems already include the fax hardware, and it doesn't take up any more room on your system, it's almost a non-issue.

Just like choosing a standalone modem, your concerns when buying a fax modem should be speed (the faster the better) and what fax protocol (that nasty word again) it uses.

The 16550 Chip Issue

Here's some more technical information that can sound a little over-whelming at first. If the 16550 (chip) had a name friendlier than a number ("I am not a number! I am a free man!"), it probably wouldn't bother you as much. If it helps, substitute the word "blivet" wherever you see "16550" and you'll probably find the subject a little less menacing.

The 16550 chip (also called a 16550 UART) is a comparatively recent technical advance in telecommunications hardware. The 16550, if you have one, is built in to your add-on serial card or the serial port in your PC. The main advantages of the 16550 are that it gives more feedback to the communications program, and it enables serial port operations to run somewhat faster.

You might not need to think about 16550 UARTs at all. First, if your computer is a name-brand, recent model (say, from 1991 or afterwards) you might already have one as standard equipment. Second, if your modem and software work just fine, there's no reason to spend extra money upgrading your system if you don't need to. (Instead, buy another computer book that increases your efficiency with the one you have.) Third, if you choose an internal modem, it will probably include a 16550 as part of its circuitry.

However, there are a few circumstances when having the 16550 matters:

℃   When your software requires it. Some programs, such as IBM's *Person to Person/2*, require a 16550 UART, or they will refuse to install. (Being refused by a piece of software is a big blow to the ego.) In the case of Person to Person/2, the software places such a demand on the modem that the higher speed and performance requirement is completely justified.

◑   When you do a lot of multitasking. Operating systems that do true multitasking, such as OS/2, can put a lot of demand on the hardware. The computer's attention is divided, so to speak, so the added performance helps the operating system manage tasks better. Faster performance matters, especially if you have more than one serial port and/or modem active in the system. Microsoft Windows does task-switching instead of true multitasking, so it needs a 16550 even more than OS/2 does.

If you find that you need to buy a card with a new serial port for your computer, make sure that you get one with a 16550. It will cost just a little more than the cheapest model, but you'll appreciate the benefits.

Single-Purpose Modems

You may need a modem for only one purpose—to communicate with one specific host, such as the computer at work or at school, or to keep in touch with a distant client.

If that's the case, consider purchasing the brand and model that the other folks use. Modems often work faster when they connect with another modem of the same make and model. Even if you aren't fond of the other brand and model, the added efficiency might be enough to change your mind.

Keeping a Balance

It's tempting for an online enthusiast to tell you to buy the fastest, newest technology modem out there. In fact, in a few places, this book tells you exactly that. But keep a balance in mind.

In the computer industry, there's value in being conservative. Buying the newest, fastest modem gives you the advantage of being able to transmit data faster than anyone else on the block (not to mention bragging rights to your friends). But it also gives you the...er...opportunity of finding the very first problems with the newest hardware. At the other extreme, for example, there are people who absolutely refuse to buy any software whose version number ends in ".0", despite the new features the product touts. Software versions that end with a zero have radical differences from the old version and stereotypically have the most errors (bugs) to iron out. So it's up to you to make the choice between a flashy new modem or a tried-and-true one.

If you're just starting out with modems, and if you really aren't sure that this telecommunications stuff is something you want to do, go ahead and get a slower modem. I'd still prefer that you get at least a 9600 bps modem, if the budget will permit it. Learning about telecommunications with a slow modem is like learning to drive in a car that isn't working properly; you won't know whether your frustration is related to the hardware (the car stalling) or to your own newness to the subject (learning how to parallel park).

In other words, don't fall prey to modem envy. Get what you need, not what's sexy.

Getting a Good Value

Most modems have identical features, such as MNP5, V.42bis, fax, etc. Most support Class 1 and Class 2 fax. Modems from different manufacturers often use the same hardware components. Unless you read packages with all the attention that a diabetic gives a sugarless-candy label, it's hard to tell the difference between one modem and another. When you look carefully, you can find variations in the power of the processor chip used and in the source of the built-in software that runs the modem. But how much difference does it make?

The real difference is in quality and support. How well does the modem work? How well does it handle phone line noise? Does it hang in there or does it lose the connection?

Is the manufacturer available to help with your problems? What do you have to do to contact the manufacturer? Can you even identify the manufacturer? Is help actually provided? Do they care? Is the company likely to still be in business later?

Happily, it is difficult to buy a bad modem. Even the cheapest modem will do an adequate job, given usual needs and average circumstances. Manufacturing quality standards are also high. In fact, you'll find that most modem manufacturers provide a three- or five-year warranty on the equipment; a few provide lifetime warranties. They can do this because their quality is generally good. A cynic might point out that you'll probably upgrade to a faster modem before the warranty runs out, but the warranty shows the commitment to support.

When you buy a quality modem, you're paying for several key things, including the following:

€   Technology. The better companies put money into research & development and work hard to move the industry forward. Many of the cheap knock-offs are just clones, adding nothing of technical value. The cheaper modems come from companies who merely assemble parts.

€   Service and support. The major modem manufacturers are there when you need them. They answer questions (no matter how "dumb" you are afraid they are), maintain BBSs and/or sections on services such as CompuServe, and fix problems quickly when they do arise.

As with any other purchase, it is never a mistake to purchase top quality. I have installed and supported hundreds of modems. Unless you happen to get a dud that is "dead on arrival," most modems will work perfectly— right up until the moment that they quit for good. A name-brand, quality modem will work, right out of the box, and it will never quit working. If there is a problem, the modem manufacturer will solve it quickly.

Personally, I have made a policy of dealing with only the major manufacturers (not the "brands" from the back of the combo sushi bar and bait shop), and I have never been sorry.

The reputation of any given vendor can vary over time, so don't feel that you have to buy a modem simply because it's on my personal list of "good guys," or that you shouldn't buy one simply because it isn't on this list.

However, I have had nothing but good experiences or have heard nothing but good things about these brands:

- ☾   Practical Peripherals
- ☾   Hayes
- ☾   Intel
- ☾   US Robotics
- ☾   Supra

Sometimes, choosing the modem brand is less important than choosing the purchase location. The least expensive options are mail-order and computer discount warehouses. You get the same equipment as you would from the more expensive computer store down the street, but if you choose that route, consider the possible lack of support and turn-around time. Make sure that a store will let you return a defective modem and will answer installation questions.

Some local stores will install an internal modem for you, especially if you buy (or bought) your computer from them. If what you read in the installation chapter makes you especially nervous, this service might be worth the extra cost. Other stores will refuse to support a modem that they didn't personally install, or they won't install the modem in a computer you purchased elsewhere. Ask first. You might also investigate asking a friendly computer consultant to install the modem for you.

But don't wimp out until you've read the next chapter. Installing a modem yourself might be easier than you suspect; it could even be fun and might make you the respected, technical wizard of all your friends. Installing an external modem is so easy that, unless you have a very strange setup, you shouldn't pay anyone extra money to install it.

If you buy a new computer that includes a modem, be sure to ask the vendor for the exact brand and model of the modem you'll be receiving.

Some companies include whichever modem they can get cheapest this quarter, so knowing the computer brand may not help you to ascertain which modem you get.

It's a good idea to join your local PC user's group at this point, if you haven't already done so. The best place to find out about local support of hardware and software—of any kind, not just modems—is from other "real users." Most user groups also have special interest groups, one of which is sure to focus on the topic of telecommunications.

Software Included with the Modem

When you buy a new modem, you almost always get a communications software package included (this is called a *bundle*). If you buy a fax/modem, you will get a fax software program as well. The quality of the software included can vary from barely-adequate to pretty good. In most cases, however, you should expect that the software that you get for free has only basic features. Don't expect more from the free software than you would from, say, the free cookbook that was included with your microwave or food processor. And, definitely, don't make your modem purchase based on the software that's included.

As with the modem recommendations made earlier, the following list is not a recipe for "the only ones to have." However, if you're shopping for communications software, these are all reliable packages from reputable companies:

- ✆   HyperACCESS/5 for DOS, Windows, or OS/2

- ✆   ProComm Plus

- ✆   ProComm for Windows

- ✆   QModem Pro

Most modems also come with free introductory subscriptions to CompuServe and other online services. If you intend to sign up with these services in any case, you'll be happy the introductory subscriptions are available.

So, Which One Should I Get?

Like every other piece of computer hardware, get the most expensive one you can afford. You won't regret it.

If you're a starving student and can't afford more than a hundred dollars, *and* you know you won't use the modem often, get a 2400 bps modem. Better yet, find someone like me who will sell you their old model cheap.

If you want to take the safe and narrow path (which is the one I recommend) buy a 14.4 kbps modem with V.42 bis. Get a modem that includes a fax, partly because it will be hard to find one that doesn't, and partly because you'll enjoy it once you play with it.

Buy one of the newer, faster modems (28.8, V.FAST, etc.) if you want to live dangerously, or if you're buying two modems and you want to be sure that you and your pre-determined remote site can transmit data as fast as possible.

Chapter 3

Installing an External Modem

So, you've decided to attach an external modem to your computer, huh? Great. (Techies call "attaching" a piece of hardware "installing" it, even when you just plug something in.) Even if you will be installing an internal modem, it makes sense to read through this chapter. The two processes include some overlap in concepts. This chapter covers hardware installation basics, and goes through the installation procedure in detail.

You learn in this chapter that you very easily can install your new external modem. Simply take the modem out of the box, then connect it to your computer with a serial cable. You plug in the power cable and the phone line and attach them to the modem, install your communications software, and you're ready to go to work.

Really, it can work that easily. This chapter goes through each step in excruciating detail, too, so the process is even easier to understand.

Preparing for the Installation

The instructions in this section apply to the installation of either an internal or an external modem. In fact, the instructions apply to installing almost anything in a computer.

First, get yourself prepared. Surround yourself with the hardware you'll need. For an external modem, that's just a small screwdriver; you'll need several sizes of screwdrivers to install an internal modem. (I'm tempted to suggest that you'll want a sledgehammer handy if you have to open up the computer, but I'm just kidding. Really—I think.)

Also, find the hardware manuals for your computer. You probably won't need them, but it's a sure thing that you *will* need them if you don't know where they are.

Making a List and Checking It Twice

Before you start to install the modem, make a detailed list of what is already in your computer. Computer people call this your *configuration*. If you have a program that can create a printout of your system settings (including how much RAM is in the system, the type of hard disk you're using, and so on), use that diagnostic program to create the list now (see fig. 3.1).

Figure 3.1

An example of a configuration report.

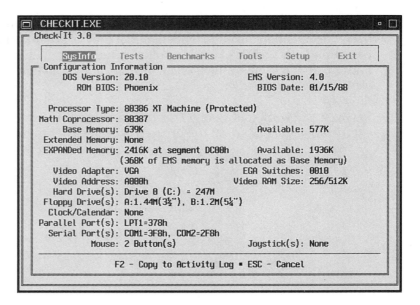

Some versions of DOS include a program called MSD (it stands for Microsoft Diagnostics) that can give you a readout of your system settings. (Under OS/2, this program is included in the \OS2\MDOS\WINOS2 directory.) You can use MSD from a DOS or OS/2 prompt to get a list of what you have, but make sure that you exit Windows (if you're running it) before you do so.

In 99.95 percent of cases, you won't need to refer to the configuration report, but having the report is kind of like having insurance. After all, you know darn well that if you have it, you won't need it. That is one simple way to ensure that things will go right. Then you'll have this technical-looking report hanging around, and you won't know where to store it. (Hint: stick it inside the hardware manual.)

A configuration report of what's in your computer is emotional insurance for this installation, but you also might want to have one around for house insurance too. I was unlucky enough to have my first computer stolen some years ago. Someone broke in and took the PC and most of the manuals. Luckily, I had registered most of my hardware and software. Had I been bright enough to own renter's insurance, I would have had an excellent record of exactly what I owned. While you're at it, pull out your house insurance and verify that your home computer is covered. You might be surprised.

If you're installing an external modem, this report probably won't be required. You'll use it only for troubleshooting, and the likelihood of needing troubleshooting on an external modem is pretty slim.

Any Port in a Storm

To get started, you should turn off your computer. You wouldn't want to shock yourself—or worse, hurt the computer. Then turn the computer around, or at least find a comfortable place to sit while you look at the back of the machine. Before you install anything, identify the parts that you'll need to pay attention to.

In computer terms, the plug into which you stick a cable is called a *port*. Your printer cable is probably plugged into a parallel port; the modem will attach to a serial port (see fig. 3.2).

Figure 3.2

The serial port, usually found on the back of your computer.

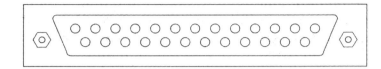

Your computer has a lot of wires coming out of the back of it. Some of them are pretty boring; it should be easy to identify the power cable, for instance. You'll also easily spot the video cable, connecting the monitor to the video card. Similarly, the printer cable connects your printer to the PC through the parallel port.

When you're installing an external modem, what you're looking for is a serial port. If you're lucky, the serial port will be labeled. You might even have two of them. The serial port might be 9-pin or 25-pin, but it will always be male. (That is, the pins will stick out. Plugs with holes instead of pins are referred to as *female*. Really! I don't make up these terms.)

While you're here, grab a pen and a few labels. Label all the plugs on your computer so that you know what everything is, the next time around, so you don't have to go through this again.

Technical Support Can Be Your Friend

Keep the modem's manual near you throughout the installation. If you get really lost, don't be afraid to call the technical support phone number. The service will be free, and the folks there can talk you through anything that isn't covered in these chapters.

The technical support service will be free, but for most modem and communications software manufacturers, the telephone call rarely is. Notice where your manufacturer is geographically located; if you live on the East or West coast, you might be able to save a few cents by calling

them at the beginning or end of your day. If you live in Maine, for example, it's cheaper to call California-based tech support in the early evening than it is during the middle of the business day.

Modem manuals sometime seem to expect you to know everything about modems before you begin reading, but the people who staff the technical support lines don't have that assumption. If you buy a decent modem, the manual will probably be detailed (if a little dull). A modem manual is not recommended for bathroom reading.

Getting Ready to Install

You've either made it this far and haven't gotten discouraged yet, or you've just jumped to this spot in the chapter to get to the really important part. Finally, everything is ready to be put together.

To connect the modem to your PC, follow these steps:

1. Locate the serial port.
2. Connect the serial cable to the serial port.
3. Connect the serial cable to the modem.
4. Plug the modem into the electric outlet.
5. Turn on the modem.
6. Connect the modem to the telephone line.

The preceding steps are discussed in more detail in the following sections.

Opening the Box

I bet you opened the box the modem came in already, didn't you? You couldn't wait; you had to see what was inside the shrink-wrap. The cat is probably already playing with the plastic.

I don't blame you. I would have done the same thing.

Riffle through the papers in the box. You should find quite a few of them, including special offers to join online services or to buy communications software. Those offers could be useful to you, but what you're looking for is the following:

- ℂ   The modem itself (it'd be a nasty thing to forget now)

- ℂ   A power cable

- ℂ   A phone cable

- ℂ   A manual

- ℂ   A registration card

A serial cable just might also be in the box, but chances are that it won't be. The only time you will find a serial cable included with the modem is when you buy a special-purpose modem (such as a pocket modem), which is expected to be used with a laptop computer. Some of those use a non-standard cable, so it's easier for the modem manufacturer to include one than to make you go shopping. Besides, you'd probably buy too much.

A *serial cable* is the heavy-duty wire that connects your modem (or another piece of equipment that uses this sort of thing) to your serial port. The serial port is also called an RS-232C connection. You will also see it referred to (throughout this book) as a com port, because it's used most often for communications.

Fill out the registration card right away, and mail it. Unlike household appliances, computer equipment should be registered with the company immediately. If an upgrade becomes available from the company, you'll want to know about it.

If you buy a new VCR or car, for example, you're stuck with what you get. Even if the manufacturer comes out with a neat new feature next year, the only way you'd be able to get your hands on it would be to buy another new VCR or car. In the world of hardware and software, however, you can often purchase the new features as add-ons. This process is called upgrading.

In modems, a hardware upgrade might make your modem run a little bit faster, or perhaps handle a poor-quality telephone line better. In software, upgrades add new features and correct defects. (If it's a major upgrade, the numbers go up a full digit. A hypothetical product called WhizBang might go from 1.0 to 2.0 in such a case. If the changes are relatively minor, the numbering only changes a percentage point.

Connecting the Modem to the PC

The first thing to do is to connect the modem to the computer so the two can "talk" with one another. The following sections take you through the process, step by step.

Serial of Champions

As mentioned previously, you need to locate the serial port. There are three kinds of serial ports. They all work the same way internally, but they come in different sizes.

At the hardware level, when the computer sends information to a parallel cable, one byte of information is sent at the same time. The information is sent in parallel. (Get it?)

When information is sent across a serial cable, however, it's sent serially, one bit after the other. Serial ports can communicate, or negotiate, with the modem (or other device). That lets them make sure that the transmission worked correctly, and that no data was lost. The process of negotiating is called hardware or software handshaking.

The three sizes (or shapes) of serial ports include the following:

- ✆ Nine-pin
- ✆ 24-pin
- ✆ DIN connector

Figure 3.3 shows you an example of nine-and 24-pin serial ports.

Figure 3.3

An example of nine- and 24-pin serial ports.

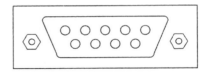

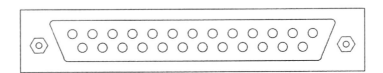

As you might guess, a *nine-pin* serial cable has nine pins for data to travel through. The *24-pin serial cable* has 24 pins and is larger than the nine-pin. When you look at the back of your computer, you might temporarily confuse a nine-pin serial port for the port for your monitor; both of those ports have about the same size "D"-shaped connector. But the serial port is male, and the video port is female. Also, the serial cable won't fit into the video port, and you probably have a monitor attached to the video port anyway.

The 24-pin serial port can look like a printer port. The printer port is female, however, and a printer cable has a strange-looking connector on one end; it looks like your worst childhood nightmare of orthodontia.

Finally, the *DIN connector* (the third kind of serial connector, as listed previously) is round and much smaller than the other connectors (it looks like a small version of the connector for a car cigarette lighter). DIN is an international standard, but to give you some idea of how little anyone cares about what it stands for, I had to look it up. (DIN is the German Standards Institute, in case you care. You never know when you'll be in a trivia contest.) Since the DIN connectors are smaller, they're used in portable modems, where size matters a lot.

From the user's point of view, none of the three types of serial connections is better or worse than the other. Some computers have smaller ports, some have larger. You simply have to check before you go shopping for a cable.

They *Name* These Things?

Without doing anything special (except perhaps spending a little extra money), you can have up to four serial ports. With some extra work, you can have eight or sixteen serial ports.

To help you keep track of each port, each one has a name. The names are pretty simple: COM1, COM2, COM3, and COM4. If you have only one serial port, it's COM1. The second is named COM2, and so on.

Your computer might have more than one serial port. If you don't know which one is COM1 and which one is COM2, you'll suddenly understand why I suggested that you label the plugs and ports on the back of your computer. There's not much advice that I can give you to determine which is which, but the COM1 port is built-in to the computer—rather than an add-in board.

Plugging It In

Now that you're certain that you have the right wire and the right places to plug them in, go ahead and do it. Plug the serial cable into the serial port on the PC, and attach the other end to the serial port on the modem.

In a few cases, you might discover that the PC takes one size of serial cable, and the modem takes another. You can either buy a serial cable made to those specifications (i.e. 25-pin to nine-pin), or you can buy a nine-pin-to-25-pin adapter; these things are really inexpensive (the adapter will cost five dollars, more or less) but it's really frustrating to get to this point and realize that you need another trip to the store. (Aren't you glad you read through this chapter first? You did, didn't you?)

If you have a serial mouse, make sure you read the section, later in this chapter, about using a modem and mouse together.

What If You're Out of Serial Ports?

Your computer almost certainly has one serial port. But that port might be in use, with a mouse, a plotter, or a printer. You might need to purchase a card with a serial port on it, and install that card before you can use your modem. (I'm sure you're thrilled to hear that.)

These cards (called *I/O boards*, which stands for input/output) can contain one to three serial ports, and sometimes another printer port as well. You can buy one cheaply (between forty and a hundred dollars), but don't get too cheap here! A slightly more expensive I/O card will have a 16550 chip, which can increase the speed and performance of telecommunications. If you have to buy a card anyway, you might as well get one that will improve your system. Besides, a really cheap one is apt to work poorly; the potential problems are just not worth the money you'd save.

It's probably outside the bounds of this book to talk about how, exactly, to add an I/O card. Otherwise, the title would have to be, Don't Panic: It's Only A Modem and Some Extra Hardware. If you do have to install another card, read through the chapter on installing an internal modem. The basic instructions are about the same, especially those concerning conflicts with IRQs, setting which com port, will be the same. (Ha! You thought you'd avoid those by getting an external modem. Wrong-o.) Then pick up a copy of Keeping Your PC Alive, from New Riders Publishing. It's designed specifically to help timid and first-time users add these sorts of pieces to their computers.

Dealing with Mice

If you have a mouse connected to a serial port, you'll need to stay aware of a few extra things. (Your mouse might be on its own card, or use a "mouse port," in which case it will use a small round connector. If that's the case, you have nothing to worry about.)

First, the mouse is probably connected to COM1, because it's probably the only com port in use. So you'll want to verify that (if you can without very much trouble), and keep in mind that you will need to tell the communications' software, later on, that you're using COM2.

If you happen to have two serial ports in use, arrange your setup so that the mouse and the modem are not both on an odd-numbered or even-numbered port number. In other words, make sure that the mouse isn't on COM1 and the modem on COM3, or a COM2-COM4 combination. If you want to know the technical reasons, read about IRQs in the next chapter. You don't want to know about this unless you have to; it's easier to simply keep the modem and mouse on an even-odd relationship.

Connecting the Phone

Connecting the phone wire is the easiest task to describe, but it can be the most frustrating in real life.

While the modem vendor won't include a serial cable (after that serial port discussion, you can probably guess why), the modem vendor almost always includes a length of phone cable. It will probably look too short to do much good, but it's intended to connect the modem to your current desk phone. The assumption is that you already have a desk phone right next to your computer, so a 6-foot length is probably plenty.

When you have the phone plugged into the modem, and the modem attached to the wall, you can still use the phone as usual—even if the modem's power is off. Just don't pick up the phone while using the modem. It's awfully easy to forget, and tell yourself, "Okay, while I'm doing this long file transfer, I'll just call...." But if (or when) you do so, you'll lose your modem connection.

In a lot of houses and offices, no one thought about connecting a computer to the phone. The single phone outlet is probably at the other end of the room. You might have to use a phone extension cord to get the wire where it needs to be. Don't jury-rig something, though. A friend who lives in an old house in Maine has only one phone plug on the first floor, and the computer is two rooms away. The entire family has to crawl around temporary webs of wires so that one person can use the modem. It isn't a pretty sight.

If you are working in an older house or office, you might not even have the standard RJ-11 connector on the phone line, and will have to do surgery on the phone wires first. "RJ-11" is the real term for the phone connection in your wall. (I have no idea what happened to RJ-1 through RJ-10, but nobody ever mentions them.)

Figure 3.4 shows the phone wire that is strung from the phone jack in the wall to the modem. If you want a desk phone nearby, you also can connect it to the modem with a second phone cable.

Figure 3.4

A connection of a telephone, modem, and wall jack.

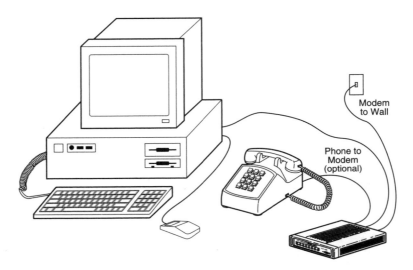

Modem to Wall

Phone to Modem (optional)

Look at your modem carefully. With some modems, it doesn't matter into which RJ-11 jack you stick the phone connector. With most, however, you have to connect the phone line from the wall jack into the RJ-11 gizmo labeled "wall;" it might have a tiny picture that is meant to look like a wall connection. The other connector will be labeled "phone" or have an icon of a telephone. A few modems, intended for portability, only have one RJ-11 connection; in that case, it's easy to figure out which plug to use.

Be forewarned that the most likely mistake you will make in installing a modem is to plug the phone lines in backwards. The way that you'll know you've done so is that everything seems to be hooked up correctly, but the modem doesn't get a dial tone when instructed (by the communications program) to do so. I'm sure this sounds like a really dumb thing to point out, but I made this exact error once.

If you panic (after your modem and phone are all hooked to the wall) because the modem doesn't work, and you call a friend for help, do not experiment with hooking the modem up an alternate way while you are still on the phone.

If you work in an office with a fancy telephone system, make modem-related inquiries first. Several of the popular office telephone systems (for example, Merlin) won't work with a modem line. If you want to use a modem line, you will have to find a bypass directly into the phone line, or use a completely separate line.

Plugging In

The last thing to do is supply electric power to the modem. Portable modems sometimes have battery packs. Most modems, however, plug into an ordinary wall socket.

One of the annoying things about external modems is that most of them require a power cable with a transformer. That puts a lump on the end of the cable, and makes it really awkward to find a place to plug the wire.

But finally, everything is hooked up. The modem is connected to the computer, to the phone line, and to the power. It's time for the moment of truth: flip the power switch.

Is the modem on?

Most of the time, the only way you'll know that the modem is alive is that you'll see a light turn on. The lights labeled MR and TR will probably turn on—MR stands for *Modem Ready*, and TR means *Terminal Ready*. That's a good sign. There might be other lights on, too, depending on the model you're using.

Nothing else is going to happen, you know. Not until you get the software working.

If something untoward happens—which, at this point, simply means that the modem doesn't seem to be on—refer to the troubleshooting chapter. (Throughout the book, you'll be referred to that chapter if you get stuck.)

Chapter 4

Installing an Internal Modem

After you install an internal modem, you will be able to hurl tennis rackets at small moving objects with deadly accuracy. You will read *Paradise Lost*, *Moby Dick*, and *David Copperfield* in one day, and still have time to refurbish an entire dining room that evening. You will know the exact location of every food item in the supermarket, perform covert operations for the CIA, and you will only need to sleep once a week.

Okay, so maybe installing an internal modem isn't quite that impressive or exciting. The goal was to get you psyched for the experience.

To install an internal modem, you have to open up the computer, and find a place to put the modem card. After you shove the card into the slot, you'll need to close up the computer. Then you need to connect the modem to the phone line, using the phone cable supplied by the modem vendor.

It isn't as bad as it sounds.

Before you get started, read through the introductory section of the previous chapter, *Installing an External Modem*. It gives some advice that will be helpful here. Use that section to create a configuration report of your system settings, if you can. That report will come in handy later.

Getting Down to Cases

Prepare yourself by collecting a few screwdrivers. (The hardware sort. Vodka isn't good for keyboards.) You'll need both a small screwdriver (the tiny kind) and a regular-sized one. You'll probably need both Phillips and flat-head screwdrivers. The equipment manufacturers seem to delight in using different sizes for different components. What the heck, grab your whole screwdriver collection.

If you have never opened up your computer before, find the manual that came with it. (Good luck. It's probably holding up a chair leg.)

Move the computer to a stable place where you can work easily, and make sure that you have adequate lighting. You're more likely to do something foolish if you're trying to balance the PC on an unsteady table, or working on the floor, surrounded by curious cats. (I bet you think I'm being hypothetical. Uh-uh. I've done empirical testing.) Unplug the power cable, just for safety.

Unscrew the case, and remove the cover from the computer. That sounds easy, but it can be harder than it looks. Most screws are in the back, but sometimes you'll find them on the sides. Some covers slide off, others lift, and yet others have a door that folds out. If you can't figure out how the machine comes apart (it probably won't be obvious), consult the computer's manual for instructions.

Figure 4.1 shows you where you might find those screws. You probably don't need to disconnect any wires besides the power plug, but every machine is different.

If you do have to remove other cables, label them. Doing so will save you a lot of grief later on.

Allow yourself plenty of time for taking off the cover. I've spent as much as an hour struggling to remove a computer cover (although, in my defense, I didn't have its manual). Opening up your computer will probably take you about 15-20 minutes the first time, however.

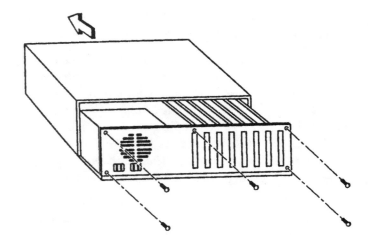

Figure 4.1

Screw locations on a typical PC.

Looking Inside

If you have never peered into the guts of a computer, you might be just a teeny bit overwhelmed. A lot of equipment is in there, and, depending on how many add-in cards you have and the general quality of workmanship, the "guts" of a computer can look like a mess.

Static electricity is the enemy of electronic equipment. So, before you do anything else, make sure you get rid of any that is clinging to you. Touch the power supply (the big gray box that's probably on one side or the other of the computer). That's the easiest way to eliminate static. (The power supply looks mysterious, but it's really boring; it's just a power supply like one you'd find in your washing machine, TV, or other electrical equipment.)

If you have never looked inside your computer before, take this opportunity to look around. This is one of the educational experiences that can make the entire subject of computers suddenly make sense. (Then again, staring under the hood of my car has never made me an expert mechanic. So don't expect too much.)

See if you can identify the computer's CPU chip, the brains of the whole operation. If you can see the chip (sometimes

continues

it's hidden by other equipment), it will probably be labeled with a number ending in 86. (80286, 80386, etc).

Also, try to identify the video card; you should be able to trace it simply by following the wire to your monitor. See if you can find the memory, or RAM, in your computer. If it's an older system, you may see a line of chips (they look like bugs, lined up for review), but in most circumstances, you'll see one or more SIMMS, cards that look like miniature add-in cards. They'll have chips on them too, but then again, almost everything you look at in here has chips.

Try to identify the purpose of every add-in card in the machine. There probably won't be very many of them. Don't worry if you don't know what something is doing there; this is just a general tour—not a comprehensive analysis.

The board into which everything else is attached is called the *motherboard*. Every PC motherboard has expansion slots—places into which you can shove add-in cards.

Add-in cards were originally called daughter-cards, which gives some explanation for the oddness of the term motherboard. The other reason for the term's strangeness is that it was made up by the kind of computer geeks whom you'd have been ashamed to bring home to Mom.

Add-in cards, sometimes called expansion cards or just *cards*, fit into the *bus*, which is the collection of slots on the motherboard.

Deciding Where The Modem Will Go

When you look at the motherboard, you'll see a collection of both short and long slots (see fig. 4.2). The longer slots are 16-bit, the shorter are 8-bit. The cards that go into 16-bit slots are faster, because twice as much data can be pumped through them in the same amount of time.

The slots are the long parallel grooves, about three inches long, that are perpendicular to the case. They look like enlarged versions of the "slot Bs" you were supposed to plug "Tab A" into, in all those kits you never got around to completing when you were a child.

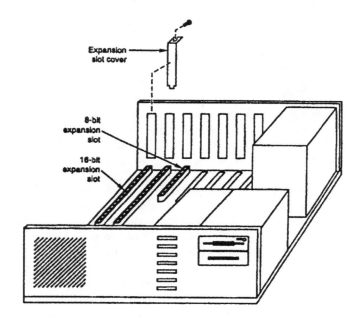

Figure 4.2

Empty slots in a PC.

The cards, too, are either 8-bit or 16-bit. You can plug an eight-bit card into a 16-bit slot without any trouble; the eight-bit card won't work any faster, but it should work. But if you plug a 16-bit card into an eight-bit slot, the card probably won't work at all.

The modem box should say, right on the outside, whether the card is an 8-bit or 16-bit card. (Don't feel terribly disappointed if your modem is "only" an eight-bit card. With modems, especially slower ones, the phone line is slower than the computer will ever be.)

Select the slot into which you're going to install the modem. Against the edge of the computer, you'll find a metal expansion slot cover; until now, that served to help keep dust out of the box. Unscrew and remove the expansion slot cover. Be careful about picking which slot cover goes with which slot, though; on several occasions, I've removed the wrong one.

After the modem is installed, you won't know what to do with the extra expansion slot cover. I've found that it does a nifty job of holding doors open on carpet. Keep it around, anyway. If you ever take the modem out of this computer, you'll want to use the cover plate again, or your computer will fill up with dust.

Taking the Modem Out of the Box

Inside the package, you'll find a modem manual, registration card, and possibly a stack of other literature. Fill out and return the registration card; these things do matter. Hang onto the manual; we'll be consulting it soon. Set the rest of the paperwork aside for now.

The modem will be stored in an anti-static bag. Even after you install the modem, keep the anti-static bag around; in case you ever need to send the card in for service, those bags do a good job of protecting the equipment. Before you open the bag, it's a good idea to touch the power supply again, to get rid of any static that you've accumulated up to this point.

Open the modem bag and carefully remove the modem card. Try not to handle it by the connectors—the part where it will plug into the motherboard. Put the anti-static bag on a table and lay the card on top of the bag. Now, take a close look at the card.

Briefly Interrupting...

Under most circumstances, you won't need to worry about anything in this section. If your computer system is a straightforward setup, then you can probably ignore the entire thing. But you won't know for sure until you read a bit further.

This is where the chapter gets a bit technical. The next section covers some of the nitty-gritty details about how a computer works and is a perfect example of why some people are intimidated by modems. Don't say you weren't warned.

Hardware Addresses

Remember that we referred to the *bus* on the computer's motherboard? On a city bus, passengers can travel to specific locations or addresses. Well, a similar situation happens with a computer's bus. The computer sends data and instructions, via the *bus*, to the different cards and devices inside the computer's system.

For city transit, the location of each bus stop has an address, such as "32nd Street and Bell Road." Similarly, each device and card in your computer is assigned an address. Those addresses aren't as easily understandable as "32nd Street," at least not to you and me, but computers can cope with much more terse instructions.

For reasons that are probably obvious, computer hardware uses standard addresses for common equipment. The only addresses we care about at this point are the ones for the com ports (also known as serial ports). You can see the standard ones in Table 4.1.

Table 4.1
Standard IRQ and Hardware Addresses for Serial Ports

Address	IRQ Setting	Usual Hardware
COM1	4	3F8
COM2	3	2F8
COM3	4	3E8
COM4	3	2E8

It Isn't Polite to Interrupt

The other technical concept that suddenly becomes relevant is *interrupts*. To understand this, think back for a moment about the analogy of the city bus.

As the city bus travels down the street, its actions are controlled by traffic lights, stop signs, and the activity of other cars and buses. The bus driver's behavior is affected by actions that interrupt the smooth flow of the bus from one place to another.

The computer is interrupt-driven, too. In this case, the interrupts are generated by electronic messages from the computer or other devices, or by the software that controls them. Interrupts can have different priorities, just as in real life. If the phone rings while you're making dinner, for instance, you'll stop what you're doing and answer it; if the dog barks, you'll notice, but you probably won't rush away from the stove to see why the dog is barking. In computer terms, the first interrupt is a high-priority interrupt; the second is low-priority.

Any device that sends an interrupt has to have a way to identify itself. *Interrupt settings*, usually called *IRQ Settings* or just *IRQ*s, are something like addresses, but not quite. At least, the computer uses addresses and IRQs differently, and that's all that matters, here.

Like hardware addresses, there are standard IRQ settings for common equipment. For example, the first printer port (LPT1) is set to IRQ7; the second printer port (LPT2), if there is one in the system, is usually at IRQ5. Serial ports also have standard IRQ settings, but you can change them if you have to. Table 4.1 shows the standard settings for both IRQ settings and hardware addresses.

Most add-on hardware can be set to different IRQs. The more choices you have, the better. For instance, one sound card will work at either IRQ5 or IRQ7. If you already own one device that uses IRQ5, and another device that uses IRQ7, you might be out of luck on getting the sound card to work. At the very least, you will have to change the IRQ settings on one of the existing devices.

To put it plainly: it's all a pain.

Why Should I Care?

At this point, your eyes are probably beginning to glaze over. Why should you care about all this? You thought the point of this book was to get past the hardware, so you can *use* this darn-fool thing!

The reason that you have to know about IRQs and hardware addresses is that you can have trouble if two devices are at the same address or IRQ. In computer terms, this is called a *hardware conflict* or an *IRQ conflict*. There are other things to call it, but not in polite company.

IRQs are like kids, all calling from different rooms in the house. You know which kid is calling by the sound of his voice, so you know who wants you to stop what you're doing and pay attention. If two (or more) of the kids who called you had identical voices, then you'd have a conflict—or cause for a vacation.

To make things more complex, a few devices share interrupts. COM1 and COM3 are at different hardware addresses, but they both use IRQ3. COM2 and COM4 share IRQ4. If you only have one or two com ports, this won't present any problem. But if you have more than two, you will have to pay careful attention to which device is on which port.

The most common problem is a mouse and a modem on the same IRQ. Because both modems and mice depend heavily on generating interrupts (you didn't know that before, but now you do), one of them—or your entire computer system—will get totally confused if they have to share an interrupt. Sound cards also present problems, because the 8-bit cards often have only a few choices of IRQ settings and these can conflict with other hardware. One of the items won't work at all, or will work sporadically. The only solution is to change the address and/or interrupt setting.

So, How Do I Change These Things?

If you do have to change the settings on equipment, then you will probably have to fool with dip switches and jumpers. These configuration switches look like teeny-tiny light switches. They usually are grouped together in banks of switches.

Depending on which way the flippers are flipped, the card will operate using a given setting. It's like the controls on a washing machine—you have to make sure the machine is set for "permanent press," "cold," and "no bleach," or you could have some nasty surprises, such as purple underwear.

When the flippers look like removable sliders instead, they're called *jumpers.* (That's probably because they tend to jump out of your hands, under the desk.) Figure 4.3 shows examples of jumpers and configuration switches.

Figure 4.3

Jumpers and configuration switches.

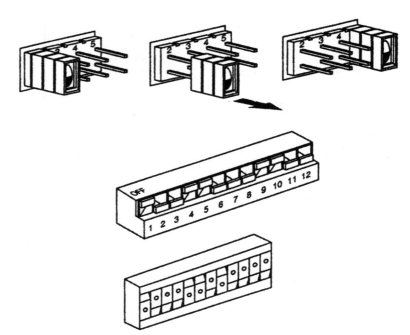

You need to check three settings on the modem: the COM port, the IRQ, and the hardware address. By default, straight from the factory, an internal modem will be set at COM1, IRQ4, 3F8. If your computer is really straightforward—a monitor and a printer, until now, nothing else—then you won't have to mess with this at all.

You can't have two devices in your computer that are labeled as COM1. Well, you can, but they aren't going to work. So, if there's already a COM1 (whether or not you are planning on using it), you can:

    ✆   Turn off the existing (internal or built-in) COM1

    ✆   Change the existing COM1 to COM2, COM3, or COM4

    ✆   Change the modem to COM2

Under most circumstances, it's easiest to set the modem to COM2. Of course, if your computer came with two serial ports, you'd have to set the internal modem to COM3. That's okay, too. If you change the COM port, make sure that you change the IRQ and hardware address as well.

Remember the diagnostic listing you generated? You did create one, didn't you? If you were able to create one, find it now. (You're probably sitting on it. Ah, there it is.) Verify that you don't have any other devices set to the IRQ and hardware address that the modem will be using. If there is, you'll have to figure out which one to change, and how to do it. It's probably simplest to change the settings on the modem, because you already have it in front of you.

The specifics of how to change the settings will be completely dependent on the brand and model of modem that you have. Follow the instructions in the manual. Now that you understand what the manual is talking about, reading it probably won't be a disheartening process.

Getting the Card In There

Finally, you've established the settings on the modem, and you're ready to put the card into the computer. You probably didn't have to change any settings whatsoever, in which case you're annoyed at me for telling you things that you didn't want to know and now, you've discovered, you didn't even *need* to know. Sorry. Maybe you can use the knowledge to impress that obnoxious brother-in-law of yours someday.

Hold the modem card over its designated slot. The face plate should point to the outside of the case, with the contacts facing toward the slot. Push the modem into the slot, making sure that it's plugged in completely. The modem should go in with a "kerchunk," and probably will take a little more effort than you think it should.

You'll discover that I wasn't merely being entertaining when I referred to "shoving" the card into the slot. Be careful, though; it might be necessary to press hard, but you don't want to break the card either. You need to strike a balance between Sly Stallone and Mother Theresa.

Replace the screw that held in the metal plate. It will help to hold the modem securely where it belongs.

Closing the Case

If you can, leave the computer open until you know that everything is working correctly. You won't really know if your setup is okay until after you install the software, so that could be another hour or two. The computer should run just fine with the cover off. In some circumstances, your room setup won't let you do this, or you might have a cat that is confused about the location of the litter box. So this is simply a convenience, not a rule.

If you lost a screw inside the case, don't leave it there. It can short out the motherboard, and make you very unhappy. You may have to get a tiny screwdriver that has a very weak magnet on it to retrieve these lost screws. Don't use a magnet out of your speaker system, however. You might not have any data left on your hard drive.

Put the computer back together, close up the case, and screw the screws back in. Plug the phone wires into the modem, with one connecting to the wall jack and an optional wire to your desk phone. The modem's plugs will be labeled, but if the lighting is poor, the writing will be hard to read.

Ideally, memorize that the "to-wall" plug is on top (or on bottom, as the case may be), because after you move the computer against the wall again you'll never be able to read it. (I've climbed under enough desks to be sure of this, so take my advice.)

Turn your computer back on, and make sure that everything starts up correctly.

Is the Modem On?

How can you tell?

You can't. You'll have to wait until you install the communications software to verify that all that work you did was correct.

Your modem might have come with a disk that has diagnostic software that will tell you if the modem is working right. If you have such a disk, go ahead and follow the directions to run the report.

You're Done—Not Really

You've successfully installed an internal modem. Congratulations! While this accomplishment doesn't exactly deserve a champagne dinner, it's something—after all, only people who know what they're doing open up their own systems. Hey, that means you understand a little about what's going on with your computer. Imagine that!

In Chapter 5, you'll receive even more technical information about modems, and then we'll get the software working. If you feel especially impressed with yourself, you can skip ahead to Chapter 6.

Chapter 5

Modem Guts

If you're really anxious to get to work, you can read ahead to Chapter 6, where you learn about communications software. This chapter covers the slightly more technical side of how modems work, to give you a better idea of what is happening when you use one.

You don't have to understand everything here before you can get started, but the more you understand a topic, the more control you have over it. (Isn't that profound? That's my profound quotient for today.)

Communicating with the Modem

You don't have to become an expert to understand what a modem is trying to tell you. In fact, I consider my knowledge of modem guts to be abysmally small, yet I manage to log into electronic services and BBSs every day.

The modem has a language of its own. You give it commands that look like short abbreviations, and the modem will reply in terse phrases. In most cases, the communications software takes care of issuing the commands (and figuring out what to do with the responses) for you.

What Are All Those Lights?

An external modem is almost certain to have external lights, usually bright red or green LEDs. Each of the lights is labeled, though the abbreviations might not mean very much to you right now. This section describes what most of the lights mean, although you only need to pay attention to a few. If you have a fax modem, it might have more lights than are listed on Table 5.1.

Table 5.1
Modem Lights for the Practical Peripherals 14.4 FXMT

LED	Description	Meaning
AA	Auto Answer	Steady—Modem will answer telephone. Flashing—Telephone is ringing.
RX	Receive Data	Data is being received.
TX	Transmit Data	Data is being transmitted (sent).
CD	Data Carrier Detect (DCD)	Steady—Valid carrier for remote modem. Flashing—retrain is occurring.
OH	Off-Hook	The telephone line is off-hook.
HS	High Speed	Modem is operating at a higher speed (4800 bps or above).

LED	Description	Meaning
TR	Data Terminal Ready (DTR)	DTR signal from the computer is asserted or forced ON (AT&D*n*).
MR	Modem Ready	The modem is switched on and ready to operate. Other people might call this an on-light.

Probably the most important thing you notice about the modem lights is that they are on (assuming the modem is turned on) and that, while you're online, something is happening. Every time you press a key when you're online (for instance, when you're logged into a BBS), you should see the TX light blink. That means that the modem is transmitting data (in this case, the key that you pressed).

If you suspect that you've lost the modem connection, or that, somehow, the hook-up isn't working correctly, you can glance at the modem to make sure that *something* is going on. If data is being transmitted and received, there probably isn't anything to worry about.

If the modem is turned on, *MR* (modem ready) *light* will probably be lit. You usually can think of the MR light as the "power switch" light.

The *OH* (off-hook) *light* means that the telephone is engaged. This is the same thing as you—or in this case the modem—picking up the phone receiver. Just because the OH light is on doesn't mean it's connected (any more than your picking up the receiver means that you're talking to Mom, or have even dialed her number).

The *CD* (carrier detect) *light* indicates that the modem is connected to another modem. That is, Mom has answered the phone. That doesn't necessarily mean, however, that she has started talking (or started giving you advice).

The *AA light* indicates that the modem is set to auto-answer and will answer the telephone. In other words, if the telephone rings, the modem will pick it up. If you use a remote communications package (such as pcANYWHERE) so that another user can dial in and use your computer, the AA light would be turned on all the time.

Under normal circumstances, leaving the modem in Auto Answer is a really impolite thing to do—unless you are presented with a sales weasel who is really persistent (and annoying). A good solid modem squeal in the ear can change anybody's mind about your suitability for that marvelous travel resort time-share opportunity.

The specific meaning of the HS light will depend on your modem. If you have an old 1200 or 2400 bps modem, the HS light will indicate that the modem is operating at 2400 bps—not what anyone else might think is blindingly fast, but it's fast as far as that particular modem is concerned.

DTR, or *Data Terminal Ready*, means that the computer is ready to talk to the modem. You'll almost never need to know about this, except when a communications program wants to know the following: "Drop DTR to Hang Up?" Dropping DTR is simply an alternate (and reliable) way for the modem to hang up the telephone.

Usually, the RX and TX work together. Under normal circumstances, while you're online, you send data ("I want to look at the new files here") expecting an immediate response ("Here are the files in the Elvis Impersonators conference"). As you send information, the TX light blinks; when you receive it, the RX will be lit. During a normal online session, you'll see these two lights blink in rapid succession.

Understanding Modem Commands

When personal computers first became popular, Hayes Microcomputer Products, Inc. pioneered the modem technology and became the de facto standard among modem manufacturers. Their modems used a set of commands, essentially a modem-specific language, that every other modem manufacturer tried to emulate. Modems that use this set of commands are called *Hayes-compatible*.

The good news is that any modem that you purchase today will be Hayes-compatible, although that standard, like most standards, has grown and evolved. (The nice thing about standards is that there are so many of them.)

Modems have two modes. A *mode* formally is a state of being, but that explanation sounds as if I've been in California too long. Think of modes like teenagers: either the teenager is hungry or the teenager is asleep. When they're awake, they're hungry. If teenagers are asleep, they can't be hungry. Similarly, modems have the following two modes:

- 🕜 **Online mode.** In *online mode*, the modem takes whatever you type and passes it through to the modem at the remote location, at the other end of the phone line. The modem isn't listening to what you type; it's just sending the data on.

- 🕜 **Command mode.** In *command mode*, the modem is listening to receive instructions. The instructions might come from you, or they might be generated by the communications program.

If you're wondering what kind of commands you might want to give a modem, rest easy. In practice, your communications program will give almost every command. Some of the commands are straightforward, such as "dial this phone number." Others are more arcane. We'll focus on just the simple ones.

Modem Commands You Might Like to Know

In Hayes-compatible modem parlance, AT means *Attention!*. Typing AT tells the modem to pay attention to the command that follows. In rare circumstance, you might have to type +++ (three pluses in a row) to get the modem's attention, so you can ask for its attention. (Yes, that's exactly as silly as it sounds.)

Table 5.2 lists the common commands that you will use.

Table 5.2
Common Modem Commands

Command	Description
AT	Attention.
ATO	Return to Online mode.

continues

Table 5.2, Continued
Common Modem Commands

Command	Description
ATD	Dial the phone number specified. Without a phone number, the modem will just pick up the phone and let the dial tone sound. T or P—tone or pulse. For instance, *ATDT 5551212* dials (tone) the phone number 555-1212.
ATH	Hang up the phone.
A/	Repeat what you did last. Usually you'd use this to redial a number.
AT&F*n*	Factory defaults. Returns all parameters to the standard default settings. AT&F1 is useful if you really screw things up.
AT$H	Ask the modem for help. The modem will display a multi-page listing of commands.
ATZ	Reset the modem.
ATA	Auto-answer mode—tells the modem to answer the telephone when it rings.
ATM*n*	Sound control. ATM0 turns the speaker off. ATM1 tells the modem to leave the speaker on until the carrier is detected.
,	A comma (,) tells the modem to wait for two seconds. You might want to use this if you have to dial out of a office where you have to dial "9" first. Sometimes, you will find that it takes a few moments to get the dial tone for an outside line. So ATDT9,123-4567 will dial 9, then wait two seconds, then dial the rest of the telephone number.

You won't use these commands often. As mentioned earlier, the communications program will probably take care of this for you. However, if you have problems with a modem or with connecting to a specific service, you'll need to look at a few sets of command strings. These are usually initialization commands and dialing strings.

Although you probably will never have to use them, Appendix C contains a list of several modem commands that just might come in handy.

Initialization commands are the set of commands that tell your modem how to behave in a given session. The initialization string might be as simple as *ATZ*—a simple reset. Or it may be more complex, depending on the nature of the connection, the reliability of your phone lines, or the control that the program needs to have over the modem.

For example, the initialization command that I have, supplied to me by one specific program, is:

```
AT&F^M?KATE1L2M1Q0V1X4Y0&C1&D2^M?K.
```

Aren't you glad that neither you nor I have to understand every piece of that?

A *reset command* or *reset string* are the commands that the modem is given (usually by your communications program) to reset itself, usually after you have hung up the phone and finished an online session.

Understanding Result Codes

Depending on the command you've issued to the modem, you might get a response. If you tell the modem to dial the telephone, the most obvious (and desired) response is that you hear the modem pick up the phone and dial. When the modem connects, the computer will give you a response of CONNECT (if it reached another modem and managed to match up), BUSY, or VOICE. Each of these is a result code—that is, a way for the modem to communicate with *you*.

In other cases, you might want to know that the command actually worked. For instance, if you type ATZ to reset the modem, the modem will respond with an OK, indicating that it followed the instruction you specified. That's the most frequent response. But if you don't get any response from a modem command—especially the more bizarre ones that we don't cover here—don't worry about it too much. The modem won't always have a result code for you.

Defining Some Terms

Like most other professions, the people who work in telecommunications have their own terms for technical subjects. We'll take a very brief look at the definitions, because you might run across them.

Error-Correcting Modems

Modem performance is measured by which standard it uses, and how well it implements that standard. In real practice, what matters most is the speed (in *bits per second* or *bps*) at which you can transfer information, and how much error correction the modem will do to cope with a poor phone line. Nearly every modem you buy today is an error-correcting modem.

Error-correction refers to how much effort the modem expends to protect you from a noisy telephone line. During every file transfer, your modem checks with the modem at the other end of the phone line. The "conversation" goes something like this:

(C)   **Your modem:** Here's some data!...Did you get that? I sent 512 bytes.

(C)   **Their Modem:** Hey, look at this neat data!...Yeah, I got 512 bytes.

(C)   **Your Modem:** Great!...Here's some more data.

The conversation between the two modems continues until the file is transferred.

If the other modem says it got 500 or 550 bytes, your modem can determine that something is amiss. Usually, your modem will tell the other modem that the data will be resent, and then your modem will again send the data (called a *packet*). Every packet of information is checked. If the line quality is poor, the modems will automatically reduce the transmission speed until the data can be reliably transferred.

Of course, modems aren't as wordy as people usually are (thank goodness). Modems use terms such as *ACK* (for acknowledgment) and *NAK* (for a negative acknowledgment—for example, if a problem or miscommunication occurs).

Understanding Data Compression

When you see references to modem hardware that uses *data compression*, it refers to the modem reducing the number of data bits used to convey a specific piece of information. Secretarial shorthand does the same thing, for those of us who still remember how to use a pencil.

How much data compression the modem can perform varies greatly, depending on the nature of the information you send. Text files, spreadsheets, word processing documents, and other "data" files compress better than do programs and files that have been compressed by other means. The amount of data that a modem can transfer is called *throughput*.

Using Modem Protocols

The word *protocol* gets bandied about a lot in telecommunications, but it's really just being used as it is in normal English. Protocols are the standards, or rules, for how something gets done. The protocol for how to address the President of the United States is very strict, as is the protocol for referring to your mother-in-law (that is, if you want to stay married).

Several protocols that are used in the world of modems include the following:

- ℂ **Modulation protocols.** Modulation protocols, such as the V.32bis protocol, define the rules for how a high-speed modem communicates.

- ℂ **Data compression protocols.** Data compression protocols, such as MNP/5, specify the rules about how a modem compresses and decompresses data as it sends and receives it.

- ℂ **File transfer protocols.** File transfer protocols, such as Xmodem and Kermit, define how data files are processed by your communications program (*not* the modem).

There are so many meanings for the word "protocol" that it's easy to get lost. The biggest difference is between file transfer protocols and everything else. In most cases, you'll be able to figure out which "protocol" is meant from the context. If the discussion is about moving files from one place to another (managed by software), the speaker is referring to file transfer protocols. If the conversation is about hardware, then the protocols being talked about are modulation or data compression protocols.

Line Settings

Communications software uses a combination of settings to determine how it will send and receive data. This section will be covered quickly, because the question of "which settings to use" has a standard answer.

It's My Parity and I'll Cry If I Want To

Parity checking is a technique used to detect memory or communications errors. The setting may be even, odd, or none. (There's an explanation for the three settings, but it's long and boring and doesn't really matter.)

Data Bits

Some services use seven bits to store each character; others use eight.

Stop Bits

A *stop bit* is a bit inserted into the data to inform the receiving system that the transmission of a byte has been completed.

A Duplex With a View

Communications can be sent full duplex or half duplex. The setting of this protocol defines if the remote computer will echo characters back to the sender. IIff yyoouu sseeee ttyyppee lliikkee tthhiiss, that means that you need to change your duplex setting.

Don't worry about this too much: there are unofficial standards for what to use. BBSs usually use 8/N/1, which is a shorthand way of saying that they use eight data bits, no parity, and one stop bit. CompuServe uses 7/E/1, or seven data bits, even parity, and one stop bit.

If you dial into any other well-known service, the software will either define these settings for you, or they will make it exceedingly clear which settings to use in their documentation. When in doubt, use 8/N/1.

S-Registers

The *S-registers* store configuration information of different kinds. You can change the settings if you need to.

Handshaking

When your modem dials the phone and connects with another modem, the two modems go through a process of meeting-and-greeting that is very similar to a business introduction. The modems have to agree on what protocol to use—for example, the speed they will use when communicating, and so on.

Two people can't talk at the same time and expect that they will communicate well. One person has to be listening while the other one talks, otherwise, information is lost. Similarly, modems have to be able to figure out when to stop sending and when to start receiving. The process of controlling the flow between two modems—a process that enables one modem to transmit only when the other device is ready—is called *handshaking*.

Part 2:

Learning about Modem Software

Installing and Using the Modem Software

Making a Call: A Quick Tour

Learning More about Communications Software

Chapter 6

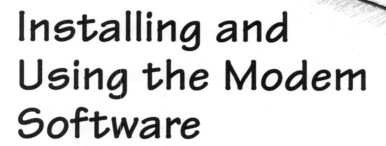

Installing and Using the Modem Software

A modem without software is about as useful as a kitchen without food. This chapter will help you to install the software that is included on the book's disk.

The instructions here are purposefully minimal; as you proceed through the next chapters, you'll find detailed instructions on how to use the software. This chapter exists just to get you started; don't worry if you aren't an expert by the end!

If you already have a modem installed, you might have skipped ahead to this chapter because you figured that you don't need to mess with the hardware. Just make sure that you know what com port your modem is using, because you'll need to have that information handy. If you don't know what I mean by a com port, read through Chapters 1 through 5 until you do.

About the Bonus Disk Software

This book includes a disk that contains a Test Drive version of Hilgraeve's HyperACCESS for Windows, a popular communications program. You can use the program to call other systems, answer calls, transfer files, and automate many everyday communication tasks. The limitations of this version won't get in your way (at least not very much) while you learn how to use your modem. After all, when you were taking Driver's Ed, you probably didn't care if the training car had a V-8 or a V-6 engine. You were kept busy enough just getting into first gear.

The purpose of the HyperACCESS Test Drive included with this book is to enable you to try HyperACCESS for Windows before you buy it. Every feature that is included in the real, commercial product is included in this Test Drive. Because the Test Drive is not intended to be used for sustained, day-to-day use, Test Drive discards user-defined settings after each session and limits sessions to 3 calls or one hour. The commercial product does not do this, of course.

If you want to order the full-blown version of HyperACCESS for Windows, or you would like to buy a DOS or OS/2 version, see the coupons at the back of this book for an exclusive offer.

The full version of HyperACCESS for Windows includes the following features, left out of this limited version:

- User's manual and application programming interface manual

- Full-blown program that enables you to save your settings and have sessions for unlimited amounts of time

- Disks

- Technical support

Installing HyperACCESS for Windows

When you *install* software, you copy it onto your hard disk and change the settings to the ones that you prefer. It's just like installing a new gas grill; you can't use it right out of the box. You have to put together the pieces and lose most of the screws under the porch before you can cook a steak. Then you have to adjust the settings so that the grill will fit into the place you have reserved for it. Putting together a new gas grill is a three-beer job. Fortunately, installing software usually doesn't take more than a small mug of hot chocolate. (Of course, "a small mug," to a chocoholic, is about the size of a beer keg.)

Throughout this installation, I'll assume that your disk drive is called drive A, and that your hard disk is drive C. If your disk drive is B or your hard disk is D (mine is; you don't have to be embarrassed), just substitute those letters in the instructions.

To install the communications program, follow these steps:

1. Start Windows, if it's not already running. If you don't have Windows, you will not be able to use the HyperACCESS for Windows Test Drive. You should, however, be able to follow along by reading the text and looking at the illustrations.

2. Put the *New Riders' Guide to Modems* bonus disk in the appropriate floppy disk drive.

3. Start Windows File Manager by double-clicking on the icon in Program Manager. It's usually in the Main group.

4. Create a new directory (use the Create Directory command on the File menu) on your system to store the HyperACCESS files in. Use any directory name that you want as long as it is no more than 8 characters long and is not the same name as another directory on your system.

   I made a directory named HYPER to store all the files in (see fig. 6.1).

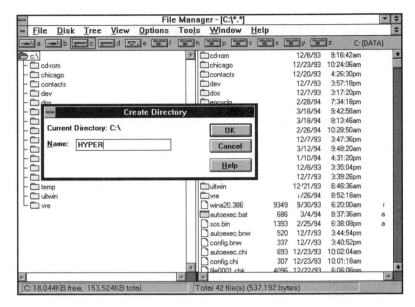

Figure 6.1

Creating a directory to store HyperACCESS Test Drive.

5. You now need to copy the HAWTD1.EXE file from the bonus disk into the new directory on your hard drive. To do this, double-click on the drive icon where the bonus disk is, such as the A icon. Next, select the **W**indow menu and choose the **T**ile command. This enables you to see both your hard drive and floppy disk windows at the same time (see fig. 6.2).

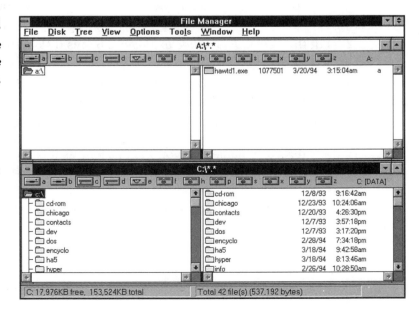

Figure 6.2

Tiling the drive windows to make copying easier.

6. Drag the HAWTD1.EXE file from the floppy disk window into the directory on your hard drive where you want to store it. In my case, I dragged it into my HYPER directory.

7. The HAWTD1.EXE file is called a *self-extracting* ZIP file, which is a fancy way of saying that it expands automatically. To expand it, double-click on the file in File Manager. Your computer should make a little noise while all the files are expanding.

8. Press F5 to refresh the screen so you can see all of the files. Figure 6.3 shows all the files that are in the HAWTD1.EXE file.

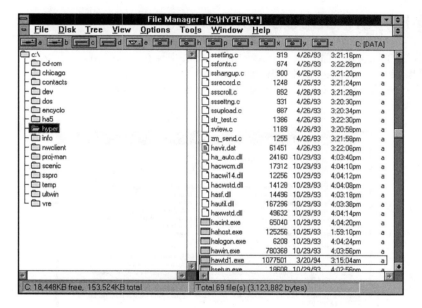

Figure 6.3

Showing the expanded files in HAWTD1.EXE.

You now can start HyperACCESS Test Drive by making a program item (icon) in Program Manager. To do this, click on a program group where you would like to have the icon reside, such as Accessories. Next, select the New option from the File menu. Click on OK to create a Program Item and type the path where you have placed HyperACCESS in the Command Line box. If, for example, you placed the Test Drive in a directory named HYPER, you need to type the following statement:

```
C:\HYPER\HAWIN.EXE
```

The file named at the end of the preceding syntax is needed regardless of what directory you place the files in. HAWIN.EXE is the main file that runs HyperACCESS for Windows. Be sure to place it in your path when you fill in the Command Line box.

After you fill in the **C**ommand Line box, click on OK. The HyperACCESS icon should appear in the selected program group.

Starting HyperACCESS Test Drive

You can start HyperACCESS by double-clicking on its icon. The HyperACCESS information screen as shown in figure 6.4 appears on-screen. This screen repeats the limitations and usage requirements for the Test Drive. Click on O**K** to remove this screen and to start HyperACCESS.

Figure 6.4

The HyperACCESS Information screen.

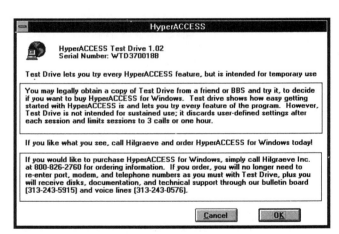

Each time you start it, Test Drive runs a setup utility that lets you set up the program for your modem and computer for that session. The following steps show you how to set up and configure Test Drive for use:

1. In the Connection dialog box (see fig. 6.5), you need to tell HyperACCESS the type of communications port, the name of the port, and the modem type that you have.

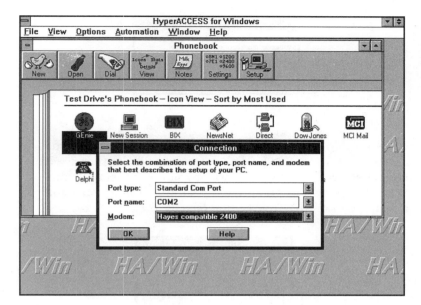

Figure 6.5

Telling Test Drive your connection information.

2. In the Port **t**ype field, click on the down arrow and select the type of port you have. If you are not sure what type you have, select the Standard Com Port setting. If you are using a laptop computer that uses a PCMCIA modem (you'll know if you're using one of these), select the PCMCIA Card with Card Manager option.

3. In the Port **n**ame field, click on the down arrow and select the COM number that your modem is set at. If you have a mouse (which you probably do since you are using Windows), your modem is probably set up for COM2. Select the appropriate port name.

4. In the **M**odem field, click on the down arrow and select the name of the modem you have. If you can't find the exact name of your modem, select one that emulates yours. You can find this information in your modem documentation. If you are still not sure, select the Hayes compatible option for the baud rate of your modem.

5. Click on OK.

6. If the Baud Rate dialog box appears (see fig. 6.6), simply click on OK. This dialog box recommends the highest speed that your modem should work at. For now, click on OK.

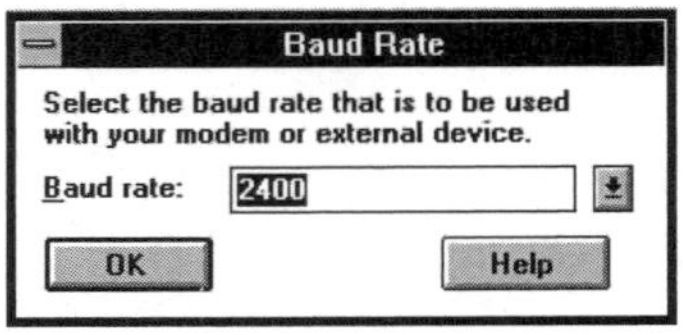

Figure 6.6

The Baud Rate dialog box, recommending the top speed for your modem.

7. You now need to tell HyperACCESS the type of dialing method your modem is using. You probably have tone dialing service (the numbers beep rather than pulse when you press them). If you have only pulse dialing, you probably know it already, so if you aren't sure, choose the **T**one option (see fig. 6.7).

Figure 6.7

You need to tell HyperACCESS the type of dialing method you have.

8. The next choice you have is to enter a dialing prefix, if you have one. Usually, businesses must dial a 9 for outside calls. If this is the case, enter **9** in the **D**ialing Prefix field and click on OK. If you don't have a prefix, simply click on OK.

9. The Transfer Directories dialog box enables you to set the directories on your computer where you want to send and receive files from and to (see fig. 6.8). If you leave these areas blank, the default directory is used, which is the one where you have the Test Drive stored. Click on OK when you are finished.

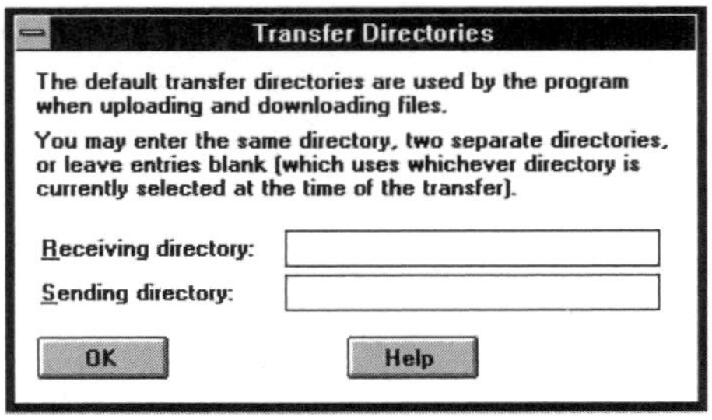

Figure 6.8

Specifying the default directories for receiving and sending files.

At this point, a dialog box appears on-screen that tells you that HyperACCESS is set up and ready to use. Click on OK.

Making a Quick Call with Test Drive

At this point, you should see the main HyperACCESS screen. In this screen is the Phonebook, which enables you to call several popular BBS systems or even to set up your own phonebook entries. As you already know, the Test Drive program enables you to set up these entries, but you cannot save them. You must order the complete copy of HyperACCESS for this feature.

Chapter 9 discusses in more detail the different types of BBS systems that are available, including CompuServe, Prodigy, and America Online.

The following steps show you how to make a quick call to a BBS, in this case the Hilgraeve technical support BBS. Note that, unless you live around Monroe, Michigan, this is a long-distance call for most readers. Use a local BBS number if you want to try out the Test Drive without paying toll charges.

1. In the Phonebook area of HyperACCESS, double-click on the HA/Win Host icon. This displays a Warning dialog box that tells you that it cannot be run. Click on OK. All you have to do is tell it its phone number.

2. In the Telephone Number dialog box, enter the number 1-313-243-5915 (see fig. 6.9). This is the Hilgraeve BBS phone number. Click on **D**ial.

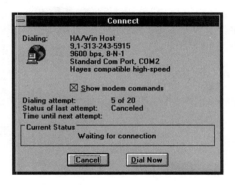

Figure 6.9

Filling in the Hilgraeve BBS phone number.

3. The Connect dialog box displays and your modem should start dialing the number.

The Hilgraeve BBS is a busy one, so you might have to try it a number of times before you get an answer. You should keep trying if you want to practice using Test Drive on this BBS system.

Chapter 7 takes you on a more complete tour of the Hilgraeve BBS using the DOS and OS/2 versions of HyperACCESS. If you are interested in purchasing a copy of HyperACCESS for Windows, see the exclusive offer at the back of this book.

About HyperACCESS/5

Not included with this book is a copy of HyperACCESS/5, which is a DOS version of HyperACCESS. This section shows you how to set up and configure this software so you can see how a DOS-based modem application is configured.

The full version of HyperACCESS/5 includes the following features, left out of this limited version:

- The full 352-page HyperACCESS/5 manual.

- Unlimited telephone support from Hilgraeve.

- Full HyperPilot script language, compiler, and documentation for complex automation tasks. (We'll mention script languages in the next chapter, though this book doesn't cover them.)

- Additional terminal emulators, including ADDS Viewpoint, ADM3A, IBM3101, IBM3278, TV925, TV950, VT220, VT320, and Wang terminal emulators. (We'll talk about terminal emulators more in Chapter 12, "Beyond BBSs and Online Services.")

- Electronic Mail in the Answer Mode.

- HyperGuard—built-in, on-the-fly anti-virus protection.

     ℭ   HyperTerminal emulator, which lets you run programs on remote PCs that also have HyperACCESS/5.

     ℭ   Zmodem file recovery.

If you decide to buy a full version of HyperACCESS/5 for DOS, see the exclusive offer at the back of this book.

If you use Windows, exit it before you install HyperACCESS/5.

Throughout this installation, I'll assume that your disk drive is called drive A, and that your hard disk is drive C. If your disk drive is B or your hard disk is D, just substitute those letters in the instructions.

To install the communications program, follow these steps:

1. Put the disk in your disk drive. Tell your computer to access drive A by typing the following, then pressing Enter:

    `C:> A:`

2. At this point, `A:>` should appear. The next step is to tell the installation program to start. (The installation program is an application, just like a communications program or a spreadsheet or word processing program; it's just a very specialized one.) Type the following, then press Enter:

    INSTALL

3. HyperACCESS/5 will start its installation program, and will ask you to specify where (on which hard disk and in which subdirectory) it should set up the program (see fig. 6.10). You can change the drive and directory if you like by typing in a different name; I changed it from C:\HA5 to D:\HA5BOOK, just because I'm ornery. You'll probably be happy with C:\HA5. Press Enter.

4. Next, you get to choose your modem from a long list. The list will be longer than the one in figure 6.11, and it's almost certain that you'll find your modem name and model on this list.

Figure 6.10

Starting the HyperACCESS/5 installation.

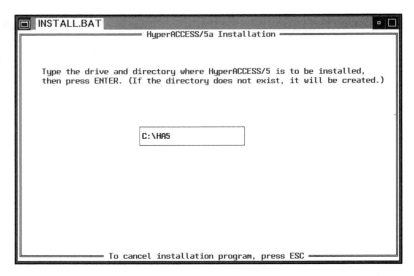

Figure 6.11

Choosing your modem.

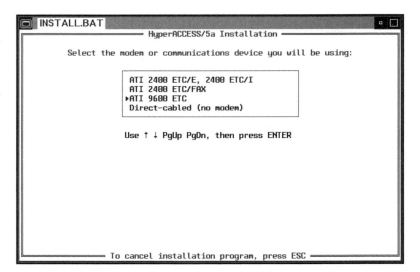

If your modem isn't included in the list of modems here, either choose a model that sounds really similar (really, really similar), or consult your modem manual to see what modem brand and model it emulates (or "acts just like"—a teenager can emulate a human being, with a great deal of effort).

If you're really stuck, choose a Hayes model that corresponds to the speed of your modem (2400 bps, if that's what you have).

To choose the modem, use the arrow keys or press PageUp and PageDn to move through the list and highlight the choices. Press Enter when you find your modem.

5. Your next choice is between tone and pulse dialing. You probably have tone dialing service (the numbers beep rather than pulse when you press them). If you have only pulse dialing, you probably know it already, so if you aren't sure, choose T for Tone, as shown in figure 6.12.

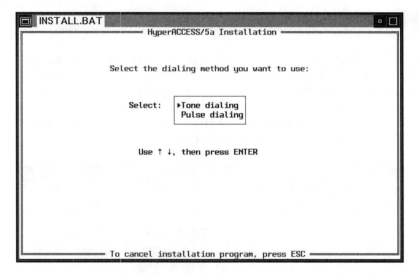

Figure 6.12

Choosing tone or pulse dialing.

6. In the next screen, HyperACCESS/5 asks you to type in the name of the communications port (also known as serial port) which you'll be using with the modem. (At this point, you can puff up your chest and feel just a bit proud; because you read through the earlier chapters, you actually understand what it's talking about!) Type:

    COM1

and press Enter (see fig. 6.13). Of course, if you're using COM2, COM3, or COM4, type the right one in instead.

Figure 6.13

Choosing a COM port.

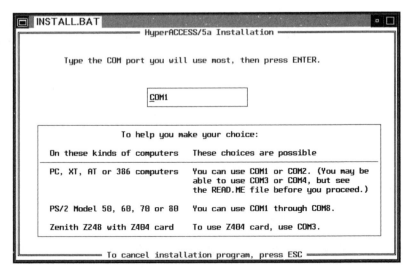

7. HyperACCESS/5 lets you set up the display in any color combination you like. In the screen shown in figure 6.14, you can choose the one to start with. When you feel like experimenting later, you can change the color combination to burnt orange on puce, if that's what makes your heart beat faster. (Look in the Preferences section, later on, if you want to do that.)

Figure 6.14

Choosing a color configuration.

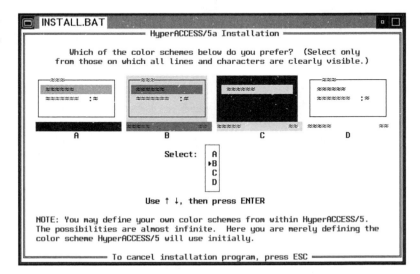

At this point, the installation program will copy several files from the floppy disk. (You can see a sample of this not-terribly-thrilling experience in figure 6.15.) It will take only a few minutes, but this is a good time to pet your cat or to refill your mug of hot chocolate.

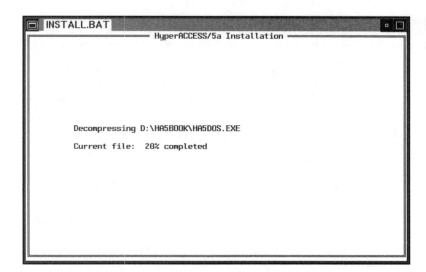

Figure 6.15
Copying files.

HyperACCESS/5 will copy several files to your hard disk. It will then display a few informative messages, and the installation program will end.

Using HyperACCESS/5

Now that the software is installed, you can put away the floppy disk. From now on, we'll use the copy of HyperACCESS/5 that you just installed onto your hard disk.

HyperACCESS/5 runs from its own subdirectory on your hard disk. You have to focus your computer's attention on that directory, or the program won't find the files it needs. Assuming that your hard disk is named C: and you installed HyperACCESS/5 in the HA5 subdirectory, type the following, then press Enter:

`CD \HA5`

To start the program, type the following and press Enter:

HA5DOS

HyperACCESS/5 will start, and will *initialize* (set up) its settings. In a moment, you'll be presented with a screen that looks like figure 6.16.

Figure 6.16

The HyperACCESS/5 Main Menu.

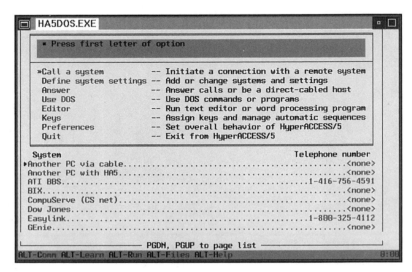

```
┌─────────────────────────────────────────────────────────────────┐
│ ▢  HA5DOS.EXE                                             ▫ ▢     │
├─────────────────────────────────────────────────────────────────┤
│  ┌───────────────────────────────────────────────────────────┐  │
│  │  ▪ Press first letter of option                           │  │
│  │                                                           │  │
│  │ »Call a system          -- Initiate a connection with a remote system │
│  │  Define system settings -- Add or change systems and settings │
│  │  Answer                 -- Answer calls or be a direct-cabled host │
│  │  Use DOS                -- Use DOS commands or programs    │  │
│  │  Editor                 -- Run text editor or word processing program │
│  │  Keys                   -- Assign keys and manage automatic sequences │
│  │  Preferences            -- Set overall behavior of HyperACCESS/5 │
│  │  Quit                   -- Exit from HyperACCESS/5        │  │
│  └───────────────────────────────────────────────────────────┘  │
│  ┌───────────────────────────────────────────────────────────┐  │
│  │   System                                 Telephone number │  │
│  │ ▸Another PC via cable...........................<none>     │  │
│  │  Another PC with HA5............................<none>     │  │
│  │  ATI BBS..............................1-416-756-4591       │  │
│  │  BIX............................................<none>     │  │
│  │  CompuServe (CS net)............................<none>     │  │
│  │  Dow Jones......................................<none>     │  │
│  │  Easylink.............................1-800-325-4112       │  │
│  │  GEnie..........................................<none>     │  │
│  └───── PGDN, PGUP to page list ──────────────────────────────┘  │
│ ALT-Comm ALT-Learn ALT-Run ALT-Files ALT-Help           8:00    │
└─────────────────────────────────────────────────────────────────┘
```

You can run HyperACCESS/5 from within Windows. You'll need to create a PIF file to do so, though. This sample version doesn't supply a pre-configured PIF file, though the full version does.

You can also run HyperACCESS/5 from OS/2. Create a program object for it by dragging a Program template to the desktop from the Templates folder. Add the file information as you normally would. Under DOS settings, however, make sure that you specify that the COM_SELECT setting should hold onto the COM port you're using until you exit the program. A few times, I've tried to send a fax during a download, and OS/2's capability to tell me that the COM port was already in use saved me quite a bit of time.

Changing Preferences

The installation should have configured the program just the way you wanted, but it doesn't hurt to double-check. Besides, you might want to change a few of these settings some day.

From HyperACCESS/5's main menu, Choose **P** for Preferences. You'll see a screen like the one in figure 6.17.

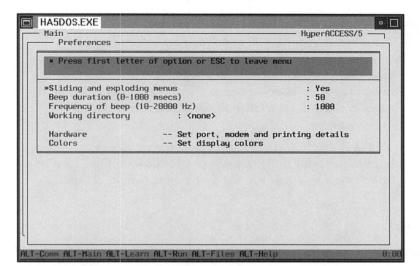

Figure 6.17

Changing options in HyperACCESS/5.

The first few settings are just fine; you don't need to change them unless you really hate the beep that the program uses.

HyperACCESS/5 lets you choose where to store files that you download. If you don't specify otherwise, it will store them in the directory where HyperACCESS/5 is running. That's messy. When you want to find that cool game you downloaded from America Online, or when you want to check on the transcript of the online conference that you grabbed from a BBS, you'll have to search through all the modem and program files.

Create a directory on your hard disk that is explicitly for downloaded files. You'll know, simply because they're in there, that they came from somewhere else.

Also, clean out that directory often. Think of it as a garage. You can store stuff there temporarily, but if you don't maintain it, you could accumulate an impressive amount of files. Worse, you won't have a clue where they came from or whether you should keep them around.

Of course, I'm most guilty of that particular sin. I have eight megabytes of stuff in my own download directory as I write this, and I have no idea whatsoever what the file named futhr.zip is doing there. On the other hand, I have boxes in the garage that have never been unpacked since we moved here.

To change where HyperACCESS/5 stores your downloaded files, type **W** for Working Directory. Then type the full path name, like one of the following:

```
C:\download

D:\HA5\files
```

To check the hardware settings, choose **H** for Hardware from the same Preferences menu. As shown in figure 6.18, HyperACCESS/5 will display three choices: Communications port, Modem, and Printer.

Type **C** to see the communications port setting. It will probably show the COM1 you chose during installation (or another com port if you picked a different serial port). If it doesn't, choose **P** for Port and type in COM1 (or whichever one you'll be using with your modem). Then press Esc to return to the previous menu.

Type **H** for Hardware again, and this time type **M** for modem. Verify that the modem selection is the one you chose during installation, and that the phone is correctly set to tone or pulse. (If you bought a new modem, this is where you'd change the settings for it.) If necessary, make changes by

typing the highlighted letter of the menu choice, as you can see in figure
6.19. To return to the previous menu when you're finished, press Esc.

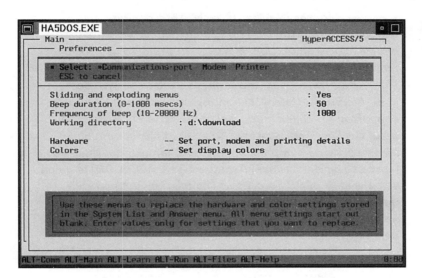

Figure 6.18

*Changing hardware
settings.*

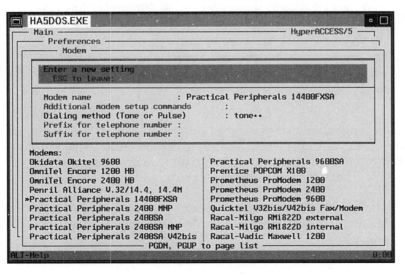

Figure 6.19

*Changing a modem
setting.*

Why does it matter so much which modem you choose? Aren't they all basically the same?

Well, yes. Mostly. It's the "mostly" that can bite you, though. Almost any modem you buy today will work with a simple Hayes emulation. However, in order to get the best possible performance out of them, each of the manufacturers has tuned their modems to work best with certain commands. That's how the manufacturers stay competitive, after all. These manufacturers make sure that they send the Way Cool settings to each of the communications software companies, so that the right settings get used at the right times. Because HyperACCESS/5 is going to take care of 99 percent of the modem command-issuing for you, it makes sense to be sure that the software and hardware can work together as efficiently as possible.

Besides, if you don't, you'll probably have a couple of nasty surprises. Nasty surprises could include modem connections that suddenly disappear, or file transfers that quit prematurely. However, these situations could be caused by plenty of other things besides the wrong settings, making the problem that much more annoying when it happens. So you might as well choose the right modem setting in the first place.

You can also change the settings for your printer by typing **P** for Printer in the hardware configuration menu. Other than demonstrating that you can print from within the communications program, you probably won't do it often in real life. There are more efficient ways to grab text.

When you're finished making changes to your setup, press Esc to return to the Main Menu. HyperACCESS/5 will confirm that you really want to save the changes (see fig. 6.20).

Is It Working?

At this point, you're ready to get to work. If your modem is hooked up correctly, and you made all the right choices in installing the software,

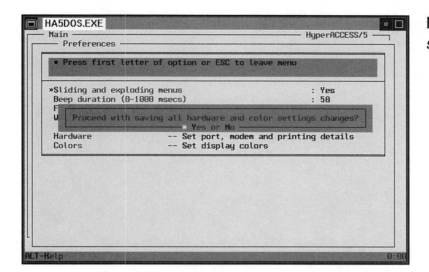

Figure 6.20
Saving changes.

you can go ahead and start calling BBSs and other services.

However, that assumes that your modem *is* hooked up correctly and that you made all the right choices, doesn't it? You'll need to check before you do anything else.

Press Alt+C to change from the menu screen to the communications screen. It's just a blank screen, with a single line at the bottom showing you some more options. Once you're actively communicating with another modem, the blank screen will fill up soon enough.

To find out if everything is connected right, type the following and press Enter. It's important that you type this in all uppercase!

    ATDT

(If your phone is pulse dial, type **ATDP** instead.)

You should hear a dial tone coming from your modem. Once that happens, hit Enter to hang up the phone. The modem will respond with OK, as you see in figure 6.21.

Figure 6.21

Testing the modem.

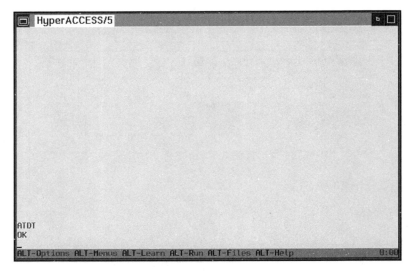

Aren't you glad you used Dial Tone?

Bummer. You tried that ATDT stuff, but you didn't get a dial tone. What's wrong?

There are three possibilities:

1. *You have the communications program set to the wrong com port. For instance, you told HyperACCESS/5 to use COM1 and your modem is really on COM2. Change the setting in HyperACCESS/ 5 and try again. There are only four choices, so trying this with COM3 and COM4 wouldn't hurt if COM2 doesn't work either.*

2. *You have the phone lines plugged in backwards. You think this sounds dumb, don't you? Check it out. It happens all the time.*

3. *You have a hardware problem. You didn't want to read that, did you? Go to the Troubleshooting Chapter. (Do not pass GO, do not collect $200.)*

This should reassure you: the problem is most likely to be either of the first two problems.

Dialing Directories

Almost every communications program comes with a dialing directory of telephone numbers. It works very much like a Rolodex; you choose the name of the service you want to dial, and the program dials the associated telephone number.

HyperACCESS/5's directory has a few BBSs and services already set up. You could dial any of these services all day long and probably have a good time. But, like the typist who placed an ad in the paper that said, "Can type *Now is the time for all good men to come to the aid of their party* at 95 words per minute. Willing to learn other phrases," eventually you will want to call a service that isn't listed here.

Adding an Entry

To add an entry to HyperACCESS/5's directory, use the following steps:

1. Choose **D**efine System Settings, then **A**dd, as you see in figure 6.22.

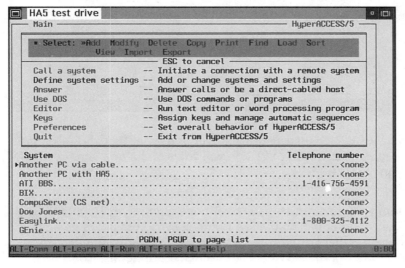

Figure 6.22

Adding a new directory entry.

2. Type in the name of the new service, **Practical Peripherals' BBS** (or as much as will fit) as you see in figure 6.14, then press Enter.

You could add any service here that you like. But since you will call the Practical Peripherals' BBS in Chapter 8, you might as well add it now.

You could type in anything here, since this name identifies the service just for you; **My favorite BBS** or **Schroedinger's Cat-Sitting Service** are just as good, if they mean something to you.

Figure 6.23

Adding the name of the directory entry.

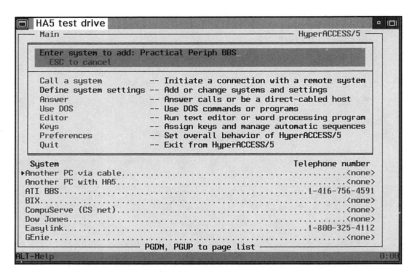

3. HyperACCESS/5 will accept whatever you type (that shows remarkable judgment, doesn't it?), and will show you a new screen, like the one in figure 6.24.

The only item you *must* adjust is the telephone number, or HyperACCESS/ 5 won't know what number to dial. (A Rolodex is useless full of names without phone numbers or addresses.) Choose **T**elephone number and type in the number of the service. For Practical Peripherals' BBS, enter **1 (805) 496-5916**, and press Enter. Notice that, as with any other long-distance telephone call, you need to add the "1". (If you're lucky enough to live in the same area code as Practical Peripherals, you could just type **496-5916**.)

Even though I just told you to enter 1 (805) 496-5916, you didn't really have to enter all of it. The parenthesis, dash, and spaces are just there to make it easier for you to read. The modem doesn't care about them. It just pays attention to numbers; you could have typed 18054965916, and it would have been just as happy.

Remember this when you're given a phone number that "spells" something, such as 1-800-WHOKNOWS. Your modem will ignore anything that isn't a number, so you have to give it all numeric digits.

Also, if you first have to dial 9 to get an outside telephone line from an office or hotel, add a comma. The modem will interpret the "," as an instruction to wait two seconds— enough time for the office or hotel phone to switch to the regular phone line. The phone number would look like this: 9,1 (805) 496-5916.

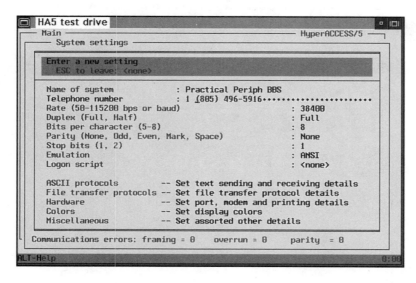

Figure 6.24

Entering the tele- phone number.

4. Choose **F**ile Transfer Protocols. HyperACCESS/5 will display something that looks like figure 6.25, with a list of the protocols available. We'll discuss what these mean in the next chapter, so don't worry about them. Just choose **Z**modem for now.

Figure 6.25

Choosing a file transfer protocol.

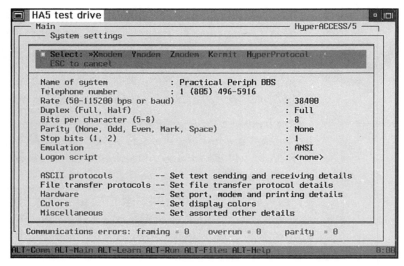

5. Press Esc to return to the previous screen. Press Esc a second time to return to HyperACCESS/5's main menu, which will now display the entry you just created (see fig. 6.26) in its alphabetized list.

Figure 6.26

Hey, great! There's a new entry here!

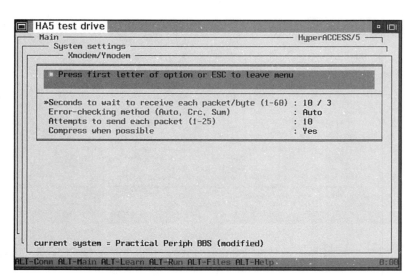

If you want to take a break, press **Q** to quit the program. (Alt+X will usually let you exit, as well.)

About the Windows Version of HyperACCESS/5

If you prefer to use Windows communications programs (they *are* prettier), call Hilgraeve at (313) 243-0576 to ask for the Windows Test Drive. (Figure 6.27 gives you an idea what it looks like.)

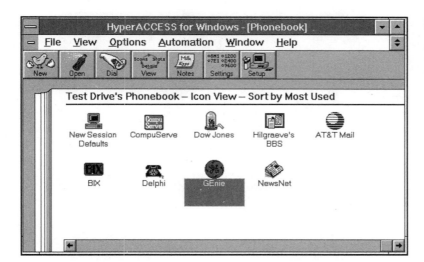

Figure 6.27

HyperACCESS for Windows.

The Test Drive disk has limitations; that's why it's only a test drive, after all. In particular, you have to reenter your modem name and other settings every time you start the program, and the test drive will work for only a limited period of time. But if you use Windows as your primary operating environment, you may be happier with a Windows communications program.

Chapter 7

Making a Call:
A Quick Tour

You have read all of the preceding chapters, and you're anxious to put your newfound knowledge to work. Or you've become impatient, and have skipped ahead. In any case, this chapter helps you get online—finally!

When you start a new job, the first things you want to learn are the location of the rest room, the time that everyone goes to lunch, and how soon payday arrives. After you understand those vital items, you are ready to get to work.

This chapter takes a similar approach, providing "the nickel tour" of an electronic bulletin board service. (From now on, we'll call a bulletin board service a *BBS*.) At this point, the idea is to get you working with the modem and the communications program. After the tour, you will have time to revisit each of the services available, and to learn in more detail about what everything means.

Dialing a BBS

If you haven't already done so, start HyperACCESS/5 for DOS. (We'll call it HA/5 hereafter, just for brevity.) You'll see HA/5's main menu (see fig. 7.1). At the top of the screen are the different features that you can use. At the bottom of the screen is the dialing directory—the electronic equivalent of a rolodex.

Figure 7.1

The HyperACCESS/5 Main Menu.

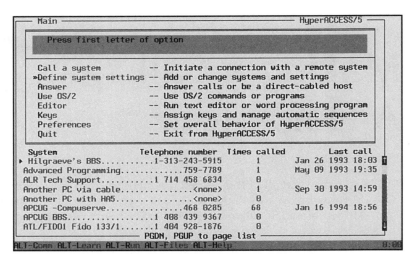

```
┌─ Main ──────────────────────────────────────────── HyperACCESS/5 ─┐
│                                                                    │
│    ░░Press first letter of option░░░░░░░░░░░░░░░░░░░░░░░░░░░░░░░    │
│                                                                    │
│     Call a system          -- Initiate a connection with a remote system│
│    »Define system settings -- Add or change systems and settings   │
│     Answer                 -- Answer calls or be a direct-cabled host│
│     Use OS/2               -- Use OS/2 commands or programs         │
│     Editor                -- Run text editor or word processing program│
│     Keys                  -- Assign keys and manage automatic sequences│
│     Preferences           -- Set overall behavior of HyperACCESS/5 │
│     Quit                  -- Exit from HyperACCESS/5               │
│                                                                    │
│   System            Telephone number  Times called      Last call │
│  ▸ Hilgraeve's BBS..........1-313-243-5915      1    Jan 26 1993 18:03│
│   Advanced Programming............759-7789      1    May 09 1993 19:35│
│   ALR Tech Support..........1 714 458 6834      0                  │
│   Another PC via cable..............<none>      1    Sep 30 1993 14:59│
│   Another PC with HA5...............<none>      0                  │
│   APCUG -Compuserve................468 0285     68   Jan 16 1994 18:56│
│   APCUG BBS.................1 408 439 9367       0                  │
│   ATL/FIDO1 Fido 133/1.......1 404 928-1876     0                  │
│ ───────────────── PGDN, PGUP to page list ────────────────────    │
│ALT-Comm ALT-Learn ALT-Run ALT-Files ALT-Help              0:00    │
└────────────────────────────────────────────────────────────────────┘
```

In the examples in this book, I am using the full version of HyperACCESS/5 for OS/2 or HyperACCESS/5 for DOS. (The text mode applications are identical.) You also can use HyperACCESS/5 for Windows, or even another program entirely. If you do, you will need to know the phone number for Hilgraeve's BBS so that you can follow along: 1-313-243-5915.

Don't forget the "1" when you add the phone number to the dialing directory; you will need that for long distance just as you do when you make a voice call.

In this chapter, you dial into Hilgraeve's own support BBS. To dial the number, simply select `Call a System`. You can do this by typing **C**, by using the arrow keys to highlight the menu option and pressing Enter, or by clicking on the option with the mouse. Any of those three options will work. Select `Data Call`. Your screen will look like the one in figure 7.2.

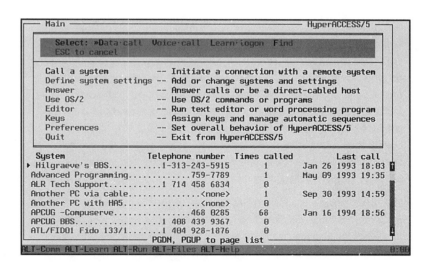

Figure 7.2
Making a data call.

Choose Hilgraeve's BBS. You might need to move the arrow keys up and down until the BBS name is highlighted, but when you have done so, pressing Enter will select it. Your screen will look something like the one in figure 7.3.

Figure 7.3
Choosing which BBS to call.

In this chapter, you use the technical support BBS of the folks who make the software you're using. Hey, it's only fair. Besides, using one known BBS means that the figures in this book will match what you see on your screen—at least approximately. As you'll learn when you get to the BBS chapter, each BBS is customized to a certain degree, and what you see on the screen of one BBS will not necessarily look that much like another. After you have seen a few BBSs, this won't bother you at all, but for your first time, it helps to be consistent.

The only problem with the idea of suggesting that you call into Hilgraeve's BBS is that, unless you're lucky enough to live in or near Monroe, Michigan (I'm not; I prefer to remain warm in the winter and snicker at people who shovel snow), the call will be a long distance one. It shouldn't cost you much if you call during evening hours or on the weekend, however. The call you make in this chapter will be a short one, so when you receive your phone bill, the charge will probably be small. If you expect to use BBSs often, be forewarned that your long distance bill might begin to look like the national debt.

If cost is an issue, you can consider calling a local BBS. Look at the list of recommended BBSs in Appendix A to see if there's one close by, or find out if your local computer user's group has a BBS (most do). It's your (ahem) call. Just realize that what you see on the screen won't look like what you see in the pictures here.

After you select Hilgraeve's BBS, the screen will clear. HA/5 will give your modem some setup codes, which will take a moment. The screen will clear again, then you'll see the modem's dialing string appear on your screen; it will probably look like the one in figure 7.4. You'll hear the phone actually dial—wow! (Look, Ma, no hands!)

The Hilgraeve BBS is a busy one, especially on a Friday night when most normal people go on dates. (I've done case studies on this topic, unfortunately.) If you do get a busy signal, HA/5 will automatically keep trying until it gets through. If you want to give up, hit the Esc key. But you've come this far; you might as well let HA/5 keep trying for a while.

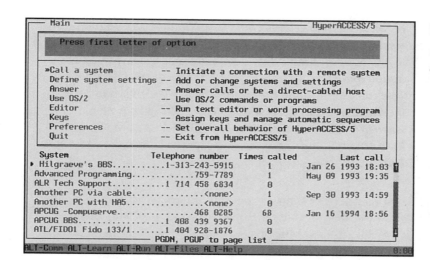

Figure 7.4

Dialing... dialing... dialing...

Dial? What Dial? Nothing happens!

If nothing happens when HA/5 tries to dial, you have a problem. If you skipped ahead to this chapter because you were bored (well! I never!), perhaps it is time to back up and read a little bit more about configuring the modem.

Watch to see if the modem responds when HA/5 gives its initialization string—you should see an OK briefly before the screen clears again. If you don't see that OK, then the modem is set to the wrong com port or configured wrong in general. If you do see the OK, but the phone doesn't make any noise whatsoever, then you probably have your phone lines plugged in backwards.

If this advice doesn't help, flip to the chapter on trouble-shooting. This also is a good point where it's handy to have a technically savvy friend nearby. And having some chocolate around can't hurt, either.

You hear the phone ring, and then hear it being picked up. The other modem will squeal. Your modem will squeal back. Then the two modems will hiss at each other for a while. (How long a while depends on the speed of your modem.) This is the process that is referred to as modem handshaking, which was defined earlier. It's a lot less intimidating than it sounded, isn't it?

Most cats believe that their True Name is the sound of an electric can opener. My cat, Max, is certain that his Name is the sound of a modem squealing—he'll run across the house and jump on my lap whenever he hears the sound. This isn't cleverness (especially from Max, who has all the intellectual prowess of a doorknob), but rather he has learned that when a modem squeals, it's a sure thing that I will sit still, and there will be a lap available for quite some time.

Within a few moments (less than 30 seconds, surely), the modems will stop hissing and will become silent. However, you'll probably see the following phrase on your screen:

```
CONNECT 9600
```

or

```
CONNECT 2400
```

or something like that. The important word is connect, because it means that the modems are connected and your computer is connected to a computer in Monroe, Michigan. Cool stuff, huh?

In this case, the connect message will scroll off your screen rather quickly. Depending on how different BBSs are set up, sometimes the message will stay on-screen long enough for you to contemplate your connectedness.

Joining the BBS

In order to use any dial-in service, you will first need to log on. *Logging on* is the process of identifying yourself to the service, as well as providing a password for access. With BBSs, your usual identification is your first and last name. With some services, your logon identification (or logon ID) is a number, similar to your telephone number.

Some BBSs permit aliases, or fake names. Aliases can be for fun, and good for privacy. (For instance, an alias would be appropriate in a BBS devoted to discussions among rape victims.) However, most BBSs expect a real name. In the examples here, I joined as Robert Tidrow because I had previously joined as me—and the point here is to learn how to join a BBS.

The BBS will prompt you for your first name. Type it in. When asked for your last name, type that in, too. Because the BBS doesn't "recognize" you (that is, it doesn't have your name in its records), you will have to join the BBS.

For commercial BBSs, joining can be a complex task. Because this is a technical support BBS, the process is pretty straightforward. (They want to make it easy for you to get help, after all.) The BBS will ask you to create a password and retype it for accuracy. (Remember your password! Write it down and keep it someplace safe.) You'll be asked for your name and address, so that the folks who run the BBS have some idea of who you are. Your screen will look similar to the one in figure 7.5. (It's cheating to use Rob's name and address; and besides, he's already joined.)

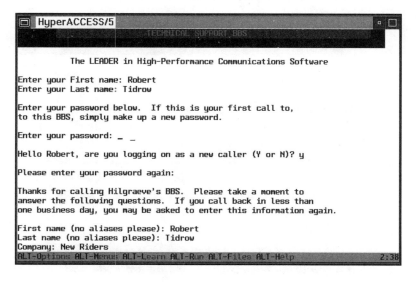

Figure 7.5

Joining the BBS.

Using Menus on the BBS

After you are a bona-fide member of the Hilgraeve BBS, the BBS will clear the screen and display a new one. (Notice that you didn't have to do anything special—the software at the other end of the phone line controls what happens on your screen.) This screen, pictured in figure 7.6, is in color, and shows the news flash. Not every BBS will have a news flash, nor will one have a flash all the time. The *news flash*, as on the radio or TV, is meant for late-breaking news or information that the sysop thinks you simply *must* have.

Figure 7.6

The BBS News Flash.

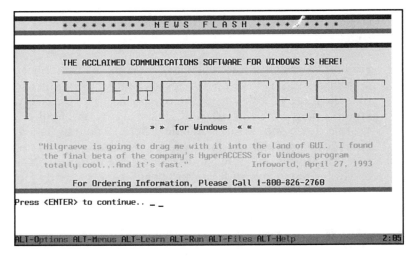

```
* * * * * * * *  N E W S   F L A S H  * * * * * * * *


      THE ACCLAIMED COMMUNICATIONS SOFTWARE FOR WINDOWS IS HERE!


      HYPERACCESS

                » »  for Windows  « «

      "Hilgraeve is going to drag me with it into the land of GUI.  I found
       the final beta of the company's HyperACCESS for Windows program
       totally cool...And it's fast."            Infoworld, April 27, 1993

             For Ordering Information, Please Call 1-800-826-2760

Press <ENTER> to continue.. _ _


ALT-Options ALT-Menus ALT-Learn ALT-Run ALT-Files ALT-Help            2:05
```

Sysop? What's a Sysop?

Sysop (pronounced sis-op) stands for system operator— the person who runs the BBS or other service. The Sysop's job is to make sure that everything is in perfect running order, that everything is exactly where it should be, and as it should be. Part of the Sysop's responsibility is to ensure that any files that are uploaded are appropriate for the service, both legally and topically.

Essentially, the Sysop is the host or manager of the electronic service. As I am a Sysop myself (though not on a BBS), it's tempting to add that Sysops are gods and goddesses, and should be treated with the same respect. Small gifts of chocolate and flowers are always welcome.

We'll cover the role of Sysops in the chapter that focuses on BBSs, later in the book.

After you read the News Flash, press Enter (just as the BBS prompts you). The screen will clear again, and this time you'll see the BBS's Main Menu.

Almost every BBS has a Main Menu of some kind. The Main Menu is where services are provided. We won't explore everything this time (in fact, we'll only skim the surface), but do take a moment to look at what's available. BBSs are usually segregated into several areas, each of which focuses on a different topic. As you can see in figure 7.7, there are separate areas for sales information, for files, and for exchanging private electronic mail with the Sysop.

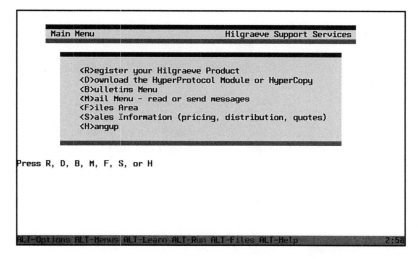

Figure 7.7

The BBS Main Menu.

In the next section, you will download a file (a short one, to keep the long-distance charges low), and sign off the BBS. When you download a file, you copy it from the remote computer (the one in the Midwest) to the one on your local computer (your own PC). We'll pay more attention to down-loading in the next chapter; right here, you'll just see what the process entails.

Downloading a File

From the Main Menu, press **F** to access the files area. The screen will clear and repaint again (this happens a lot on BBSs, and it takes longer to read here than it does to happen), this time displaying a screen that looks like the one in figure 7.8.

Figure 7.8

The Files Menu.

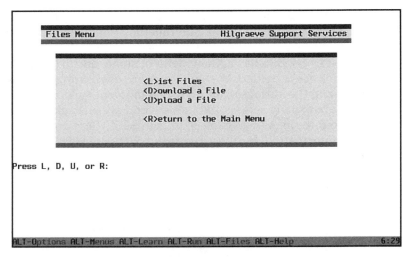

The screen shown in figure 7.8 enables you to choose between listing the files available, uploading or downloading a file, or backtracking to the previous menu (the Main Menu). Because we don't yet know what files are available to download, press **L** to tell the BBS to list the files. The screen will scroll (that is, text will be added at the bottom and disappear at the top of your screen), and display a list that looks something like the one in figure 7.9. (Depending on what files the BBS maintains, the screen may look somewhat different.)

Figure 7.9

Available files on a BBS.

```
                  Files available for Downloading
   * These are file batches.  You will receive more than one file when you
     download these names.  Receive into a directory name, not a filenme.
=======================================================================
                          HyperAccess/5 Files
=======================================================================

1   - * MODEMS1       100472  7-09-91  Latest call and answer scripts, Ver 1.x
2   - * MODEMS2       126769  9-11-92  Latest call and answer scripts, Ver 2.x
3   - * MODEMS3       134904  2-23-93  Latest call and answer scripts, Ver 3.0
4   - * MODEMS31      147708  8-30-93  Latest call and answer scripts, Ver 3.1
5   - * HA5BBS          2344  3-07-90  A set of scripts for this HA5BBS
6   - * EMAIL          35059  9-04-90  Email scripts for the HA5 Host
7   -   GETMAIL.DOC     7224  7-25-90  Retreives your mail from MCI
8   -   SWITCH.DOC      4016  2-25-91  HA5 Host example for dialing
9   -   HA-PIF.DVP       416  2-15-91  PIF file for HA5 running under DESQview
10  -   TOHA5DOS.EXE   17740  5-06-91  For HA5DOS, Version 2.x :Import PC+ info
11  -   TOHA5OS2.EXE   17576  5-01-91  For HA5OS2, Version 2.x :Import PC+ info
12  -   CAP3101.HP       241  7-24-91  Capture utility for 3101 emulation


ENTER to continue, C for Continuous, or Q to Quit:
ALT-Options ALT-Menus ALT-Learn ALT-Run ALT-Files ALT-Help          7:25
```

You can list the entire selection if you like, but let's assume that we immediately see the exact file we want: GETMAIL.DOC. Type **Q** to quit listing the files (this could continue for quite a while), then type **D** to download a file. The BBS will ask for the file name, as shown in figure 7.10; type in the full name: getmail.doc. (Capitalization doesn't matter here, although it may matter on some BBSs.)

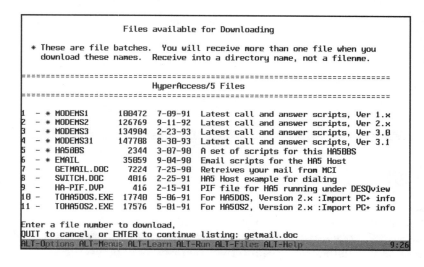

Figure 7.10

Specifying which file to download.

So far, so good.

The next thing that the Hilgraeve BBS needs to know is which file protocol to use. (We'll describe exactly what this is in the next chapter; at this point, just follow along.) The BBS will display the screen you see in figure 7.11, asking which of the available protocols to use. Type **Z** for Zmodem.

HA/5 will take over from here. Because we've chosen Zmodem as the file protocol, the software at both ends of the modem can take control. HA/5 and the BBS will establish some initialization information between them, and then a new window will open on your screen.

The numbers you see in the window will vary, depending on your modem speed and how good a connection you've established. A few minutes later (HA/5 will tell you about how long to expect), the file will complete its transmission. If everything worked well, you'll find a copy of getmail.doc on your local hard disk. (What you'll want to *do* with it, I don't know. Perhaps you'll find a reason to dial into MCI, someday.)

When HA/5 is done, the BBS will return you to the main menu.

Figure 7.11

Specifying which protocol to use.

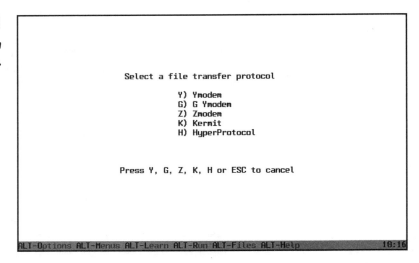

```
                    Select a file transfer protocol

                         Y) Ymodem
                         G) G Ymodem
                         Z) Zmodem
                         K) Kermit
                         H) HyperProtocol



                    Press Y, G, Z, K, H or ESC to cancel




ALT-Options ALT-Menus ALT-Learn ALT-Run ALT-Files ALT-Help          10:16
```

Ending the Call

That should be enough as a short tour—after all, you've successfully joined the BBS, interacted with the software, and downloaded a file. Now, it's time to log off. *Logging off* is the procedure of gracefully leaving the service. Just as you usually say, "Good-bye" before you hang up the phone, you need to tell the system that you're leaving, so that it can clean up after you. (If something untoward happens—you lose the connection and aren't able to log off—it isn't a terrible thing. You just want to avoid that, for the same reasons that you don't want to hang up on your boss without warning.)

Logging off is usually a very simple procedure. Here, on the Hilgraeve BBS, all you have to do is type **H**, for Hang up, at the Main Menu. When you do so, you'll see a screen much like the one in figure 7.12.

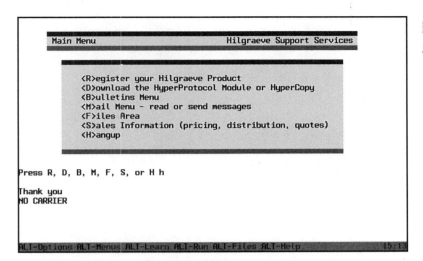

Figure 7.12
Saying good-bye.

The BBS's modem will usually disconnect from yours, and you'll see the message: NO CARRIER. In some cases, the BBS won't drop the connection. If you don't see NO CARRIER, press Alt+O (for Options), then choose **H**ang up (or type **H**), to ensure that the modem has disconnected. Then you can exit the program by typing Alt+X. You've completed your first online session!

Chapter 8

Learning
More about
Communications
Software

This chapter explains the fundamentals of modem software, including the terms that "everyone" seems to know. After you understand what's going on, your online sessions will be much more meaningful to you.

In Chapter 7, you learned to dial into one BBS and had a brief tour of what was available. When the concepts begin to make sense, you move on to apply the information in another online session, calling a different BBS.

Understanding the Hardware/ Software Relationship

Communications hardware and software each have different roles. This section explores which each does.

What the Hardware Does

In regular use, communications software tells the modem hardware what to do. By itself, a modem does absolutely nothing. It's just like a car without a driver. Like a car, the modem has built-in capabilities. A car might have four-wheel drive or air bags or a V8 engine; your modem might be 14,400 bps with V.42bis. But neither of them is going to do anything until someone or something tells it what to do.

What the Software Does

You use communications software to connect with other computers and to communicate with them after you make the connection. (The cool techie term is that you *interface* with the other computer.) So that you can reach this lofty goal, the communications software gives specific commands to the modem—under your direction. You take a look at these commands in a few minutes.

Although this setup sounds rather technical, it really isn't. You drive a car every day, which is a lot more technical than using a communications program. But you don't think about the mechanics of turning right—you just do it. Using communications software is also much safer; no matter what kind of mistakes you make, at least you can't wrap yourself around a tree.

Exploring Communications Software Concepts

Every communications program can perform several elementary tasks. More expensive programs expand on these tasks by providing more options or more control over these tasks, or they might add to the basic set. But the basic tasks are the absolute requirements.

Controlling the Modem

Any communications program enables you to give commands to the modem, either directly or through more human-understandable instructions. If you want to get down-and-dirty, you can always type

    ATZ

just to see the modem say:

    OK

(This conversation probably doesn't give you much of a thrill.) In more normal circumstances, however, you let the communications program handle the modem, and you tell the program what you want to get done. The two most usual commands you give the program are to call a service, and to hang up the phone when you're done with the call.

Almost every communications program has a dialing directory. Just like the Rolodex on your desk, a *dialing directory* keeps a list of phone numbers. Each program keeps the directory in a slightly different format, but most of them store the name of the system (a BBS or other service), the phone number, and the communication parameters for each service. You can see examples of dialing directories in figures 8.1 through 8.3.

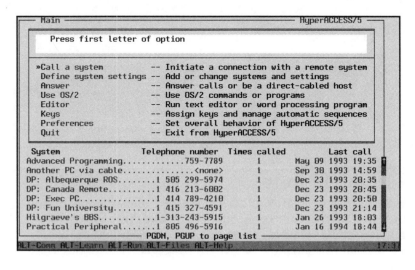

Figure 8.1

The dialing directory in HyperACCESS for OS/2.

Figure 8.2

The dialing directory
for Zap-O-Com for
OS/2.

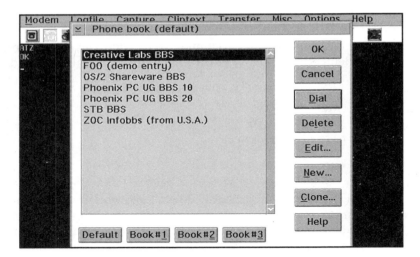

Figure 8.3

The dialing directory
for ProComm Plus.

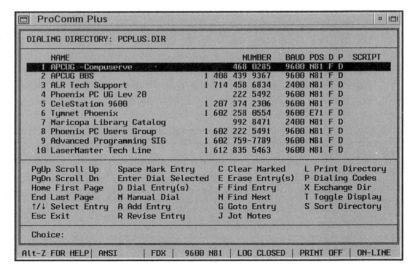

Entering Terminal Mode

Usually, after you connect with another computer and modem, you want
the communications program to stay out of your way. You want it to be
there when you need its services, of course, but in general you simply
want to pretend that the software isn't there. When you're working with
the communications as if you were sitting in front of the remote computer, the program is said to be in *terminal mode.*

You work this way with your word processor. Most of the time, you want to have your attention on the text that you're typing. That's the equivalent of terminal mode. When you want the program to come forward (to index the text or do a spelling check, in this word processing example, or to record keystrokes or download a file when you're working with a communications program), the application is only a few keystrokes away.

Capturing Text

Sometimes, when you're online, you find some text that you want to keep. Perhaps it's a message from a friend, giving directions to her house; maybe it's instructions on the best way to use the service. If you want to keep information that scrolls across your screen, you use the *text capture* facility within your communications program.

When you capture text, the program saves every character that is sent and received, storing it in a file on your local disk. The stored file contains everything: the text as well as any special characters that you type (including backspaces, which the computer considers a strange-but-acceptable character), and the text and special characters that your system receives. Compare figures 8.4 and 8.5 to see the difference between what you see on-screen and what is captured to the file.

Figure 8.4

What you see on-screen.

Figure 8.5

What is captured.

```
   9. Network gating
      From: Scott Hellewell #1 @1208005 VirtualNET
      To:   Cavalier #1 @1805013 VirtualNET
  10. VBBS/2 and Dos doors
      From: Robb Lightfoot #1 @1916005 VirtualNET
      To:   DoomsDay #1 @1407008 VirtualNET
  11. questions answers
      From: John #328 @8305 WWIVnet
  12. I would like to know..........
      From: Trail Rider #1 @8775 WWIVnet
  13. VBBS/2 and Dos doors
      From: Hired Gun #14 @8607 WWIVnet
  14. Ami pro
      From: Pegasus #153 @3308 WWIVnet
  15. Utilities
      From: Clark #14 @1703007 VirtualNET
      To:   ~HD~ #1 @1619060 VirtualNET
  16. Norton's SpeedDisk.
      From: Ice Man #1 @1609008 VirtualNET
      To:   Trail Rider #1 @8775 WWIVnet

Scan: Read (1-84) Q)uit [Enter] to Continue Scan: 15
```

Notice that the file starts capturing information after you tell your communications program to turn on the capture feature. The file doesn't capture what's already on-screen. If you want to capture a note that you've just read, you have to turn on the capture and then read the message again.

Capture files can be extremely useful because you can grab whatever information you need. When you see long or involved instructions, or a filthy joke that you think your best friend might appreciate, turn on the capture feature and seize the information for posterity. (If it's really funny, send it to me at my CompuServe number: 72241,1417.)

Transferring Files

Text capture enables you to grab text that comes across the screen. *File transfer* enables you to move entire files from one place to another.

When you *upload* a file, you transfer a file from your computer to the remote computer. To *download* a file, you copy it from the remote computer to your system. Confusing uploading with downloading is easy to do, so take a look at figures 8.6 and 8.7.

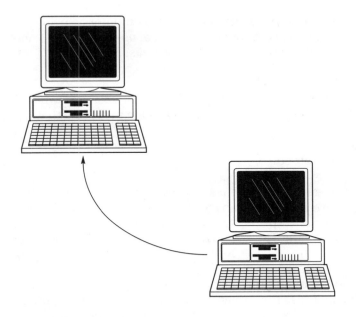

Figure 8.6

Uploading a file: transferring it from your computer to the remote computer.

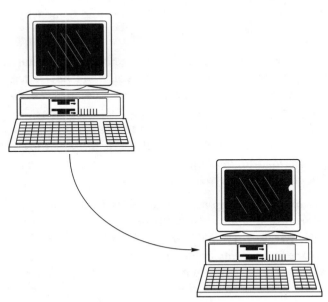

Figure 8.7

Downloading a file: copying it from the remote computer to your local PC.

This concept might help: I visualize the remote computer as being "above" me in some way. That way, I can think of *up*loading a file. Another way to remember is that you dial *up* other systems, so *up*loading files makes sense.

Every communications program enables you to upload and download files. Programs vary, however, in the number of file protocols that they support.

Huh? What's a file protocol?

Remember that when you capture text, as described in the preceding section, you capture both the ordinary characters and the characters that the computer considers "special" (for example, the code that the computer uses to indicate the Tab key). This set of characters is called the ASCII character set.

If you try to send binary information (such as the contents of a program file) by scrolling it across the screen, however, you see nothing but junk— or at least, characters that look like junk. Transferring the information that way also would take a long time, and the data would be susceptible to errors introduced by line noise.

You've all probably experienced a bad phone connection at one time or another. On a voice line, you don't notice the line quality unless it's really bad; it has to sound like the other person is talking from inside a bucket before it becomes bothersome. Line noise is the same thing as a bad phone connection. Because of the density of the data being transmitted, modems are much more picky about the line quality than are human life-forms.

Your communications program does its best to interpret any information that arrives. Often, when you encounter line noise (or "a dirty line"), and you aren't in the middle of a file transfer, the line noise appears as weird or random characters. (For a real-life example of line noise, flip ahead to fig. 8.20. The strange characters at the end of the note are line noise—I certainly would never have typed them!)

A *file protocol* is a set of rules, or an agreed-upon scheme, for how computers relate to each other. The protocol defines the organization of how the data is sent, which error-checking rules should be used, and so on. In other words, a protocol is a method of sending or receiving a file.

File protocols let you send binary data—that is, any information that isn't straight text. In real life, you'll use file protocols to send text files as well—they're faster and more reliable than capturing a file to disk.

Most communications programs support at least a handful of protocols. Many packages support more than a dozen protocols. In general, the more protocols the better—but only a few are absolutely necessary:

- ℂ **Xmodem.** Xmodem is one of the "original" binary file protocols, invented by Ward "X" Christensen around 1977. You sometimes hear it referred to as the Christensen protocol. Xmodem is slow by today's standards, but it was the first widespread file-transfer protocol. It uses blocks of 128 bytes, and after each block is sent, it sends a 1-byte checksum to check for errors. If an error is encountered, the block is re-sent. Almost every communications program offers this protocol. Xmodem/CRC is the same as Xmodem but is somewhat more reliable. In general, Xmodem works when other protocols don't.

- ℂ **Zmodem.** Zmodem is fast. It also has the capability to transfer information about the files it sends, so you arrange to upload or download files in a "batch mode." A batch mode upload or download enables you to transfer a group of files in one fell swoop. It's like transferring all your groceries from the car in one paper bag, instead of bringing each item into the kitchen separately. Batch mode, when it's available, can save you a little bit of time, but most of the savings are in convenience. Zmodem has crash recovery and is almost error-free. You can find Zmodem in almost every communications package you buy, and you probably shouldn't buy one if it doesn't include Zmodem.

Crash recovery is a nifty feature. If your upload or download is interrupted for any reason, and you call the BBS back and try to redownload the same file, Zmodem continues from where it left off. That can save a lot of time (and money)!

C **CompuServe-B.** CompuServe has its own binary protocol, called CompuServe-B, CIS-B, or CIS-B+. CompuServe B+ is most similar to Zmodem. Like Zmodem, it's a streaming protocol (it doesn't wait for one block to be acknowledged before sending the next), and it enables you to resume interrupted downloads. The performance of CIS-B+ is pretty good, and it's certainly the fastest and most reliable protocol to use on CompuServe.

Several other file-transfer protocols are available, with varying degrees of support. Xmodem is reliable but slow; Ymodem is faster than Xmodem but slower than Zmodem. Kermit is dismal, but you can find it on many older BBSs.

Automating Frequent Actions

Most communications programs provide a *scripting* feature, which enables you to automate the things that you do most often. If you find that you often repeat certain tasks, a script can make your communications faster and more enjoyable. That sounds much more complicated than it is. Just think of the stereotypical husband who grunts whenever his wife chatters at the breakfast table; the stereotypical husband is running a "morning script." Scripts (and similar functions called macros) can enable you to do the following:

C Produce many keystrokes when you type a single key

C Wait for prompts from the remote system and respond when the prompt arrives

C Wait until a particular time or for a given length of time before following the steps you provide

C Create special menus or functions

One common script is a login script. You usually can assign a login script to a specific service so that when you log in to a BBS, the communications program waits for the "What's your name" prompt before the script provides your name and password. Figure 8.8 shows a sample login script. They can look rather arcane, but many programs make creating them an easy job.

```
type("<ALT-M><ALT-C>")
wait tenths(7)
type("<ENTER>")
wait prompt("e:/xA0/xA0", 30)
type("apcug1<ENTER>")
wait prompt("/x00/x00? ", 30)
type("a<ENTER>")
wait prompt("me? ", 30)
type("esther schindler<ENTER>")
wait prompt("rd: ", 30)
type("chocolate<ENTER>")
end()
```

Figure 8.8

A sample script for logging in to a BBS.

Don't spend much time studying the previous example. Every communications program uses different rules for how to create scripts; learning the ins and outs of the one that you plan to use makes more sense. (Scripts are not covered in this book.)

Knowing about Other Options

The features described in the previous paragraphs are common to almost every communications program, even those that are included with your computer for free. The better communications programs add to these features considerably: they offer built-in virus checking, access to the operating system, archiving tools, and so on.

Participating in the Communication Process: An Online Session in More Detail

Now that you have learned more about the online process, your next online session should make more sense.

This time, you use the Practical Peripherals BBS. Practical Peripherals provides support for its modems through this BBS, as well as in its forum on CompuServe. This sample session uses this particular BBS because it's an easy and straightforward one.

Dialing

Start HyperACCESS/5 for DOS, if you haven't done so already. This time, choose the Practical Peripherals BBS, as shown in figure 8.9. (The phone number is (805) 496-5916 if you find that you have to enter it yourself.) Press Enter, and watch as HA/5 sets up the modem, then dials the phone and connects.

Figure 8.9

Preparing to dial the Practical Peripherals BBS.

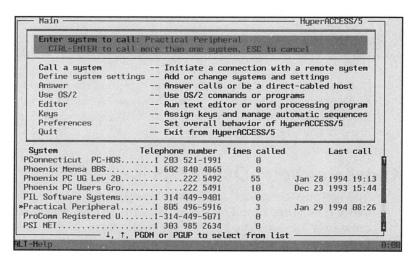

Logging In to the BBS

You can see from the first sign-on screen (see fig. 8.10) that the Practical Peripherals BBS looks different from the Hilgraeve BBS. Although the inconsistency might be slightly disconcerting at first, it shouldn't bother you. In fact, the variety in online demeanor is how BBSs differentiate themselves from one another. After all, most restaurants look different from each other, yet they all serve food. And, as in restaurants, you can expect to find the same several items on a "standard" menu.

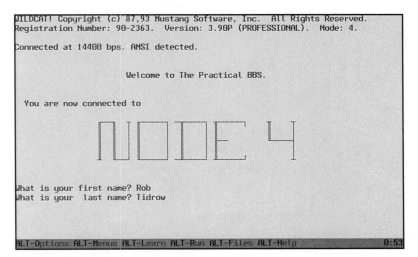

Figure 8.10

Another login screen.

I logged in to this BBS previously, as Rob. When you connect to the BBS, you have to join it and answer similar questions to those you answered for the Hilgraeve BBS. After the initial session, you simply are asked for your name and password, just as it shows in figure 8.10.

After you've logged in (or joined, as the case may be), the Practical Peripherals BBS displays a *splash screen* or *news flash*, another kind of announcement menu. You often see the kind of display shown in figure 8.11, letting you know what kind of hardware and software the particular BBS is using. Sometimes, the reason is that the sysop is incredibly proud of the stuff he or she has accumulated; other times, the sysop got the stuff cheaply, in exchange for a free plug.

Following the instructions on-screen (you soon learn, the hard way, that reading the instructions is the *only* way to use an online service!), press C to continue reading the announcements. Sometimes these announcements are important; sometimes they aren't. When you're done reading the announcements, the BBS might display a listing of bulletins like the one in figure 8.12.

Many BBSs don't force you—well, *encourage* you might be a better expression—to read the bulletins unless one of them has changed. Some BBSs require that you read some, or all, of the bulletins before you can become a registered user. That's their way of making sure that you can never whine, "But I didn't know those were the rules!" That isn't the case in this example. Here, you read a bulletin but capture the contents to the hard disk—as was discussed earlier in this chapter.

Figure 8.11

Hey! You've managed to log in!

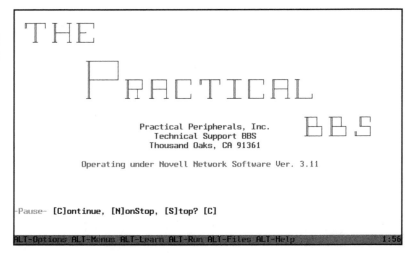

Figure 8.12

A typical Bulletins menu.

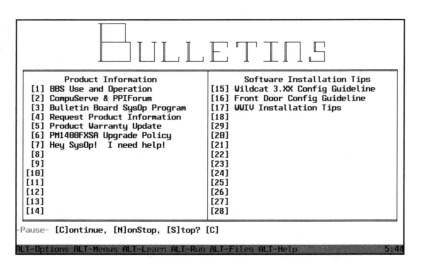

Notice that HA/5 has stayed out of the way ever since the modems connected; control has been left to you and to the BBS. But now you need to get HA/5's attention again. First, press **1** to indicate that you want to read bulletin #1, but *don't press Enter*. Press **Alt+O** to bring up the Options menu, and **C** to start the Capture. Press Enter or **B** to begin the capture, as shown in figure 8.13. Press Enter again to accept the default file name of CAPTURE.TXT.

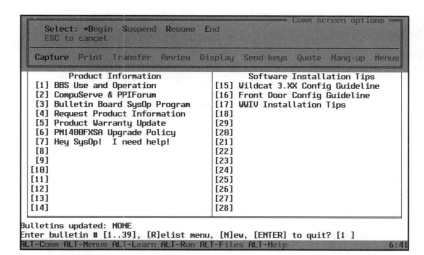

Figure 8.13

Starting a text file capture to disk.

It's Default of the Other Guy

A default or default value is what you get when you don't specify otherwise. Around my house, if you say that you want ice cream but don't say exactly which flavor you want, you get chocolate. (Is there another flavor?)

A lot of computer stuff depends on defaults; the programs assume that you want something one particular way unless you insist otherwise. Here, for instance, the text is captured to a file with the default name of CAPTURE.TXT (not a sexy name but not a dumb choice either) unless you give it a name you prefer, such as PRACTBBS.TXT or WAYCOOL.CAP.

As soon as you specify or accept the file capture name, HA/5 returns you to terminal mode—the focus goes back to the online session. Press Enter to finish telling the BBS that you want to look at bulletin #1 (remember, you didn't press Enter before). HA/5 captures whatever you type and whatever text scrolls across the screen. (When you look at the CAPTURE.TXT file later, you can see that the first character in the file is the Enter you just pressed.) Notice the small cpt displayed in the lower-right corner of figure 8.14, which indicates that a capture is active.

Figure 8.14
Capturing text to disk.

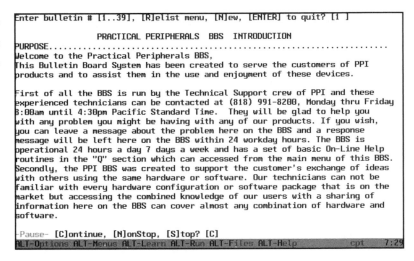

When you've captured enough text (presumably, after you've read the entire bulletin), remember to turn text capture off; otherwise, your entire online session is recorded to disk! Turn the capture off in a manner similar to the way you turned it on: press **Alt+O** to bring up the HA/5 menu, then press **C** to Capture and **E** to End (see fig. 8.15).

Figure 8.15
Ending the text capture.

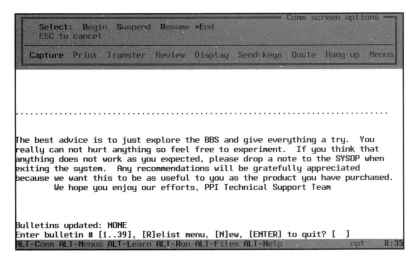

That should give you an idea of how bulletins work. From the bulletin menu displayed at the bottom of the screen, press Enter. The BBS might tell you a "fortune cookie"—that is, an amusing or pithy quote of the day—and check your electronic mail. Because you're new here, you're unlikely to have mail waiting.

Interacting Online

After you have checked out the bulletins, the BBS displays its main menu. As you can see in figure 8.16, the Practical Peripherals BBS Main Menu looks quite different from the Hilgraeve BBS Main Menu and offers some different services.

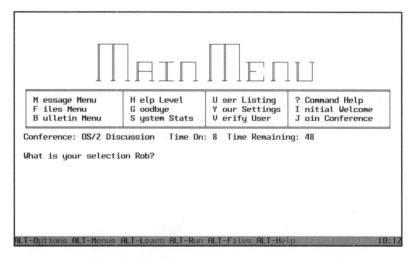

Figure 8.16

The Practical Peripherals BBS Main Menu.

The Practical Peripherals BBS is a typical one: it focuses on messages and on files.

Press **M** to choose Message Menu and thus read some messages. The BBS then displays another menu, the Message Menu.

Most BBSs have more than one message area. Message areas are often called conferences or forums. (Just to make life interesting for you, several different terms often describe the same thing. They start to make sense after you use them a little bit.) Each conference specializes in a different topic. On some BBSs, all the message areas are available to you automatically. In other cases, most of the message areas are visible, but you have to request access to one or two areas explicitly. Still other BBSs require that you specify one message area at a time and work through them one by one.

The Practical Peripherals BBS is in the last category. To *join*, or access, a conference, press J at the Main Menu to choose Join Conference, and indicate the number of the conference you want to examine. Because, as shown in figure 8.17, you don't know what the conference choices are, request a list of available conferences by pressing L.

Figure 8.17

Choosing a message conference.

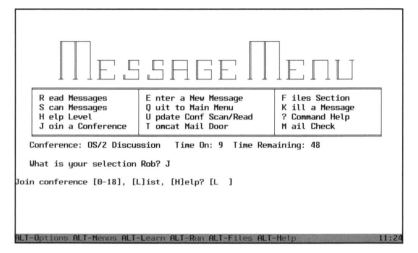

The BBS displays a list of conferences, as you can see in figure 8.18. Although a reasonable number of conferences are listed here, on the active, exciting BBSs you can find hundreds of conferences! Choose whichever conference you want by typing the associated digit and you'll return to the Message Menu.

The Message Menu reflects the conference you've chosen. From the Message Menu, press N to read messages that are new to you. Now the fun really starts!

The BBS displays messages one at a time. Read them, savor them, enjoy them, ignore them. Take a close look at figure 8.19 to see what information is included in a message. You see a sender (who wrote it), a recipient (to whom it was written—which might be All, meaning that everyone is invited to respond), and a subject. Each message also is assigned a number and other information that you can use for tracking. You can find out, for instance, whether the message was read or to what message this one was a reply.

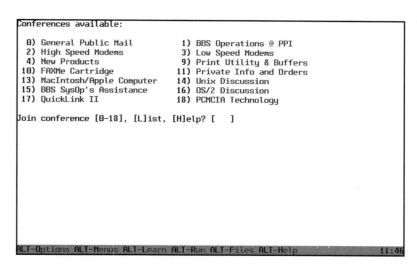

Figure 8.18

Listing available conferences.

```
Conferences available:

  0) General Public Mail          1) BBS Operations @ PPI
  2) High Speed Modems            3) Low Speed Modems
  4) New Products                 9) Print Utility & Buffers
 10) FAXMe Cartridge             11) Private Info and Orders
 13) MacIntosh/Apple Computer    14) Unix Discussion
 15) BBS SysOp's Assistance      16) OS/2 Discussion
 17) QuickLink II                18) PCMCIA Technology

Join conference [0-18], [L]ist, [H]elp? [   ]




ALT-Options ALT-Menus ALT-Learn ALT-Run ALT-Files ALT-Help        11:46
```

Figure 8.19

Reading a message.

```
[T]hread, [ENTER = next]?

From    : EUGENE ASTADAN (SysOp)      Number    : 367 of 1155
To      : DANIEL BROWN                Date      : 11/07/93 8:02pm
Subject : BBS LOGON LONG DISTANCE     Reference : 359
Read    : 11/08/93 10:57am (REPLIES)  Private   : NO
Conf    : 000 - General Public Mail

DB>>IN EACH CASE THE SYSTEM WOULD EITHER LOG ON AN DROP OUT "NO CARRIER"
DB>>OR TIME OUT .

Daniel,

It sounds to me like their system is not running with error-correction
or data compression enabled.  Please issue an AT&Q6 to your modem (or
incorporate it into your initialization string) and re-test your
connection.


Eugene Astadan, SysOp

Read mode : (SELECTED) (367 +)
Msg Read [346-1155], [F]orward, [H]elp, [N]onstop, [Q]uit, [R]eply,
[T]hread, [ENTER = next]?
ALT-Options ALT-Menus ALT-Learn ALT-Run ALT-Files ALT-Help        14:22
```

And, of course, you can see the text of the message itself. Hopefully, this part is the most exciting. (Granted, figure 8.19's message isn't all that exciting, but what do you expect of a technical support BBS—UFO sightings?)

At the end of each message, you are presented with several options:

ⓒ   **Forward.** Sends a copy of the message to a recipient you specify.

ⓒ   **Help.** Asks the BBS for help on what these options mean.

©   **Nonstop.** Enables you to read messages nonstop, without a prompt at the bottom of each message. This option is especially useful when you want to capture the entire text of a conference to a file and read it off-line, when you aren't making the phone company richer.

©   **Quit.** Tells the BBS that you want to quit reading messages in this conference.

©   **Reply.** Enables you to reply to this message.

©   **Thread.** Enables you to read the messages in this message thread. A *message thread* is a set of messages and the replies to those messages. (Message threads are covered in more detail in Chapter 11, "Cutting Costs with Your Modem.")

©   **Read Next.** Enables you to read the next message, in numerical order. This choice is the default—if you just press Enter, you see the next message.

Your screen probably doesn't show the same messages that are shown in the figures in this chapter. Most online services, including BBSs, keep only a fixed number of active messages.

If you want to reply to the message you see on your screen, press R. Then compose a reply; an example is shown in figure 8.20. The message editor works like a simple word processor. Okay, so maybe it's a brain-dead word processor, but you don't need much, after all. Your lines wrap just as in your word processor, so you don't have to press Enter at the end of every line. If you want to leave a blank line between paragraphs (I recommend that you do), press the spacebar once, and then press Enter.

When you're done composing your response, press Enter on a blank line, without any other character. You then see a menu like the one at the bottom of the screen in figure 8.20. Because I'd be embarrassed to leave as dorky a reply as the one I wrote here, I'd press **A** to choose Abort and back out of the entire thing. Ordinarily, you would press **S** to save the message—and, magically, you have left lurker status.

```
Daniel,

It sounds to me like their system is not running with error-correction
or data compression enabled.  Please issue an AT&Q6 to your modem (or
incorporate it into your initialization string) and re-test your
connection.


Eugene Astadan, SysOp

Read mode : (SELECTED) (367 +)
Msg Read [346-1155], [F]orward, [H]elp, [N]onstop, [Q]uit, [R]eply,
[T]hread, [ENTER = next]? r
            Subject? [BBS LOGON LONG DISTANCE   ]
     Enter your text. [ENTER] alone to stop. (72 chars/line, 150 lines max)
   (----+----1----+----2----+----3----+----4----+----5----+----6----+----7--)
 1: If I had anything to add, here, I would say so now.
 2:
 3: --Esther⌐ ⌐U
 4:

Edit Message [A]bort, [C]ontinue,      [I]nsert, [L]ist, [E]dit
[U]pload,     [Q]uote, [F]ull Screen, [D]elete, [S]ave, [H]elp? [ ]
ALT-Options ALT-Menus ALT-Learn ALT-Run ALT-Files ALT-Help            15:44
```

Figure 8.20

Composing a reply.

A lurker *reads messages but never responds to one.
Lurkers, sometimes called read-only members, are electronic eavesdroppers. We all have sat in restaurants and
listened to the fascinating conversation at the next table;
lurking is like that.*

*As a lurker, you can learn a lot; sometimes, other people
ask the questions that hadn't occurred to you yet. But
online life is a participatory sport. You can get only so
much pleasure from watching—if you don't dive in and
participate, you're missing most of the fun!*

Read a few more messages if you find them interesting. If the messages
are boring, don't automatically assume that all messages on every BBS are
dull. You wouldn't judge all parties by the conversations you heard at
only one, would you?

When you're done reading messages, press **Q** to quit and return to the
Message Menu. Then press **F** to switch to the File Menu.

Downloading a File

To find out which files are available on this BBS, press **L** to display a list.
The BBS displays a listing of files similar to the one in figure 8.21. This BBS
shows more detail about each file than did the listing in Hilgraeve's BBS,

including the number of times each file was downloaded (which can be a sign of its popularity), the size of each file, and when it was uploaded.

Figure 8.21

Listing the files available.

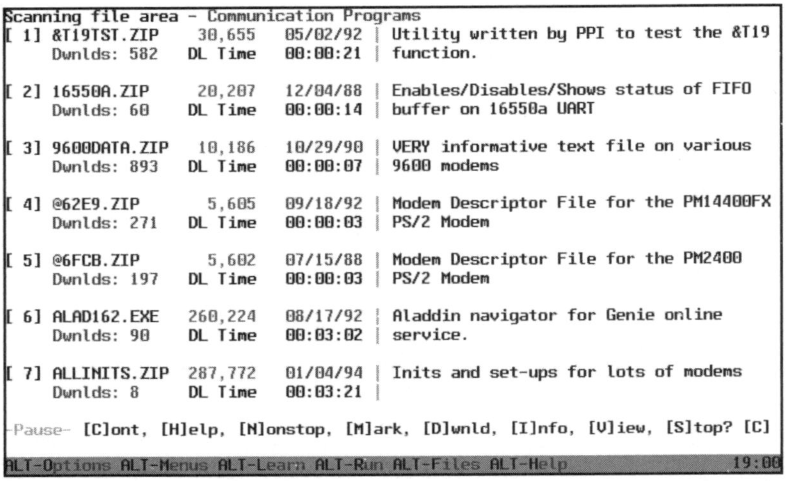

```
Scanning file area - Communication Programs
[ 1] &T19TST.ZIP    30,655    05/02/92 | Utility written by PPI to test the &T19
     Dwnlds: 582    DL Time   00:00:21 | function.

[ 2] 16550A.ZIP     20,207    12/04/88 | Enables/Disables/Shows status of FIFO
     Dwnlds: 60     DL Time   00:00:14 | buffer on 16550a UART

[ 3] 9600DATA.ZIP   10,186    10/29/90 | VERY informative text file on various
     Dwnlds: 893    DL Time   00:00:07 | 9600 modems

[ 4] @62E9.ZIP       5,605    09/18/92 | Modem Descriptor File for the PM14400FX
     Dwnlds: 271    DL Time   00:00:03 | PS/2 Modem

[ 5] @6FCB.ZIP       5,602    07/15/88 | Modem Descriptor File for the PM2400
     Dwnlds: 197    DL Time   00:00:03 | PS/2 Modem

[ 6] ALAD162.EXE   260,224    08/17/92 | Aladdin navigator for Genie online
     Dwnlds: 90     DL Time   00:03:02 | service.

[ 7] ALLINITS.ZIP  287,772    01/04/94 | Inits and set-ups for lots of modems
     Dwnlds: 8      DL Time   00:03:21 |

-Pause- [C]ont, [H]elp, [N]onstop, [M]ark, [D]wnld, [I]nfo, [V]iew, [S]top? [C]

ALT-Options ALT-Menus ALT-Learn ALT-Run ALT-Files ALT-Help                19:00
```

To download a file, press D. The BBS software used here enables you to mark several files for download at one time, which is extremely convenient. Type in the name of the file you want to download (you certainly don't have to pick the same one that I did), and the BBS estimates how long the download will take, in minutes (see fig. 8.22). Because I've connected to this BBS at a high speed, downloading even a large file doesn't take long. If you're using a 2400 bps modem, the required time probably is significantly longer. Press Enter when you're done selecting files, and the download begins.

Throughout the download (displayed in fig. 8.23), HA/5 keeps you updated with the percentage complete, any error messages, the length of time elapsed, and the download *throughput*, or number of bps actually transmitted.

Working with Compressed Data

The file I downloaded here, MDR401.ZIP, is a compressed file. What can you do with it?

File compression is covered in more detail later, in the chapter on making the most of your online dollar. This section gives you just a short introduction.

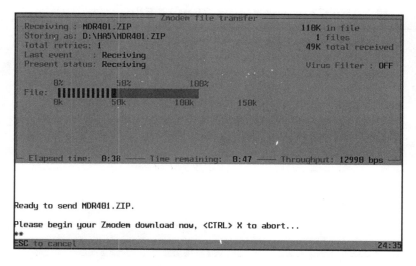

```
    Dwnlds: 215    DL Time   00:00:17 | to be used with TXMDM2
[ 3] MDR401.ZIP     112,444   02/02/93 | Modem Doctor 4.01 Diagnostics for UART
    Dwnlds: 409    DL Time   00:01:18 | and Modem up to 2400

[ 4] MODEMS.EXE      14,433   04/18/93 | Latest modems.dat file for Procomm.
    Dwnlds: 687    DL Time   00:00:10 | Includes FXSA & FXMT

[ 5] MSK313.ZIP     302,936   07/12/93 | MS_Kermit 3.13 for DOS.
    Dwnlds: 6      DL Time   00:03:32 |

[ 6] MSVIBM.ZIP     305,745   08/07/93 | MS-Kermit V3.13
    Dwnlds: 6      DL Time   00:03:34 |

[ 7] PCPLUS11.ZIP   176,834   03/30/88 | PCPLUSTD ver 1.1 ARCive
    Dwnlds: 147    DL Time   00:02:04 |

Enter up to 99 files. Press [ENTER] alone to stop.

                         Bytes      Time    Total Bytes  Total Time
                         -------    -------  -----------  ----------
File # 1? mdr401.zip     112,444    1.3      112,444      1.3
File # 2?
ALT-Options ALT-Menus ALT-Learn ALT-Run ALT-Files ALT-Help              23:19
```

Figure 8.22

Preparing to download a file.

```
----------------------- Zmodem file transfer -----------------------
 Receiving : MDR401.ZIP                          110K in file
 Storing as: D:\HA5\MDR401.ZIP                    1 files
 Total retries: 1                                 49K total received
 Last event    : Receiving
 Present status: Receiving                        Virus Filter : OFF

      0%        50%          100%
 File: |||||||||||
      0k        50k          100k          150k



 - Elapsed time:  0:38 ----- Time remaining:  0:47 ----- Throughput: 12990 bps -


Ready to send MDR401.ZIP.

Please begin your Zmodem download now, <CTRL> X to abort...
**
ESC to cancel                                                          24:35
```

Figure 8.23

Monitoring the download.

Consider an average text or word processing document. Most of it is spaces, tabs, and other "white space," right? But each character stored is a byte, and when you're transmitting across long-distance phone lines or using services that charge by the minute, sending such information in its native format, uncompressed, can get expensive.

File compression is the process of fitting ten pounds in a five-pound bag. Through some nifty use of technology and an impressive amount of brain sweat, files can be squished before transmission and unsquished at the other end.

If you need a more visual example, imagine that you wanted to move the contents of your living room. You could set up your living room, as is, in the back of the moving van—including the rugs, the TV set across from the couch, and so on. (Frankly, I'd get rid of that lamp.) That's what sending information uncompressed is like. In contrast, think about how much less space is needed to box up everything and pile the boxes in the back of a van. It's the same stuff, but stored more compactly. That's what file compression is all about.

Another advantage of compressed files is that several files can be contained, or grouped together, in one file. The following table, for instance, describes the files zipped into MDR401.ZIP. Notice that the zipped file is 110K in size, but when it's uncompressed, 315K are stored. When you unzip the file, you get 315K worth of data and programs.

Table 8.1
The Contents of a Zipped File

Length	Method	Size	Ratio	Date	Time	CRC-3 Name ("^==>case conversion)
1156	Deflate	486	58%	03-01-92	20:59	6442e581 ^!
118345	Deflate	49659	58%	03-01-92	20:54	2f5edf25 ^mdr.exe
52	Deflate	43	17%	01-04-91	10:38	97fc1da1 ^mdr.mnu
140281	Deflate	42215	70%	10-09-91	20:27	49c11331 ^mdr4doc.txt
3881	Deflate	1422	63%	10-09-91	20:31	516fb33a ^mdr4ordr.frm
3081	Deflate	1473	52%	03-01-92	20:00	7224983d ^mdrbeta.txt
34286	Deflate	10460	69%	10-09-91	20:36	709abd23 ^mdrfirst.txt

Length	Method	Size	Ratio	Date	Time	CRC-3 Name ("^==>case conversion)
1627	Deflate	808	50%	03-01-92	20:02	665fc1c0 ^mdrpack4.lst
12853	Deflate	4302	67%	03-05-93	16:30	c5ee0f54 ^sysbbs.txt
———		———	—			———
315562		110868	65%			9

The most popular file compression format used is the ZIP format, or PKUNZIP. To use a file that ends in .ZIP, you need an unzipper. A copy of PKUNZIP is included on the *New Riders' Guide to Modems* bonus disk.

Ending the Session

To log out of the BBS, press G to choose Goodbye. The BBS verifies that you do want to log out, and then hangs up. You might see some line noise as it does so (see fig. 8.24).

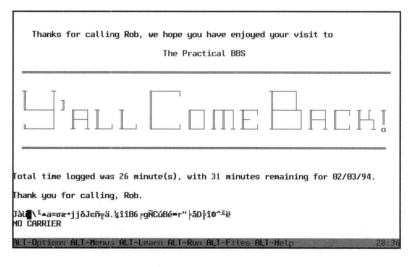

Figure 8.24
Logging out.

You've finished another online session! Congratulations!

Part 3:

What You Can Do with a Modem

What Do Online Services Provide?

Using Bulletin Board Systems (BBSs)

Cutting Costs with Your Modem

Beyond BBSs and Online Services

Journey to the Internet

Chapter 9

What Do Online Services Provide?

Online services let you access or share information with other people. Most online services provide an *incredible* number of services. A BBS is like the corner grocery store; an online service is a supermarket—the kind that sells tennis shoes and blenders, as well as green peppers and baker's chocolate.

You probably won't know it, as a customer, but most of the online services run on mainframes or minicomputers, rather than microcomputers. Most online services are available internationally, or at least within North America. To access them, you usually dial a local phone number or a toll-free number.

Finding Out What's Available

Several different kinds of online services are available, including electronic mail services, information banks, and more.

An *electronic mail service*, as its name implies, specializes in sending and receiving personal electronic mail, called *e-mail*, and doesn't do very much else.

Information banks are essentially dial-up collections of data. These include NewsNet and the Dow Jones News/Retrieval service, as well as the BRS database. Another example is the national database of health-related papers and journals. (The best thing about the service, for those of us not in the health-care field, is that the access software is named *Grateful Med.*)

In many cases, you can access these information banks through another service. For instance, you can reach Dow Jones through CompuServe.

Consumer-oriented services are the department stores of the electronic world, trying to serve a wide variety of needs. These include CompuServe, America Online, GEnie, and Prodigy.

Learning About Cost

One attribute shared by all of these services is: It ain't free. Some of them charge you a monthly or yearly fee. Some charge by the minute. A growing number of these services charge a nominal monthly fee, with additional charges for the "extra stuff." Not surprisingly, the really cool services are the ones they consider "extra stuff," luring you into a spending spree.

What Does It Take to Sign Up?

In order to use any of these services, you will need to get an account with them. That won't cost much. In many cases, signing up will be free. Most of them follow the razor blade rule: give away the razors and charge for the razor blades. When you purchased your modem, there was probably at least one *"Sign up free!"* kit included.

User IDs and Passwords

When you sign up with any of these services, you will receive a user ID and a password. The user ID is similar to a telephone number—some of them even look just like one.

Guard your password! Remember that your credit card bill is attached to its use. Never tell someone your pass-word—it's your online and financial security safeguard.

Determining What You Need from an Online Service

You should investigate each of the services before you sign up with any of them, especially if there's a sign-up fee. Find out what the service offers, its cost, and how the service is accessed. A less expensive service that requires that you make a long distance call to access it won't seem inexpensive for very long.

Think about what you want to do online and sign up with the service that best suits your purpose. What kind of information do you need access to? If you don't need anything except database information, sign up with those services directly. If you access them through a consumer service such as CompuServe, CompuServe will add a charge of its own.

Each service has a different "personality." For instance, GEnie and America Online are chattier than CompuServe, which has a reputation of being more technical. (Of course, you can find plenty of technical information on America Online, and an overwhelming amount of chatter on CompuServe. I've told myself a million times not to exaggerate like that!)

When you evaluate the different consumer services, remember the old adage, "You get what you pay for." Because the less expensive services require a smaller commitment from members' checkbooks, they're willing to chatter more. The quality of the information exchanged may reflect that fact.

For instance, I find the Literary Forum on CompuServe to be one of the most useful opportunities for peer-to-peer discussion—there are conversations about everything from properly preparing a manuscript to "Underwear of the Keep." (Look, when you're writing a novel, accuracy is important! How much do you know about corset covers?)

In contrast, a writer friend confided to me that her experience with the writers area on a competing service was "full of advice from little old ladies writing romance novels set in the 15th century, with heroines named Tiffany." Your mileage may vary, of course; the point is to find a place that is comfortable and worthwhile for you.

What is CompuServe?

It's really difficult for me to give an unbiased picture of CompuServe. I've been a CompuServe junkie for most of the last ten years, and a CompuServe Sysop for the last three. I met many of my best friends through CompuServe—and there are several of them I've never met in person. I'll try to be fair, but forgive me if I get a little wistful and the fondness shows through.

Some of CompuServe's services include:

- ℂ   Private **e-mail**, so you can correspond with your buddies.

- ℂ   **Electronic mall and shopping services**. You can buy almost anything in the mall, from a refrigerator to a computer book to flowers. This is great when you live in a rural area, or when you suddenly remember that Mother's Day is two days away. (Those flower delivery services work great!)

- ℂ   **Interactive games**. You can play games with people on the other side of the planet!

- ℂ   **Investment information**, such as stock prices.

- ℂ   **Updates** about news, weather, and sports.

- ℂ   **Travel information**. You can make reservations online, find out if flights have arrived on time, and ask other people for recommended restaurants in distant cities.

- ℂ   **Over 350 public forums**, each devoted to a different topic. Each forum is like a BBS conference and is subdivided further into ever-more-specific areas of interest. Each forum has a message area, a files area, and a conference section. There are forums devoted to any subject you can imagine, from crafts to spreadsheet technical support to computer consulting. (Yes, in fact there are *two* forums about sex. I knew you were wondering!)

Because you obviously have the fine discrimination and taste to have read this far, I'd like to personally invite you to visit my forum on ZiffNet. The motto of ZiffNet is All About Computing, Online. It's run by the same folks who

bring you PC Magazine, Computer Shopper, and several other computer-related periodicals. I'm the primary Sysop of the Executives Online forum, which hosts computer industry luminaries for week-long visits discussing the latest-and-greatest in the computer industry. I try to keep it a merry place. There's usually a pot of electronic hot chocolate on the stove, and you're welcome anytime. GO ZNT:EXEC will get you there.

Another place to check out is the forum devoted to support of Macmillan Computer Publishing. GO CIS:PHCP will take you right there. In the MCP forum, you can find the files related to books from New Riders (as well as its sister publications). For instance, if you buy an AutoCAD book from New Riders, you can find the drawing files associated with the book in the MCP forum libraries. You'll also find some of your favorite MCP authors "hanging out" in the MCP forum, so you can ask me directly how to double the recipe for chocolate silk ice cream that I included in another book. (How's that for a plug to read everything I've written?) Or you can tell the editors just how helpful this book has been to you.

Using CompuServe

Frankly, if you use one of the standard communications programs (such as HA/5) to access CompuServe, it's...well...ugly. Because CompuServe supports so many kinds of computers (there are people dialing in with Macintosh, Atari, and UNIX systems), it has to be based on the lowest common denominator. And that is low indeed.

As figure 9.1 shows, CompuServe in its "vanilla" form is based on text menus. You choose the number of the item you want, which leads you to another menu. That leads to another menu, and another, etc. Although you can always get where you want to go, you may not always know where you *are* while you're getting there. If you know what CompuServe service you want to access, you can jump there directly by typing **GO COOKS** or **GO WEATHER** or **GO**—well, you get the idea.

Figure 9.1

The text mode of CompuServe.

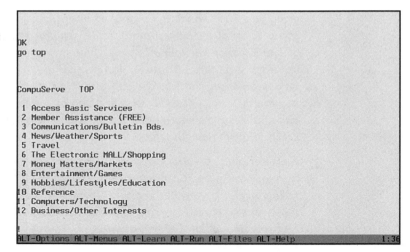

```
OK
go top


CompuServe    TOP

 1 Access Basic Services
 2 Member Assistance (FREE)
 3 Communications/Bulletin Bds.
 4 News/Weather/Sports
 5 Travel
 6 The Electronic MALL/Shopping
 7 Money Matters/Markets
 8 Entertainment/Games
 9 Hobbies/Lifestyles/Education
10 Reference
11 Computers/Technology
12 Business/Other Interests
!
ALT-Options ALT-Menus ALT-Learn ALT-Run ALT-Files ALT-Help          1:36
```

Online Help

CompuServe can be a bit daunting at first, simply because it's so big. (If you were used to a corner grocery, you'd be a little intimidated by the size of a Mega store, too.) Fortunately, there is plenty of help available. You can type **HELP** anytime, and there are a few forums devoted to providing help to new CompuServe users. The PRACTICE forum and HELPFORUM are among the best, and they're free of connect-time charges.

Making CompuServe Easier

Although you can access CompuServe with any general communications program, there are several programs written specifically to access the service. Their intent is to make the service easier and to minimize costs.

CompuServe's Pretty Faces

When you join CompuServe, your start-up kit will probably include a copy of CompuServe Information Manager, or CIM. CIM is available in DOS, Windows, and Macintosh versions, though we won't cover the latter here. Figures 9.2 and 9.3 show the aesthetic differences between the DOS and Windows versions; the programs have nearly identical features.

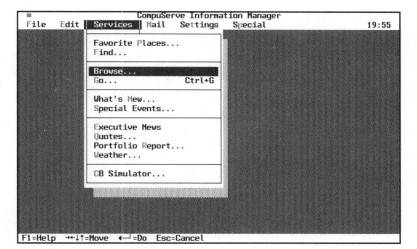

Figure 9.2
The DOS CIM screen.

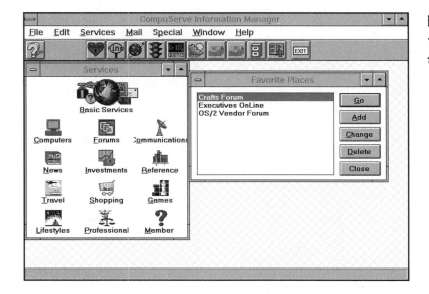

Figure 9.3
The Windows CIM front end.

CIM puts a pretty face on CompuServe, and it makes it easier to navigate the service. It helps you to create a phone book of your online correspondents, gives you access to online graphics (such as current national weather maps), and makes it easy to wander around the service. CIM is a good way to get started.

How do you get one of the CIM packages?

If you buy a CompuServe kit from your local software store, it will probably include a disk with CIM or WinCIM on it. If you became a CompuServe member because a membership brochure was included with one of your hardware or software purchases, you'll have to go a little further out of your way.

You can call the phone number for CompuServe, listed at the end of this section, to request a copy. Alternatively, dial into CompuServe with HyperACCESS/5 and type GO ORDER at the ! prompt. By following the instructions on the menus, you can download a copy of CIM or WinCIM directly onto your hard disk. CompuServe charges you about $10 for the download, but they also credit your account $10 the first time you use the software, so it comes out free.

Offline CompuServe Navigators

Although CIM makes it easy to explore CompuServe, it is not usually the best tool for using the service—especially if most of your online activity is in CompuServe's forums. There are several *offline navigators* that help you to use CompuServe, but minimize the time you spend actively online. Their intent is to automate your use of the service, so that you can efficiently find and download files, and read and respond to messages without the online clock ticking.

Offline navigators are available for nearly every hardware platform. Figures 9.4 and 9.5 show two of the popular programs, one for DOS and one for OS/2.

How to Reach CompuServe

This section barely scratches the surface about the number of CompuServe services available. If you want to learn how to make the most of your CompuServe online dollar, I highly recommend another New Riders book: *Inside CompuServe*, by Richard Wagner.

To find out more about CompuServe services and their products, call CompuServe at (800) 848-8199 or (614) 457-8600. You can write to them at:

CompuServe
5000 Arlington Center Blvd.
P.O. Box 20212
Columbus, OH 43220

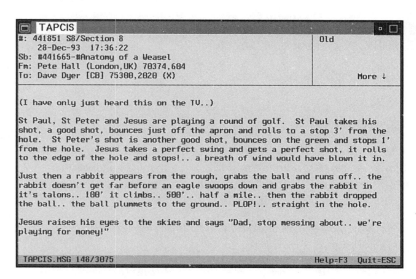

Figure 9.4
The TAPCIS DOS-based interface.

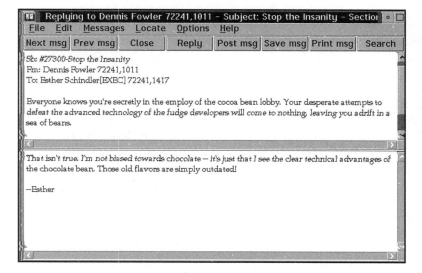

Figure 9.5
Golden CommPass is an offline navigator for OS/2 that takes advantage of OS/2's multi-threading.

What is Prodigy?

Prodigy is intended for less avid computer users, geared more to home and family users with shopping, communications, advertisements, and other consumer service interests.

Unlike CompuServe, you must have Prodigy's software in order to access the service. The system is graphics-based, and it displays everything (even text) graphically. You can get Prodigy access software for Macintosh or IBM PC-compatible computers.

Prodigy offers several kinds of services:

- ℂ   The **Information** service updates you throughout the day on news, weather, and sports.

- ℂ   **Stock Quotes and News** provides you with updated stock quotes and articles on companies and industries from the Dow Jones News/Retrieval service. You can store a personal portfolio of securities and market quotations.

- ℂ   The **Brokerage** section enables you to buy and sell stocks, options, CDs, and mutual funds.

- ℂ   **Banking and Bill Paying** enables you to automatically pay bills without writing checks. You can pay recurring payments, such as a mortgage, and check your bank account statements, which are revised daily.

- ℂ   With **Travel and Leisure**, you can make your own travel arrangements.

- ℂ   **Consumer Information** provides you with over 700 product evaluations from publications such as *Consumer Reports*, *Home Office Computing*, and *Road and Track*. You can also find out information about movies, articles on parenting, cooking, pet care, and other topics.

- ℂ   The **Encyclopedia** service puts the Academic American Encyclopedia online. Over 33,000 articles are cross-referenced, making it easy for students to look up necessary information. (Those of us with a cynical streak contemplate how technology has advanced the state-of-the-art in last-minute, 8th-grade-history-report plagiarism.)

© **Bulletin boards** enable users to exchange information on hundreds of topics, from scuba diving to rock music.

Didn't I warn you that different providers use different names for the same services? A CompuServe forum is the same thing as a Prodigy bulletin board, each of which is similar to a BBS conference.

© **Shopping** lets you choose from major catalogs, enabling you to stay at home and order.

Using Prodigy

It doesn't require much effort to log onto Prodigy. After the software is installed (and they make it really easy, I promise), you simply type **PRODIGY**, enter your Prodigy account ID, and press Enter. The software asks you questions about your configuration—a topic about which you're an expert, now, because you made it through Part I of this book.

After you finish with the software installation, you see a screen similar to the one in figure 9.6.

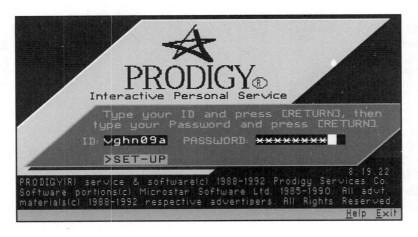

Figure 9.6

The Prodigy Log-In Screen.

When you begin using Prodigy, you may find yourself captivated by the graphical advertisements, information, and displays. The screens are fairly simple to move around in, but very different from other available online services. You can move from screen to screen by using commands or your mouse. To make a selection, you either select the item on the screen or use the menu bar at the bottom of the screen, as you can see in figure 9.7.

Figure 9.7

Prodigy's opening screen.

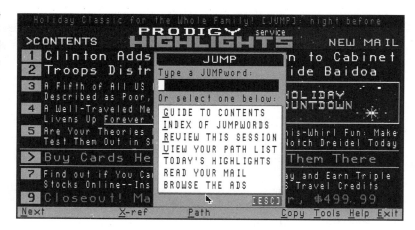

How to Reach Prodigy

If you want to sign up as a user with Prodigy and obtain the necessary software, you can call Prodigy Service Company at (800) 822-6922 or (914) 993-8000. Or write to:

Prodigy Service Company
Membership Services
445 Hamilton Avenue
White Plains, NY 10601

Other Consumer Services

Although CompuServe and Prodigy are the largest consumer online services, they are certainly not the only ones around. Here's a brief look at two other services: GEnie, from General Electric Information Services, and America Online.

GEnie

GEnie offers a vast array of services for the home computer user as well
as the professional user. It was established in 1985 and has grown rapidly,
in part because it's among the most affordable consumer services. GEnie's
menu structure and services are similar to CompuServe's, though they
aren't quite as extensive. GEnie is particularly strong as a medium for
special interest groups that are involved in roundtable discussions on
topics of interest. (Yes, just as you suspected—*roundtable* is yet another
term for forum or conference. Delightful, isn't it?)

GEnie offers its users information retrieval centers, e-mail, a gateway to
the Dow Jones News/Retrieval service, headline news, and columns by
well-known people in the computer industry. GEnie has also established a
link with the Internet, which has increased its popularity dramatically. To
get more information about GEnie, write to or call them at:

GE Information Services
401 N. Washington Street
Rockville, MD 20850
(800) 638-9636
(301) 340-4000

America Online

America Online is another inexpensive service with an impressive list of
features. America Online uses a graphical user interface, with icons and
drop-down menus, to access its basic services such as e-mail, bulletin
boards, multi-player games, travel reservations, and stock quotes. Figure
9.8 shows just one of the services available.

To get more information on this service, write or call them at:

America Online
8619 Westwood Center Drive
Vienna, VA 22182
(800) 227-6364

Figure 9.8

America Online's interface.

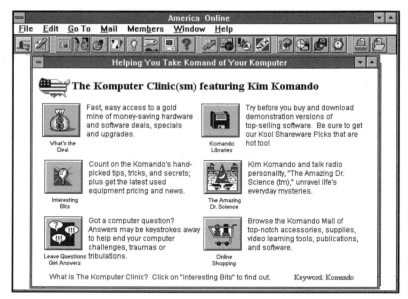

Using Online Mail Services

If your primary purpose in using a modem is to correspond with other individuals using e-mail, you may not need a consumer service at all.

E-mail services enable you to send and receive messages from other members of the service. It's okay if your correspondents are not all using the same service; most of the consumer services exchange mail with the others. If you're using MCI Mail, for instance, you can send and receive messages from your friends on CompuServe.

E-mail received or sent via one of the mail services includes the time and date that the message was sent, the names (or IDs) of the sender and recipients, and, of course, the text. You usually have options for alternate delivery, and you can ask that the message you send be faxed to the recipient, or printed and mailed. If international support is important to you, make sure that you confirm what services overseas are available from the vendor; they can vary quite a bit.

Access to these services is usually driven by commands, although, like the other online services, there are third-party commercial products that attempt to make the job easier.

Unlike the consumer and database services that charge by the minute, most of the e-mail services charge by the number of messages you send, with surcharges for documents over a certain size.

Who owns electronic mail?

If you're at work, and you write an e-mail message that travels on the service paid for by your employer, who owns the message?

This topic is the focus of a recent court case between prominent members of the computer industry. One company executive, who was quietly corresponding with another company about a job move, left copies of his MCI Mail messages (including company-proprietary information) on his hard disk. The employer maintains that because the information was sent using the account paid for by his company, the "private" mail belongs to the company. What do you think?

Several businesses depend on MCI Mail, SprintMail, or one of their competitors. Here's a brief overview of what they provide.

MCI Mail

MCI Mail is part of MCI Telecommunications Corporation. Of all the e-mail services, MCI Mail is probably the most popular because of its rates, its ability to link to other services, and its large user base. You can send mail at the same rates to MCI Mail subscribers overseas.

MCI Mail services—besides simply sending and receiving your messages—include receipt notification of your message, multiple addressee and mailing lists, and a message filing system. You can upload and download messages, and have messages delivered via fax, the US Mail, and Telex. You can exchange messages with subscribers to CompuServe, AT&T Mail, and SprintMail.

To access MCI Mail, you dial a toll-free number. To become a member of MCI Mail, contact:

MCI Mail
1111 Nineteenth Street, NW
Washington, D.C. 20036
(202) 416-5600
(800) 444-6245

SprintMail

SprintMail is a service of SprintNet, one of the largest packet-switching networks in the U.S. The network is run by US Sprint, which markets SprintMail to businesses of all sizes. Like MCI Mail, you can create messages with the standard options that include receipt notification, multiple addresses, carbon copies, and mailing lists.

Using SprintMail, you can mark messages urgent, private, and registered. You can also save a copy of the message in the file area, grant the message a specific date and time for delivery, or repeat a delivery at certain times. (This would be a good way to let the boss know, at exactly 5 p.m. on Friday, that you've taken the company jet to Rio.)

SprintMail uses local access numbers for modem access. To contact the company, contact:

US Sprint
12490 Sunrise Valley Drive
Reston, VA 22096
(800) 877-4646

Chapter 10

Using Bulletin Board Systems (BBSs)

The easiest online service to access is an electronic bulletin board. Bulletin boards, or BBSs, give you access to thousands of files, enable you to exchange messages with other people, and provide an electronic community. This chapter looks at BBSs in detail—how they work, how to use them, and the tacit rules of behavior followed on BBSs and other online services.

Understanding BBS Features

BBSs are run by individuals or by companies. They are run on a single microcomputer or, for the large systems, over a microcomputer network. You can usually exchange messages with other BBS members, as well as upload and download files. Some BBSs have additional services—everything from ordering books to performing a nationwide job search.

Types of BBSs

Several different types of BBSs are available, including the following:

(**Technical support BBSs** on which hardware and software manufacturers answer questions about the use of their products and provide support files such as device drivers. (The two BBSs you called in earlier chapters, Hilgraeve's and Practical Peripherals', were both technical support BBSs.)

(**For-profit BBSs** are businesses. The people who run and maintain the BBS charge you for access, and they intend to make a profit. The for-profit BBSs are often among the best; because there's a charge involved, the owners need to make the service worth the membership fee. No one will want to fork over $20 or $50 to a BBS that provides poor service. It's that supply-and-demand thing again.

(**"Just for fun BBSs,"** are BBSs on which organizers run their services simply for the joy of it. These BBSs fit into either of the following categories:

(**Community BBSs** include those that are run with a local focus or to serve a specific group of people. Community BBSs include user group BBSs.

(**Special interest BBSs** pander to a specific interest or topic. These can be among the most fascinating to explore. There are BBSs devoted to computer consulting, to parenting, to computer graphics, to folk music, to model trains. The U.S. Government maintains a Consulate BBS so that you can find out about the status of Americans overseas in case of an emergency. Figure 10.1 shows some services provided by a BBS devoted (mostly) to farming and agricultural issues. With over 50,000 BBSs out there, it is certain that there's at least one focusing on your favorite topics.

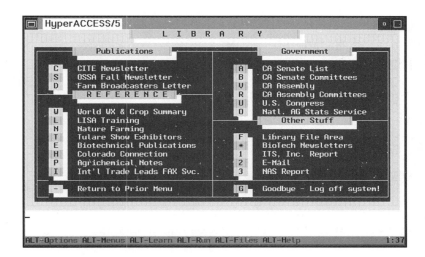

Figure 10.1
FarmNet is a BBS specializing in farm issues.

In each case, the manager of the BBS is called the *Sysop,* which stands for system operator. Despite what some of them will tell you, Sysops are not god-like, omnipotent beings. They just act that way.

Comparing BBSs and Consumer Services

Some of the distinctions between BBSs and the big online services seem arbitrary. As a user, you probably don't care if the service is run on a mainframe computer or a minicomputer. Some of the biggest BBSs have services that rival the "biggies" and provide telephone access from out-of-state that isn't too painful (expensive). So, how do you choose?

The real difference between them is that most BBSs don't try to be all things to all people. Except for the largest BBSs (some of which have over 150 phone lines), BBSs are small-scale operations run by enthusiastic volunteers, serving a dedicated but limited audience.

Another distinction between the big services and BBSs comes from their business philosophies. The big services are owned by mega-companies such as H&R Block, Sears, and IBM. BBSs are, by their nature, something that individuals create. Randy Seuss and Ward Christensen (yes, the same guy who invented Xmodem), started the first BBS in Chicago in 1978. From their earliest days, BBSs have been a way for users to help other users—with no rules except those that they set themselves.

BBS Services

As you saw in the online introductory chapters, most BBSs share a basic set of services. Most BBSs will include the following:

- ♣ File areas where you can upload and download files
- ♣ Bulletins with BBS-specific and community updates
- ♣ Message areas and electronic mail
- ♣ Utility features

The utility features enable you to modify your password, switch between novice and expert modes, and change other online options. (Don't worry about expert mode for a while. By the time you're ready for expert mode, you won't need this book anymore.)

You might have noticed that Hilgraeve's BBS didn't support electronic messages, except private ones to the Hilgraeve staff; that isn't unusual for a technical support BBS, because they don't want to take up online time on idle chatter between users, when others are frantic for help. Hilgraeve, like most other computer companies, provides support forums on the big services as well (CompuServe, in their case), so there's plenty of opportunity for users to interact on the larger services.

Depending on the BBS, you might find some other services as well.

Messages Passing In The Night

Some services enable BBSs to exchange messages and electronic mail. Using a *FidoNet* BBS (and usually for an extra fee), you can send e-mail across town or to the other side of the world with *Echomail*. The note you write in Phoenix about your favorite musicians might be read—and answered—by someone in Florida, Moscow, or Melbourne. Your message will travel through a circuitous modem path, passing from one BBS to the next, until it reaches the Fido BBS where your friend expects to read it.

Messages posted in one conference on a Fido BBS might be copied (or *echoed*) to BBSs all around the planet.

FidoNet dates back to the early 1980s, when hobbyists and software authors wrote utilities to automatically share files, messages, and electronic mail among various BBSs. The original Fido BBS software was written by two programmers living on opposite coasts who needed an easy way to exchange updates. FidoNet grew on an informal basis as more BBS operators, both public and private, began linking their systems.

Other BBS message exchange services (sometimes called Echomail) include the Relaynet International Message Exchange (RIME) and VirtualNet. (Figure 10.2 shows a message posted in Alabama, but read in Phoenix through VirtualNet.) There's no single "best" message exchange service any more than there's a "best" restaurant.

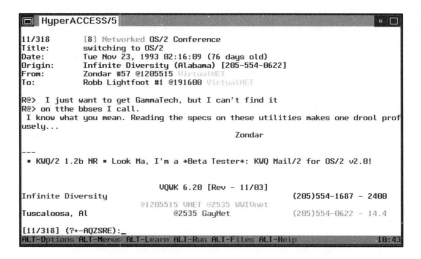

Figure 10.2

A message that's gone through one of the BBS networks shows where it originated.

A-door-ation

Quite a few BBSs support doors. A *door* is a sub-program to a BBS. Doors are usually game oriented; you can play online versions of Global War or Saratoga Raceway or BBS Chess. Online games can be solo, where you play by yourself, or they can be multi-player. In multi-player games, you can play the game with—or against—the other BBS users. Figure 10.3 shows me winning at a betting game.

Figure 10.3

You can play games online with doors.

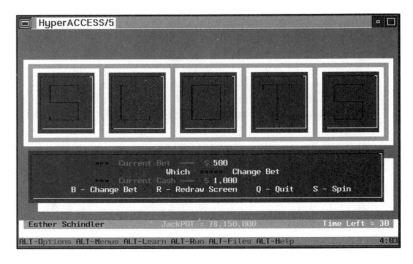

Doors are not limited to games. The variety of door services is simply stunning. There are loan analysts, searchable databases, questionnaires, voting booths, and so on. To use a door, you select a command such as Open to produce a menu of available doors on the BBS. (See figs. 10.4, 10.5, and 10.6.) The door is almost a small BBS in itself, with its own menus and options. When you're finished using a door, control passes back to your original BBS.

Figure 10.4

What's behind the door...

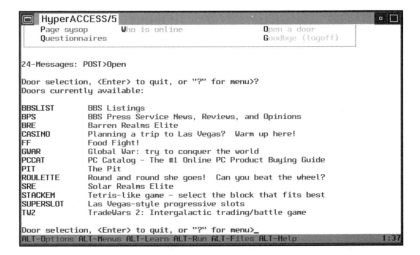

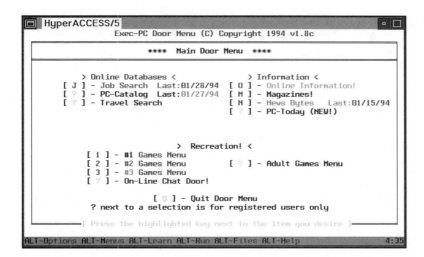

Figure 10.5

Another BBS door selection.

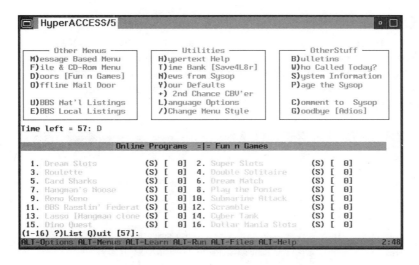

Figure 10.6

Another BBS door selection.

One common door supports an offline mail reader (see fig. 10.7). *Offline mail readers*, which are covered in more detail in Chapter 11, let you do most of your correspondence offline, on your own time, without the use of phone lines. You download a *mail packet* from the BBS, containing the messages addressed to you, as well as the new messages in the BBS conferences you mark as interesting. Using the mail reader, you can read your mail and compose replies to messages for a later upload. Once you upload the reply mail, it becomes part of the stream of messages in the conference.

Figure 10.7

*The door to an
offline mail reader.*

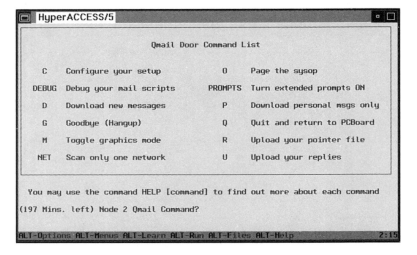

Figure 10.7

*The door to an
offline mail reader.*

Chatting Online

Some BBSs support *teleconferences*, open areas where the people who are
currently logged in can indulge in online chatter. You can usually see who
else is logged in to another node (another phone line that accesses the
service) with a menu command. Figure 10.8 shows a sample screen of
activity on a popular BBS.

Figure 10.8

*Looking at who's
currently online.*

```
┌─□─ HyperACCESS/5 ─────────────────────────────────────────── □ □─┐
│ W H O   I S   O N   T H E   N E T W O R K                        │
│ #  Time    DL  UL Current Activity Name & Location   02/07/94  14:59:05 │
│                                                                  │
│ 31 14:59            Logging on                                   │
│ 40 14:56  1087   5 Hyperscan(tm)    JOHN WUNDERLIN WAUWATOSA WI  │
│ 48 14:50  1835  83 External Door    PETE FANNING MILWAUKEE WI    │
│ 52 14:39  2827  41 Batch downloadZ  VERNON FRAZEE MIAMI FL       │
│ 100 14:30  431   0 External Door    PAUL HIBBARD BROOKFIELD WI   │
│ 101 14:55  941   1 Accessfile       STEVE DISTAD SOUTH MILWAUKEE WI │
│ 102 14:57  751   3 Batch downloadZ  JEFF DRISCOLL ORLANDO FL     │
│ 103 14:58  746   0 Bulletins        JACK ROOSA ROMEO MI          │
│ 104 14:44 1958   0 Batch downloadZ  SCOTT MAYORGA BEVERLY HILLS CA │
│ 105 14:52   23   0 Full Screen Edit JON WILCOX WAUKESHA WI       │
│ 106 14:51  352 144 Download prep    RICK OWEN IDAHO FALLS ID     │
│ 107 14:40  958   1 Full Screen Edit DUANE RUGG MILWAUKEE WI      │
│ 108 14:58  330   0 Reading messages LIZ DARING MILWAUKEE WI      │
│ 109 14:30  252   0 Listing Files    DENNIS BECKER WAUKESHA WI    │
│ 110 14:49  923   0 Batch downloadZ  STEVE NICOLOFF LAKE ZURICH IL │
│ 112 14:48 4534  34 Listing Files    JOHNH GORMAN CEDARBURG WI    │
│ 113 14:52 3581  96 Reading messages STEVEN MCCOY CARMEL IN       │
│ 114 14:57  565   6 Listing Files    JAMES FISH GERMANTOWN WI     │
│ 115 14:54 8364  36 Listing Files    JIM BOOS BROOKFIELD WI       │
│ 116 14:40 3568  18 Batch downloadZ  BOB NOVAK WEST ALLIS WI      │
│ >> More? ([Y]/(S)top/(C)ontinuous/(T)his screen/(W)ho           │
│ ALT-Options ALT-Menus ALT-Learn ALT-Run ALT-Files ALT-Help  1:56 │
└──────────────────────────────────────────────────────────────────┘
```

Teleconferences are most popular where the BBS community is local, minimizing long-distance phone charges for the members. I belonged to one BBS that had a "Koffee Klatch" teleconference at 11 p.m. every Sunday night. Participating in an online teleconference is a great way to interact with people in real-time. (Check out my poor victim in figure 10.9.)

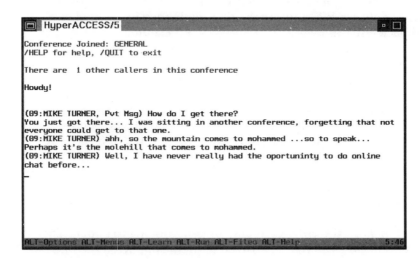

Figure 10.9

An online teleconference.

If you participate in a teleconference, you will learn the importance of improving your typing speed because much of your time is spent waiting for other people to type. As a result, you often wind up with two or more overlapping, interwoven conversations. It's usually more interesting than it is confusing.

Using Teleconferences for Business.

For several years, I participated in a weekly teleconference with 14 other user group officers spread all over the world. We had real business to discuss, and we managed to discuss it. However, there was plenty of idle chatter that turns acquaintances into fast friends (how fast? 9600 bps, of course!). I learned about Cincinnati chili, Australian slang, and Memphis barbecue. We also managed to get real work done—a fact which, because you know me by now, probably amazes you. It certainly amazes me.

BBS Costs

When BBSs were a new phenomenon, they were free. While there were business-related reasons to start a BBS (to create an internal company BBS, for instance), most of the people who set up and maintained the BBSs did so from the goodness of their hearts and the joy of experimentation. Some people ran BBSs during the day, while they were off at work. It was a laid-back environment, hard to predict but exciting.

Obviously, that couldn't last.

There are still many BBSs out there that are absolutely free, but it's getting hard to find them. Most of the free BBSs are sponsored by another agency. For instance, the equipment for a user group BBS is paid for by the membership dues of the user group. Many of the free BBSs are excellent—but quite a few are not.

Individual BBSs gained in popularity because they had the most files available for download or the best message conferences. The people who ran those BBSs had to pay for the hard disk space, as well as telephone lines, a place to keep the computer, and air conditioning to cool it. Then BBSs began to network so that several computers supported the BBS and more phone lines could be supported. As the services grew, so did the expense. It simply couldn't stay free.

For example, here's the equipment owned by one large national BBS, as of a few years ago: 25 Anchor 2400-bps modems, 58 US Robotics Dual Standards, 24 CompuCom 9600 Speedmodems, 5 Hayes V-Series V.42bis modems, and 16 direct telephone lines. These were networked together, and hooked up to 10 batteries that supplied 16 kilovolts of uninterruptible power. They had a four-ton air conditioning unit, the type that is ordinarily used for a 4,000 square foot house Three large humidifiers strained to keep up the humidity, to minimize static discharges that shot down the system, but they weren't always enough. Six people worked full-time to keep the BBS running.

Someone has to pay for all that!

When you join a BBS that charges for membership, you are put into a "demo mode." As a visitor, you can't use all of the services until you plunk down your cash, though you can usually see that they are present (it's the nyah-nyah form of marketing). Just like any other service, the cost of membership can vary from dirt-cheap to gasp-inducing expensive.

Most BBSs charge on a subscription basis (for example, $35 per year) or based on actual usage ($1 per minute). Some, however, charge based on how many files you download and the modem speed you use. In the latter cases, they often give you "credit" when you upload files. This is just one way a BBS can get more files to make available to its members.

BBS Customization

There aren't many standards in the world of BBSs. Every BBS menu looks different from every other BBS menu, even if they're based on the same software. The commands that you give the BBS to list files or to read messages can be convoluted, arcane, and arbitrary.

As a result, using a BBS can be incredibly frustrating to a novice. It's hard to remember that to read all the new messages on a PC Board BBS you type **R**, **A**, but to read the new messages on a Galacticom BBS, you type **M**, **R**, **S**.

BBS software packages are like word processors, spreadsheets, or any other type of software. People get religious about these things. Some Sysops swear by one brand of BBS software; others swear at it. Also, the people who write the BBS software make it easy for the Sysop to manipulate the menus—and it's clear that there are some Sysops out there who flunked kindergarten art.

Learn to embrace the differences between BBSs instead of getting frustrated with them. Remind yourself that customization is how BBSs distinguish themselves from one another. Notice the differences between the main menu screens shown in figures 10.10 and 10.11 and appreciate how different they can look, while supplying the same basic services.

If that positive attitude doesn't work, and you really hate the inconsistency in BBS interfaces, you will probably be happier on one of the larger consumer services. In any case, don't be afraid to experiment! You aren't going to blow anything up. I promise.

Figure 10.10

The main menu of a BBS.

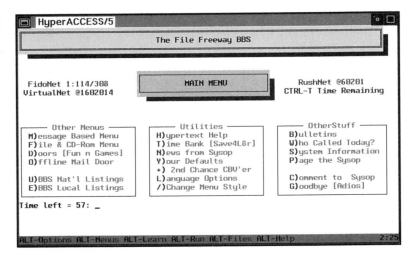

Figure 10.11

The main menu of another BBS.

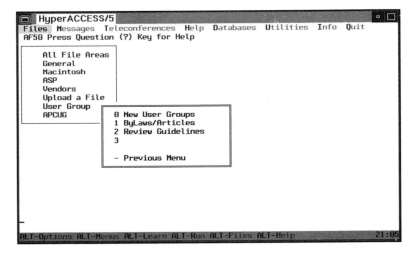

Using a BBS for the First Time

As you learned in earlier chapters, the first time that you dial into a BBS is a special case. Because the BBS doesn't know you, or anything about you, you have to provide that information. If it's a paid BBS, you have to learn about the subscription rates and so forth. And, because you're new to the neighborhood, you have to find out what the rules are.

Most BBSs provide different levels of access for each class of user. For instance, a hypothetical BBS might have levels such as the following:

- ℂ **New User.** We won't trust them with anything except filling out the questionnaire, peeking at what they aren't allowed to use (for example, can list files but not download them), and telling them what to do to graduate to the status of regular user. Assumed to be pond scum until they prove themselves worthy.

- ℂ **Regular User.** These folks are okay. They can do the "normal" stuff. Are no longer pond scum.

- ℂ **Privileged User**. They have access to special areas, extra time allotted, and are permitted on the super-way-fast new modem that the Sysop just installed. They can earn privileged status through higher fees or by bribing the Sysop with chocolate. Are definitely not pond scum.

- ℂ **The Sysop.** God.

Call-Back Verifying

In the BBS examples used in earlier chapters, you were automatically accepted as a new user. You were asked to provide your name and address, and not very much more; then the BBS registered you without any fuss. Presumably, when the Sysop looked at the records for new sign-ons for the day, she would raise an eyebrow, at least, if someone joined with a name like "Chaos Reigns"—that's not a good sign that a new member will be well-behaved on the board.

Of course, that's less of a problem on a technical support BBS; people don't tend to log in to make trouble, partly because most technical support BBSs are on the boring side. (Hey, face it. Did I ever promise you that those two were going to be *exciting*?) Other BBSs have to be more careful. Some accept credit cards of payment and, in any case, nobody likes a disturbing element.

To minimize deadbeats, many BBSs have a registration process that is much more complicated than the ones explored earlier. One of these is *call-back verification*.

When you reach a BBS that uses call-back verification, you go through something similar to the "regular" new user process—you fill in a questionnaire, choose a password, and so on. One question will ask you for the telephone number of your *data line*, that is, the telephone you're using for the modem as opposed to the one you use with your mouth. The BBS will give you instructions that inform you that it will hang up shortly and call *you*. You have to issue the proper commands to put your modem in auto-answer mode. When the BBS calls your computer a few minutes later, your modem will answer. The BBS will ask you to retype the password that you chose. Then, *voila!* the BBS will register you as a user, and you will no longer be considered pond scum. Provisionally.

Using a BBS that implements call-back verification might be the only time that you need to put the modem in auto-answer mode. It's really simple—honest. Your communications program might make it easy to do this by providing an option that says, "Auto-answer." (How simple!) If you have to do it from a terminal screen, type:

ATA

If the modem responds with OK, you're in business.

Frankly, I'm not too thrilled with BBSs that require call-back verification. For one thing, there are too many problems with it. What if you're dialing from a phone extension at work where modem access goes through the local area network? Someone will be peeved to hear a modem squeal in the ear, and you'll probably have to buy lunch for everyone because it was all your fault.

Also, call-back verification can be confusing for novices. It isn't too confusing for you, but then you're not a novice anymore. (You know what *bps* is, don't you? Has it occurred to you that you actually understand what is meant by those weird terms mentioned at the beginning of Chapter 1?)

Thankfully, call-back verification doesn't seem to be the wave of the future. At least, not *my* future.

Understanding Questionnaires

Most BBSs require that you fill out a questionnaire when you join. These can be brief and straightforward, asking simply for your name, address, and phone number. (Figure 10.12 shows a portion of a reasonable questionnaire.) Or, they can be long and detailed, requesting your marital status, astrological sign, and personal philosophy.

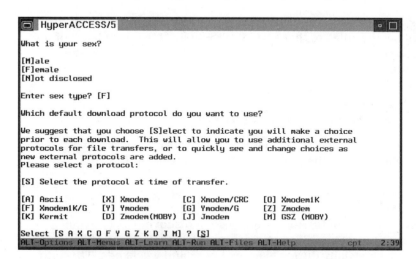

Figure 10.12

BBSs collect information about you in the membership questionnaire.

Some BBSs store the more personal information in a *registry* so that people of like interests can find each other. You never know; there might be someone out there who shares your obsession with embroidered pictures of Tom Cruise. The more personal information is usually optional; don't fill it in if you don't want to.

The Sysop might call the phone number you give, to confirm your identity. BBS Sysops have to be wary; after all, there's no way of knowing if you *are* a crazy person, or if someone joined the BBS with your name as a fake identity.

A Handle on the Situation

Most BBSs request that you join with your real first-and-last name. Others, particularly special-interest boards or those whose major purpose is chatting, encourage the use of *handles*, or aliases. If you're old enough to remember the CB-radio craze, you'll remember the term "handle"—it's exactly the same thing.

As with any other community, the appropriateness of a handle, and the use of one at all, depends on the environment. There are BBSs on which it would seem right to have a handle such as *Feisty Wench* or *Stud Muffin*.

Then again, you might find yourself in the electronic equivalent of show-ing up in blue jeans for a formal ball. Look around, first. Err on the conser-vative side.

In any case, if the Sysop requires a full, real name, supply it. If you don't want to follow the rules of that BBS, don't join it. There are plenty of other BBSs where you're sure to find people whose rules (or lack thereof) match your own.

Normal BBS Operation

You only join a BBS once, but you will probably use it again and again. This section addresses the day-to-day issues in using a BBS.

Busy signals

If you become active in BBSing, you will soon discover the constant companion of the active BBS participant: busy signals. Good BBSs are in high demand, especially during evening hours and weekends. The auto-matic redial feature of your communications program is certain to be-come a close friend... or at least a frequent one. Frequent busy signals usually indicate that the BBS is a popular one, implying that there is a reason for its popularity. As your favorite BBS grows, it will undoubtedly add more telephone lines and more services.

Some BBSs have a "standard" phone number, for the general public. If you pay extra, you can gain access to a limited access phone number, which will make it easier for you to get in.

You'll know that you've reached the BBS junkie stage when the following things happen:

- ✆ You recognize the tones mailed by dialing your favorite BBS. (The original BBS run by the Capital PC Users Group, in the mid-1980s, sang "Stronger Than Dirt." Really, it's true. 8848!)

- ✆ You justify an additional home phone line so that you can use the modem without disturbing the other members of your family.

- ✆ You write to your online best friend three times a day, but it's been two months since you called your mother. (Sorry, Mom!)

Understanding Online Graphics

There are at least three ways to view BBS menus:

- Text only
- ANSI graphics
- RIP graphics

Using color and graphics on a BBS slows down your online session. The BBS has to transmit those colors and characters to your computer over the modem, taking loads of time to do it. Thus, the fastest way to use a BBS is text-only, such as shown in Figure 10.13. If your intention, in using a BBS, is to acquire information and get off-line, then use text. When a BBS prompts Use Graphics? choose No.

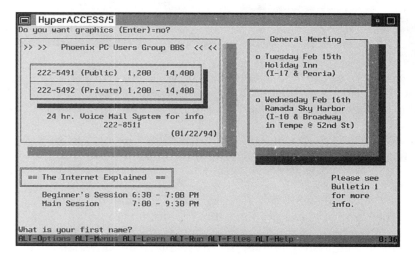

Figure 10.13

A BBS screen using simple text.

To use ANSI graphics, you will need to examine the CONFIG.SYS file on your hard disk. See if the CONFIG.SYS includes the following line:

```
DEVICE=ANSI.SYS
```

If it does, you can use ANSI graphics on any BBS. (If you're using OS/2, you will need to check the DOS settings for the communications program object.) ANSI stands for the American National Standards Institute, which developed standards defining how information is displayed on a computer screen. Using ANSI graphics, you will be able to see menus in color, and the screen can even blink (see fig. 10.14).

Figure 10.14

A BBS using ANSI graphics.

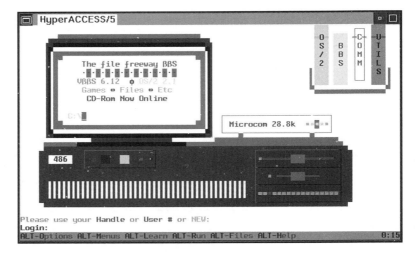

However, all of the "graphics" are created with the keyboard. Some people can do astounding things with ANSI graphics, a few of which are not suitable for discussion in a family book.

There's a new BBS graphics standard call *RIP graphics*, for Remote Imaging Protocol. It's just starting to gain acceptance on BBSs, so you will probably see it more and more. The results, as you can see in figure 10.15, are really pretty.

There's another type of online graphics that has nothing to do with BBS menus. Some BBSs, and CompuServe in particular, let you view graphic files interactively, if they're stored in the GIF graphics format. Some BBSs specialize in GIF images, which are also available for download. More than a few pay attention to adult-oriented graphics; others include a more prosaic variety, including pictures of Star Trek characters and a space shuttle.

Figure 10.15

RIP Graphics is a new standard that brings the graphic user interface to BBSs.

Messages

If the BBS is halfway decent, there's quite a bit of traffic in the message area. As a result, most Sysops break the message area into several topical sections. This way, you can read messages on topics you care about and ignore everything else. Figure 10.16 shows how one BBS subdivides the message area into conferences. Just to keep you on your toes, some BBSs refer to the sections as *conferences*, others as *message areas*. Before very long, someone else is sure to come up with another term for the same thing. You wouldn't want to get complacent, would you?

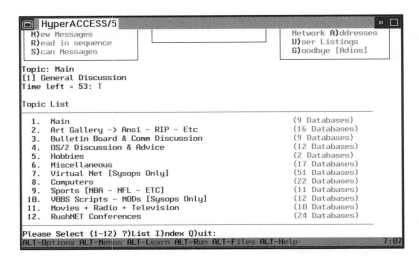

Figure 10.16

Message areas are subdivided into sections or conferences.

Reading Messages

You can read messages in several ways. First, you can scan messages, examining the subject, author, and date before you decide if you want to read the full message. You can read messages in the order that they were posted. Or you can read the message in thread order.

A message *thread* is the collection of a message and its replies... and the replies to the replies, and the replies to *those* replies. If you write a message that says, "Which desktop publishing package should I buy?" which gets five responses, and each of those responses gets a few responses, the entire collection of messages is called a *thread*. If you made a graphic representation of the thread, it would look something like an organization chart, as you see in figure 10.17. (This particular example is from CompuServe, not a BBS, but the theory is the same. It's just that Windows CIM makes it easy to view a map of the thread.)

Figure 10.17

A WinCIM message map.

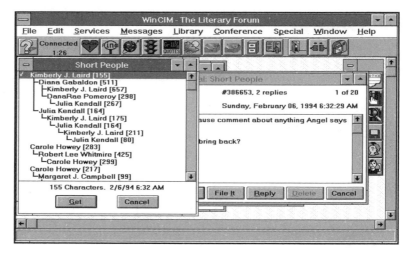

It usually makes the most sense to read messages in thread order. However, some BBSs make it awkward to do so.

Using an Online Editor

When you compose a new message or a reply on a BBS, you use an *editor*. Editors are similar to word processors, but they have a few features that word processors lack (such as the capability to attach a file to your message) and they leave out features that are standard in a word processor.

For instance, there's nothing in an online editor that makes it easy for you to spellcheck your message, and nobody cares that much about layout.

The standard online editor is called a line editor. A *line editor* (shown in fig. 10.18) lets you type or change just one line of text at a time. Using its user interface is as much fun as being trapped in an elevator for three hours with an enthusiastic accordionist.

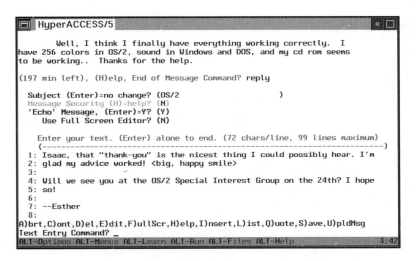

Figure 10.18

A BBS line editor.

You can also use a full-screen editor. A *full-screen editor* lets you work with your message as if it were a simple word processing document. Depending on the BBS software (and how elaborate the Sysop felt when he set up the system), you can add color and other ANSI characters to your message. Full-screen editors are still not a joy to use, but they are much more comfortable than line editors.

I continue to use a line editor when I'm writing interactively. Why? Firstly, I'm a geek, and I have been using BBSs for so long that I actually understand the arcane commands. (They tell me that psychiatry might be able to cure this.) Also, line editors are faster than full-screen editors because the BBS doesn't have to update the entire screen when you change one line. Okay, okay, at the bps rates I'm using, I shouldn't care about speed. It's habit, all right? And full-screen editors are more susceptible to errors from line noise.

When I really care about writing a lot on a given BBS, I use an offline mail reader.

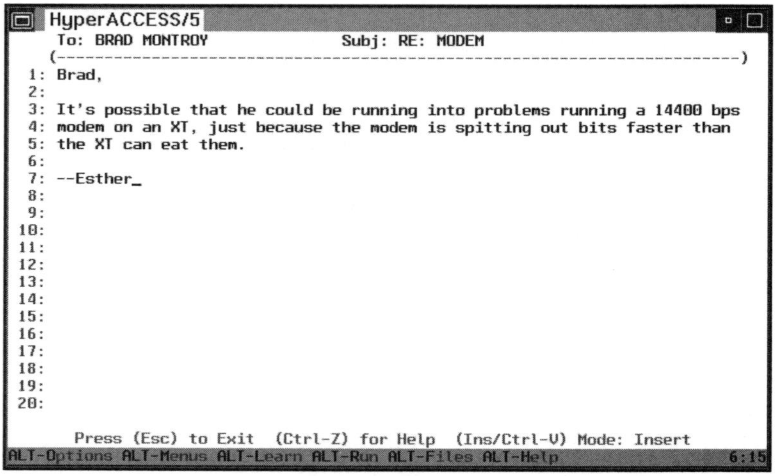

Figure 10.19

*A full-screen editor
on a BBS.*

```
┌─────────────────────────────────────────────────────────────────────────────┐
│ ▣ HyperACCESS/5                                                        ▫ □   │
│    To: BRAD MONTROY                      Subj: RE: MODEM                      │
│   (─────────────────────────────────────────────────────────────────────)   │
│ 1: Brad,                                                                      │
│ 2:                                                                            │
│ 3: It's possible that he could be running into problems running a 14400 bps   │
│ 4: modem on an XT, just because the modem is spitting out bits faster than    │
│ 5: the XT can eat them.                                                       │
│ 6:                                                                            │
│ 7: --Esther_                                                                  │
│ 8:                                                                            │
│ 9:                                                                            │
│10:                                                                            │
│11:                                                                            │
│12:                                                                            │
│13:                                                                            │
│14:                                                                            │
│15:                                                                            │
│16:                                                                            │
│17:                                                                            │
│18:                                                                            │
│19:                                                                            │
│20:                                                                            │
│                                                                              │
│       Press (Esc) to Exit   (Ctrl-Z) for Help   (Ins/Ctrl-V) Mode: Insert    │
│ ALT-Options ALT-Menus ALT-Learn ALT-Run ALT-Files ALT-Help           6:15    │
└─────────────────────────────────────────────────────────────────────────────┘
```

Thinking About E-mail Privacy

On most BBSs, the only difference between a public message in a conference and a private electronic mail message is that the e-mail message is
marked "private"—only the writer and the recipient can read it. Usually.
On some BBSs, the Sysop has the ability (though rarely the interest or
time) to read the content of private messages. If you're concerned about
the privacy of messages you leave on the BBS, *ask* before you post any
truly confidential information.

In contrast, messages sent as electronic mail on most of the national
services (particularly, MCI Mail and CompuServe) are truly private. The
staff can't read the messages even if you want them to do so. (Prodigy is a
notable exception to this rule.)

Tagging Along

You will often see a *tag line*, or a signature line, at the end of a BBS message. Most tag lines are amusing—or, at least, intended to be so, though
they can be used as advertising. Tag lines have recently gained in popularity because most off-line readers provide their own self-identification and
add a tag line at the end. See the following list for some examples of
taglines. (Figure 10.20 shows a message with an extravagant tag line.)

✆   All hope abandon, ye who enter messages here.

✆   —T-A+G-L-I+N-E—+M-E-A+S-U-R+I-N-G+—G-A+U-G-E—

✆   If this were an actual tagline, it would be funny.

✆   Unable to locate Coffee—Operator Halted!

✆   It's only a hobby ... only a hobby ... only a.

✆   Chicken heads are the chief food of captive alligators.

✆   I'm in shape ... round's a shape isn't it?

✆   Proofread carefully to see if you any words out.

✆   Mental Floss prevents Moral Decay.

✆   All wiyht. Rho sritched mg kegtops awound?

✆   Back Up My Hard Drive? I Can't Find The Reverse Switch!

✆   This tagline is umop apisdn.

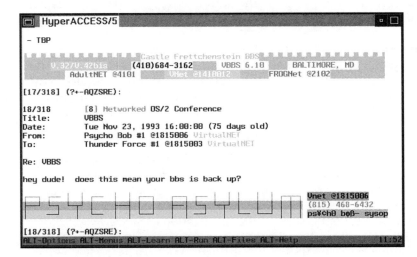

Figure 10.20

An extravagant tagline.

File Libraries

The file areas of most BBSs, like the message areas, are usually separated into sections based on the topic. Many BBSs contain an automatically-updated file that contains a list of every file on the BBS; it's usually named ALLFILES.TXT, or something similar.

BBSs can have hundreds or thousands of files in their file areas. Some of these files are informational, such as "how to install a second hard disk" or "the basics of genealogy." Others are graphics, such as the GIF files discussed above. There might be demonstration versions of popular programs. But the largest number of files, on most BBSs, are shareware or public domain applications.

About Shareware and Public Domain Software

Shareware is copyrighted software which is distributed on a "try before you buy" basis. You can share the program with other users and, in fact, you are encouraged to distribute it. Shareware programs permit you to use the program, without paying up-front, for a specified amount of time. If you continue to use the software, you are then honor-bound and legally-bound to *register* the software by mailing payment to the author. Shareware applications are almost always bargains because the author's effort has gone into improving the program instead of marketing costs. When you register the application, the author usually sends you the latest version, often including a printed manual.

There can be differences between the shareware version and the registered version of a program. Some authors encourage users to register by adding more advanced features in the registered version; other do so by taking away or limiting a feature in the shareware version. You usually get more functionality with the registered version, as well as a clear conscience.

Registering shareware is easy. You will find a file called ORDER.FRM in the compressed file, or there will be a registration form at the end of the electronic manual. Fill it out and mail it to the author with your check.

Many shareware authors belong to the Association of Shareware Professionals (ASP), an organization that tries to manage the enormous shareware industry. Some BBSs are "certified" ASP boards, which usually indicates that they have the latest version of the software.

Register your shareware, or you will burn in hell. (I don't know how I can put it more plainly.)

Public domain software applications don't have a copyright and are absolutely free. There are also programs that are copyrighted but free, such as the programs distributed by IBM in the Employee-Written Software (EWS) service. Not surprisingly, there aren't all that many public domain or free programs out there. They are usually small utilities, but they can be quite good!

Copyrights and Wrongs

If you upload a file to a BBS or other service, you *must* have the legal right to do so. Even if you think that *Slug Patrol* is the greatest game in the world, if it's commercial software, you do not have the right to distribute it. Distributing copyrighted software, without legal permission, is considered software piracy and is punishable by law. So is distributing any other file that you do not have the legal right to copy, such as a recording of the Terminator saying, "I'll be back."

Downloading Can Be a Batch

Several BBSs support batch file transfers. You can mark a number of files as you browse through the file listings and download them all at once. Your file transfer protocol must support a batch download format, however. (Zmodem and Kermit do.)

Uploading a file

Uploading a file to a BBS can be confusing, the first time. Here's the general sequence of events. These instructions assume that you are already connected to a BBS, logged in, and are sitting at a menu or a prompt line on that BBS.

1. Inform the BBS that you want to upload a file. Type **U** for upload.

2. When the BBS asks you for the file name, type the name: **frodo.zip** or **recipe.txt**. Don't include the full drive and directory name (the path name) where it's found on your disk.

3. The BBS will ask you for a description of the file, either before or after the file is transferred. On some BBSs, the file description is 40 characters long; on others, you can type a whole paragraph. You'll have to read the instructions online.

Please do your best to make the file description meaning-ful. "Newest version of a cool game" doesn't mean any-thing, a year down the road. How do I know it's really the newest version? If it's version 3.4, say so. If you don't know the version number, at least include the date of the program's release.

4. Choose a file transfer protocol when the BBS prompts you to do so. It's vital that you specify the same protocol at both ends of the connection. If you tell the BBS that you're going to send the file with Xmodem, and you tell the communications program to send it with Ymodem, you will have nothing but trouble.

Some BBSs record your protocol preference when you join, or remember the last one you used. If you need to change this, check the BBS utilities area.

5. When the BBS says something like, "Start the file transfer now," it's time to tell HA/5 (or whichever communications program you're using) that you want it to send the file. Using HA/5, press Alt+O for the options screen. Choose Transfer, and then select a file proto-col. Type the name of the file—this time with the full path name, for example, *d:\fantasy\frodo.zip*. The upload should start, with a status screen updating you of the file transfer progress.

If you have to stop the transfer for some reason, you can usually escape by pressing the Esc key on your end. You will probably have to press some key combination to interrupt the BBS, which is still waiting for a file transfer; the standard is Ctrl+X but you should read the BBS screen before blithely trying that.

The first few times you upload a file, you will probably be fascinated by the information on the status screen. (Don't be embarrassed—the first time I defragmented my hard disk, I thought that status screen was fascinating, too. What? Me, a nerd? How could you say such a thing!) Don't be alarmed if you see a few errors creep in during the upload; it just means that the communications software and the error-correcting mo-dems are doing their jobs. If you see a lot of errors, however, you might want to consider logging off the BBS, and trying again later, with a better phone connection.

If the error count starts with the very first block sent and counts up all the way, there are three probable causes:

- The BBS wasn't waiting for the upload yet.

- Some character (such as the 9 on the numeric keypad) was sent in front of the first block.

- The BBS and your communications program were using incompatible file transfer protocols. Some BBSs misname a protocol now and then. Watch out for Ymodem on many BBSs; on many boards, it's actually 1K-Xmodem.

Exploring BBS Software

When you access a BBS, you are actually calling and using another computer using BBS software. BBS software is just another application, one that happens to manage phone lines as well as files, messages, and the other features discussed in this chapter.

There are many BBS software packages available. Some of them are shareware. The most popular BBS packages, in no particular order, include:

- Wildcat

- TBBS

- PC Board

- RBBS-PC

- Galacticom

Most of the time, you won't care which software a particular BBS is using. Just like a book, you probably care more about the content than the layout. However, you might discover over time that there are BBSs whose interface you prefer, and others which you hate.

Finding BBSs To Access

It usually isn't difficult to find out about BBSs. There are over fifty thousand of them out there! Here are a few different ways to find out about BBSs in your area, or which specialize in areas of interest to you:

- ℂ   **Word of mouth.** Word of mouth is, of course, the most informal and most common way to find out about popular BBSs. Ask other people for advice at a computer user group meeting. They'll be happy to tell you about their favorites!

- ℂ   **BBS Messages.** You will find mention of other BBSs in BBS Messages. Some BBSs have a door that lists nearby BBSs. The quality of these lists varies widely because BBSs don't necessarily stay in business for very long. But because most of the phone numbers are local, it's worth calling them.

- ℂ   **Computer-related periodicals.** Some computer-related periodicals, both local and national, provide BBS listings. *The Computer Shopper* magazine, in particular, has a monthly listing of BBSs around the world, as well as a column dedicated to BBSing (and another one which discusses online life in general). If there's a local computer newspaper, find out if they can provide you with a list.

- ℂ   **Special interest periodicals.** If you're interested in a special topic, whether it's chile pepper cooking or genealogy, look in the special interest periodicals that you already subscribe to. There are often several BBSs listed or advertised.

- ℂ   **Computer hardware and software companies.** Computer hardware and software companies often have technical support BBSs. Find out what the telephone number is by looking in the user manual.

- ℂ   **This book.** You will also find a listing of popular BBSs and selected user group BBS in the back of this book.

The Online Community

The people that you meet online form a community, one that extends around the world. The world becomes a smaller place because it's so easy to correspond with people about any topic whatsoever. Some people refer to the online universe as *cyberspace,* a universe that exists in a virtual (or un-real but created) world.

The only thing that matters when you communicate on a BBS or on an online service is what you have to say—what you think, what you feel, what you choose to talk about. Some people are all-business; others are terminally chatty. When you're online, your identity is who you present yourself to be. Your race, creed, color, geographic location, and other minutiae don't matter unless *you* make them matter.

I have talked about everything from earthquakes to managing volunteers, without discovering the gender of my correspondent. (Eventually, I discovered that Chris was Christine, not Christopher. The mind does an indescribable, odd little mental twist when that happens.)

One online friend never mentioned, in three years of online acquaintance, that he had cerebral palsy and was wheelchair bound. His "disability" (it's hard to imagine that Howard was disabled in any way) mattered just as little as we all wish it would matter. Only when I was planning a trip to his city did Howard's physical attributes become relevant.

Had I initially met him in person, I would have noticed the wheelchair before I noticed the kind, funny, giving person who shared my appreciation of puns and chocolate. Online, Howard was able to be Howard, not some disabled guy. That's a really cool thing.

Because it's so easy to become involved with online friends, it's possible to forget about the lurkers. When you're involved in a discussion in a public forum on CompuServe, or loudly proclaiming your personal preferences on a BBS, your attention is focused on the people with whom you're corresponding. You think you're talking in a living room, but you're really standing on a stage, with the spotlight turned on. I have been startled when I meet people at conferences, and utter strangers tell me about my life—the name of my new kitten, my fondness for chocolate (I bet that's a revelation to you, huh?), and my choices in software. Remember that you are in a public place. Don't say anything that you wouldn't say at a crowded party.

The Rules of the Road

As in any other community, behavior is bound by manners and many spoken and unspoken rules. In "real life" we spend most of our childhood learning those rules. Because you're new to the online community, it helps to have an introduction so that you don't embarrass yourself unnecessarily. These should warm the cockles of your heart. (Nobody likes cold cockles.)

Many new users type their messages in all uppercase because it seems easier. Don't do it. Using "all caps" is considered to be SHOUTING and is very difficult to read.

When you post a new message on a BBS, don't post it in every section of the board. You might think that you're reaching the largest possible audience by doing so, but most people read every section on a BBS or in an online forum if they care about the subject at all. You're just wasting time and money for other people. This makes them cranky.

Also, when you post a message, make your subject meaningful. If you post a message to ask for help in the Fax Software Conference, don't give the message a title of "Fax Software." That's a given; try "Which package to try?" or "FaxWorks - WordPerfect Problem." The more specific you can be, the sooner you will get your question answered and the more accurate the answer will be.

Remember that everyone involved in a discussion online is there as a volunteer. The online community is formed of people who really care, who will help you with technical and non-technical problems just because they want to help. Very few people get paid for this. Be grateful, and let the gratitude show. Even better... the best way to thank someone who helped you is to be there for the next person who needs help. Help someone else. Be a giver as well as a taker. It's a lot more rewarding.

Keep the nature of the specific community in mind. If you visit an adult BBS, don't be startled by the adult content. Most BBSs are family-oriented in nature, however, so be aware of the language you use. Avoid using words that would be excluded from the nightly news.

Respecting Other People

In the heat of an emotional argument with someone else, it's easy to let your emotions get involved. That's good. What isn't good—and is rarely permitted by the Sysop—is to attack another individual personally. You can say that someone's opinion is wrong, or that they have a stupid opinion. You cannot say that the other person is stupid. There's a subtle but important difference.

The point of all our conversations (online or not) is to make the world a better place, to increase understanding (whether about the star of a movie or about the best programming language to use). Accusing people of stupidity doesn't move us in that direction. Trying to understand why someone has "a stupid opinion," and offering facts to back up your point of view, *does*.

Every one of us has done dumb things. Repeatedly. We have all made mistakes. Do you consider yourself a hopeless jerk as a result? Or, rather, do you figure that there's still plenty to learn in life (from oneself as well as from others)?

Give others the same benefit of the doubt. Provide compelling, logical reasons to prove your side of the story—*that* can convince others to agree with your viewpoint. Nobody is going to agree with you (publicly at least) that he is a blithering idiot; he is not going to listen to you particularly well when you engage in name-calling. If you're down to name-calling, it's because you feel helpless to change the situation in some other, more-meaningful manner.

Flame Wars

There are some experiences that everyone needs to experience for himself. No amount of "good advice" will prevent you from falling in love with the wrong person, will teach you to back up your hard disk regularly, or will keep you from getting involved in a flame war. You just have to learn the lesson the hard way.

A *flame war* is an online discussion that generates more heat than light. While you can have emotional tirades about any topic, the key to a flame war is that *nobody will change his mind as a result of the conversation*. Is there anything that someone could possibly say that will change your mind about computer architecture, the moral issues regarding abortion, or the rights of smokers? No? Then don't get into a discussion on the topic!

You aren't going to listen to me—you know it. You're going to get into at least one flame war in your online existence (with someone who, I'm quite sure, is an absolute jerk—after all, *he* didn't buy this book). Hopefully, you will get it out of your system quickly, like your first love affair gone-bad.

Don't say I didn't warn you.

Understanding Online Jargon

People who work together in any business develop a shared jargon. The online community is no exception. There are many words and terms that online junkies use which can be confusing to the newcomer.

Back when online access was much more expensive (CompuServe was $21/hour at 1200 bps 10 years ago) and everyone was much more conscious of every character transmitted, people developed an online short-hand. BTW is *by the way*, for instance. Even though they're no longer strictly necessary on the grounds of cost, the abbreviations have stuck. Then again, maybe it's because most people don't like to type. Table 10.3 shows a few of the most common:

Table 10.3
Common Online Abbreviations

Online Jargon	What It Stands For
BTSOOM	Beats the S**t Out Of Me
BTW	By The Way
FWIW	For What It's Worth
GD&R	Grinning, Ducking, and Running

Online Jargon	What It Stands For
IAC	In Any Case
IANAL	I Am Not A Lawyer
IMHO	In My Humble Opinion
IOW	In Other Words
OTOH	On The Other Hand
PITA	Pain In The A**
PMJI	Pardon My Jumping In
ROFL	Rolling On Floor Laughing
RSN	Real Soon Now
RTFM	Read The (expletive deleted) Manual
TIC	Tongue In Cheek
TPTB	The Powers That Be
TTFN	Ta Ta For Now
WTH	What The H***

When people talk on the telephone or in-person, they depend on nonverbal cues to improve communication. Sometimes, it's hard to tell if someone is pulling your leg, or being facetious, until you look at her face.

Those nonverbal cues don't exist in cyberspace. Because we still need those cues, people include *emoticons* in their messages to serve the same purpose. Emoticons are a direct description of a physical action, usually in brackets: *<grin>* or *[blushing]*, for instance. They, too, can have their own form of shorthand: *<g>* (for <grin>) or *:-)* (turn your head sideways to the left, and it will look like a smiley-face). There are hundreds of emoticons, some of which incorporate abbreviations.

Learning to communicate well online can make you a much better writer. If it is possible to be misunderstood online, someone absolutely will misunderstand what you say. As a result, you will learn to be more rigorous and careful in what you say and how you say it. If you care about the topic you're writing about, you will quickly discover that you learn to express yourself well. Don't be afraid to use emoticons liberally, if they help your message. The important thing is to let yourself show, and to be clear about what you say. Following the rules in Table 10.4 will help you do this.

The following appeared on Kanto Central, a popular BBS that used to operate in Tokyo, Japan:

"THIRTY WAYS TO LOVE KANTO CENTRAL" (Or Whatever Bulletin Board System You May Happen To Call)

1. Thou shalt remember thy name and password.
2. Thou shalt check thine facts and name thy sources that all may verify.
3. Thou shalt not POST IN ALL CAPS!
4. Thou shalt use thy real name.
5. Thou shalt not monopolize a topic.
6. Honor thy moderator.
7. Thou shalt not covet thy neighbor's password nor handle.
8. Thou shalt not post messages that are stupid, worthless, or lack meaning.
9. Thou shalt use the English language properly.
10. Thou shalt spell thy words correctly.
11. Thou shalt not use a "handle" unless thine computer is a portable.
12. Thou shalt delete thine olden messages.
13. Thou shalt help other users.
14. Thou shalt not post anonymously when offering criticism.

15. Thou shalt keep thy foul language to thyself.

16. Thou shalt not occupy thy favorite system with thine arguments, for verily, I say unto thee that thou shalt make a fool of thyself.

17. Woe be unto the user who attempt to crash a system, for he or she shalt be cast out from the sanctuary of the hobby and must repent by doing 40 days and 40 nights of penance of voice-only communications.

18. Thou shalt first dial modem numbers during the day by way of voice line to assure correct numbers.

19. Thou shalt not beg for e-mail.

20. Thou shalt not post messages while drunk, stoned, or bent out of shape.

21. Thou shalt confine thy messages to those of friendship, requests for assistance, aid to the needy, advice, and advancement of thy hobby; and thou art obligated to repel any who wouldst transgress upon those commandments.

22. If thou doth promise to reply to a message and thou doth not, then surely thou shalt spill coffee into thy keyboard and burn out thy central processing chip.

23. Thou shalt not giveth any false information when applying for membership, for verily it is written that whosoever shall do so will surely be found out and thy welcome on all boards will be terminated forever and ever.

24. Thou shalt log in properly and in accordance with the system rules.

25. Thou shalt observe length limits.

26. Thou shalt not upload "worm" programs.

27. Thou shalt not ask stupid questions that are already fully explained in the topic or instructions.

28. Thou shalt not exchange copy protected software through the BBS.

29. Thou shalt not violate applicable local laws and regulations affecting telecommunications, or ye shall will feel the wrath of thy judicial system.

30. Thou shalt not hack.

Care & Feeding of Your Sysop

Despite my jokes about Sysops, they deserve your fullest respect. Sysops usually invest their own time to make the board a success, and much of their work is invisible to the membership. There is no job so thankless as reviewing newly uploaded files at midnight. Oh, okay, changing a diaper is more thankless. Just barely.

Remember, too, that the Sysop's word is law. Sure, they wield some power, but they also have responsibility to go with it. If someone posts a copyrighted file or a credit-card number on the board, it's the Sysop that takes the heat.

Say "thank-you" to the Sysop, occasionally. Those two words are the most powerful in the universe.

It won't take you long to discover that most BBS menus have an option that says, "Page the Sysop." That option makes the BBS beep until the Sysop answers. You can usually engage in a live "chat" with the Sysop, which is extraordinarily useful when you're new and confused, or you need some specific help. However, don't misuse this feature. If the Sysop is present (and, in most cases, they aren't), he might be busy in a task that's really difficult to escape. Don't be afraid to ask for help if you need it, but don't be a pest either.

BBSs have to get the files they distribute from somewhere. In most cases, they get shareware programs and other files because members upload them. Some BBS software is configured so that you get credit every time you upload a file. Others don't enforce rules like this (it can lead to a BBS full of useless files as people want the free credit), but do remember that both the BBS universe and shareware are based on users helping users. Contribute what you can. If you find a good shareware program, and a good BBS, do your part to make it better.

Chapter 11

Cutting Costs with Your Modem

By now, you have discovered how cool modems can be. You have made a few friends and found a storehouse of shareware programs dedicated to your favorite hobby. A congenial stranger even helped you figure out the cause of the strange sound in your computer. (How *did* the kitten get in there?) Then the bad news arrived.

You got the bill.

If you dive into online life wholeheartedly, that first phone bill or credit-card bill can be a killer. On CompuServe, people who participate actively until the Visa bill arrives are called "forty-day wonders." After the first bill arrives, those people disappear from the service faster than ice cream on a hot July day.

It doesn't need to be like that, however. With some good tools, a bit of knowledge, and common sense, life online can be affordable as well as fun.

Saving Money with Hardware

One quick fix is to buy a faster modem, or to improve the performance of the one you already own, but there are many methods people use to save time and, therefore, money.

Using a Faster Modem

If most of your online activity is uploading or downloading files, you will save money by switching to a faster modem. If you are making long-distance calls, spending less time online translates directly into less time using the expensive phone line.

If you use one of the consumer services, however, check the difference in rates before you run out to the store for a faster modem. Accessing the larger services at 1200 bps or 2400 bps costs the same, but the hourly charge for 9600 bps or 14400 bps is higher. It probably *will* be cheaper to use a faster modem, even at a higher hourly rate, if your major activity is file transfer. It will also be worth the upgrade if you're using one of the online navigators (discussed later in this chapter).

If you're using an online service for exchanging interactive messages, the upgrade won't make that much difference. When you type interactively online, you're just idling faster.

Modem Hardware Features

Make sure that you're using the error-checking and data compression that is built into your modem. This implies that you have to learn more about the setup and initialization strings used by your communications program, but doing so is free—if it makes a difference in your phone bill. (Say, *how* big did you say that bill was, again?)

This would be a good time to dig out your modem manual as well as the manual for your favorite communications software. It's possible (though not likely) that you have the data compression or another time- or data-saving device turned off in your initialization settings. With a little experimentation, however, you might be able to tweak your settings to get just a little bit more performance out of the equipment. (If you admit that you actually enjoy doing this, you'll be getting your Official Computer Geek card in the mail in no time at all.)

Saving Money with Software

There are several software tools that help you to maximize what your communications software does and to minimize the amount of time you actually spend online.

How File Transfer Protocols Can Save You Money

Obviously, the fastest way to get your files is to use the fastest file transfer protocol available on the service. In general, the newer the protocol, the faster the data will flow. You can get some clue of its age from the name of the file protocol—Xmodem is oldest, Ymodem is slightly newer, Zmodem is among the newest. Kermit, which is named after the muppet, is an older, fairly slow protocol.

If the BBS supports the feature, use batch mode for file transfers. *Batch modes* enable you to select several files and download them all at once. Not only do you save time because the modems are able to devote their attention to one another, but you don't have to hover around the computer—waiting for one download to finish so that you can type in another file name.

You probably wouldn't hang around, anyway, as you probably have better things to do than watch a download status screen. So the major time savings comes from the fact that you aren't wasting time in the kitchen, making yet another cup of hot chocolate, while your forlorn modem sits in the office and blerps that it's done with that download, and what, oh master, should it do now?

File Compression

File compression has two purposes:

- ℂ   To save disk space

- ℂ   To group together related files

Ten Pounds in a Five-Pound Bag

Imagine that your file is a down sleeping bag. You can squish the sleeping bag into a really tiny backpack, but you can't sleep in it when it's squished. You have to take the sleeping bag out of the pack before you can use it for its normal purpose.

Similarly, after you *archive* or *compress* a file, you have to de-compress the file before it can be used. The process is also called unzipping (for files compressed with PKZIP) or de-archiving (*Archiving* originally referred to a file compressed with ARC, but has evolved into a generic term). You might also hear the process referred to as *packing* and *unpacking*.

You archive a file to squish it into a compressed format. You de-archive it or un-compress it to get it back into its original format. Because file compression reduces the file size necessary to store the information, you spend less time downloading, and thus you save on online charges.

The first compressed files used a process called "bit packing" and had file extensions such as .LIB or .SQZ (e.g. *modem.lib* or *modem.sqz*). As computers got faster and memory and disk capacity increased, the various file compression methods continued to improve as well. There are several different file compression formats—ARC, ZIP, ZOO, LZH, SIT, and probably a half dozen more that I can't remember. Although the details and the efficiencies of the various compression methods differ, the central idea remains the same.

The original compression or *archive* format, developed by System Enhancement Associates (SEA) used a file extension of ARC. Other compression formats were developed that were faster and created smaller files, but you might still find an occasional ARC file. The ARC format is available for most hardware platforms, so it's the lowest common denominator. The most popular compression format on IBM PC-compatibles, however, is PKWare's PKZIP.

You can't run a compressed file directly. If you downloaded MODEM.ZIP from your favorite BBS, you will have to de-compress the file before you can run the program (or programs) stored inside. To de-compress a file, you need the de-compression utility that matches the compression program; PKZIP uses PKUNZIP, for example. Without the program to de-compress the file, the zipped file is completely useless.

Some archive programs can create a special form of compressed files called self-extracting. A *self-extracting* file does not require a decompression utility. When you run the file (MODEM.EXE), it will decompress itself.

Any of the compression utilities will enable you to group together, in the one compressed file, all of the support files belonging to a specific program. Any kind of file can be included: a spreadsheet file, word processing document, a graphics file, or program files.

The exact amount that any file can be compressed will depend upon the actual content of that file. For example, certain text files can be compressed to as little as 35 percent of their original size, although GIF graphics files will not compress at all.

Using File Compression

Most archiving utilities will provide a short help screen if you type the program name without any parameters. For example, typing:

```
PKUNZIP
```

displays the following options:

```
-c[m] = extract to screen [with more]  -t = test zipfile integrity
-d = create directories stored in ZIP  -l = display software license
-n = extract only newer files          -o = overwrite existing files
-q = enable ANSI in comments           -s<pwd> = unScramble with password
-p[a,b,c][1,2,3] = extract to printer [Asc mode,Bin mode,Com port] [port #]
-j<H,S,R> = mask off Hidden/System/Readonly attributes upon extraction
-J<H,S,R> = don't mask off Hidden/System/Readonly attributes
-v[b,c,d,e,n,p,s,r] = view ZIP(s) [Brief listing/sort by Crc/Date/Ext
   /Name/Percentage/Size/sort Reverse (descending) order]
zipfile = ZIP file name, wildcards *,? ok.  Default extension is .ZIP
file    = Name(s) of files to extract. Wildcards *,? ok. Default is ALL
files.
```

Compression programs are extremely flexible and powerful, so you should read the documentation carefully before you try anything fancy. Remember that these programs are shareware; if you use them, make sure you register them!

With the PKZIP program, you can create a new ZIP archive of all the files in the current directory by typing the command:

```
PKZIP -MZEX FIZZY.ZIP *.* [Enter]
```

This will create the archive FIZZY.ZIP and will move all the files in the current directory into the new archive, using maximum compression. PKZIP will pause before it compresses each file to enable you to type in a comment identifying the files that will be in the archive.

Figure 11.1 shows what happens when you unzip a file. The program identifies each file during the de-compression.

Figure 11.1

Unzipping a file.

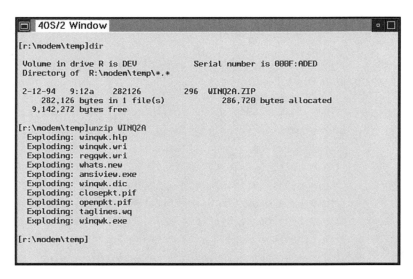

As a file is added to an archive, the program identifies the file, and lets you know how much the file was compressed. See figure 11.2.

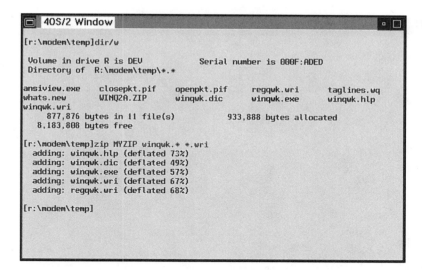

Figure 11.2
Zipping files into a new archive.

You can use the command-line decompression program to find out what files are in a specific archive (What was that *futhr.zip*, after all?). However, there are several handy utility programs that make it easier to look at the contents of your zipped files, and, in some cases, do the archiving and de-archiving from within the program. It's certainly a more understandable process. Figures 11.3 and 11.4 show you archive file viewers for OS/2 and Windows.

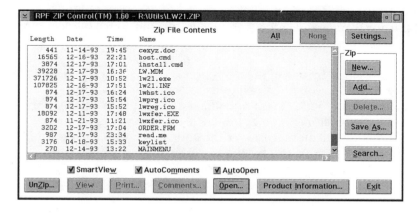

Figure 11.3
An archive file viewer for OS/2...

Figure 11.4

...and one for Windows.

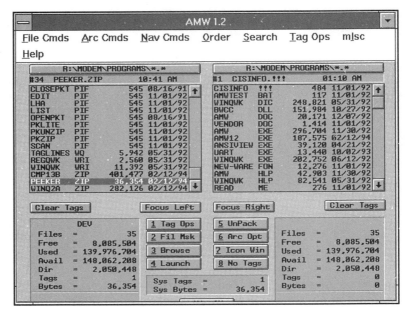

Offline Readers

The purpose of an offline reader or navigator is to automate the use of the BBS or online service and, in the process, to reduce connect time to a minimum. The time-consuming tasks of reading or replying are done using the facilities of your own computer where the computer time is "free." The programs for BBSs are called *offline readers*; for the consumer services such as CompuServe, they're called *navigators*.

The efficiency provided by one of these programs can save you a great deal of money. If it takes you fifteen minutes to compose a message online, that might cost you $2. Prepared offline and sent with a navigator or offline reader, the cost might be as low as 22 cents for the same message. Multiply this by 100 messages over the course of a year (or even a month) and you start to get a feel for the savings that one of these programs can provide. They make it possible for you to participate without busting your budget.

Using an Offline Reader

Most BBS interaction is like wandering around the student union at a college. You look around at the bulletin board to see if there are any interesting notices, and you hang around the social area to see if anyone you like wanders by.

Having an offline mail reader is like owning a post office box. Although you can still hang around the post office if you like (our rural Maine post office was the best place to hear the local gossip), most of what you do is pick up and drop off mail. You still correspond with people, and you still send them the same information; you just don't take as much time to do it. Because you're actively online for less time, you save money—and you also free up the BBS so that it's easier for someone else to dial in.

Another advantage to using an offline reader is that you gain a consistent user interface for reading and responding to messages. Because so many BBSs have different menu structures, it's much easier to be able to read and respond to messages using a program that you already know.

In order to use an offline reader, the BBS you call must have a "QWK" mail door, because it's the BBS's responsibility to create the mail "packets" that it sends to you. A mail packet almost always includes messages. It can also include bulletins, a list of new files posted on the BBS since your last call, and a newsletter file from the sysop, announcing changes and updates to the BBS.

Mail packets are created and stored in a compressed format (which often uses, or incorporates, PKZIP), allowing many small files to be packed into a single larger file. These programs are referred to generically as Packers and Unpackers. In many cases, you can choose which compression program you want the BBS to use. The offline reader uses the packers and unpackers to process mail packets. You must use the same tool as the BBS did. If the BBS packed the file using PKZIP, the offline reader will require that you have PKZIP (and PKUNZIP) on your computer.

The offline reader reads the packets, stored in a standard format called "QWK," and lets you use its built-in browser and editor to read and respond to messages. Depending on the program, you can also select files to be uploaded or downloaded, or use the word processor or editor of your choice.

After you're done reading and responding to messages, the offline reader will assemble your replies and commands into a mail packet. Then you can get back onto the BBS, online, to upload the reply packet.

Here's the process:

1. Log onto your favorite BBS and select its mail door.

2. Check your configuration options. For instance, you probably want to verify the file transfer protocol (which the door may or may not "remember" from the main BBS), and select the BBS sections you want to download.

3. Tell the BBS to send the mail packet. The BBS software will bundle the new or selected messages into a file, archive that file, and then send you the file, as shown in figure 11.5.

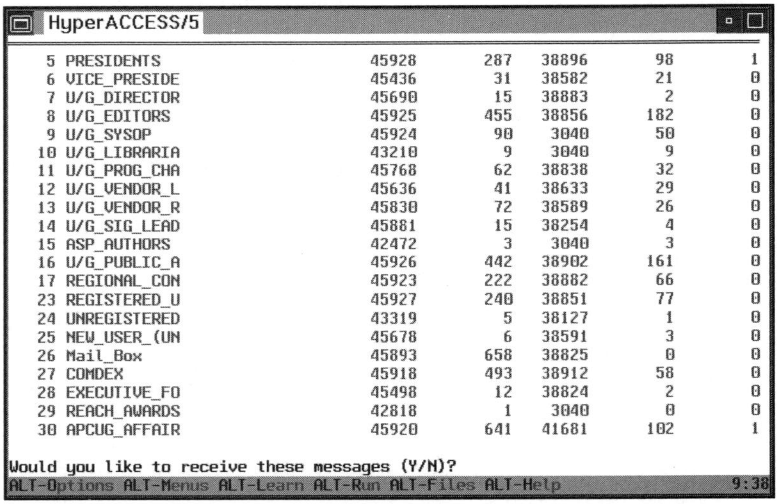

Figure 11.5

Selecting messages to download in a mail packet.

```
┌──────────────────────────────────────────────────────────────────┐
│ ▣  HyperACCESS/5                                           □  □   │
├──────────────────────────────────────────────────────────────────┤
│     5 PRESIDENTS           45928      287    38896      98       1 │
│     6 VICE_PRESIDE         45436       31    38582      21       0 │
│     7 U/G_DIRECTOR         45690       15    38883       2       0 │
│     8 U/G_EDITORS          45925      455    38856     182       0 │
│     9 U/G_SYSOP            45924       90     3040      50       0 │
│    10 U/G_LIBRARIA         43210        9     3040       9       0 │
│    11 U/G_PROG_CHA         45768       62    38838      32       0 │
│    12 U/G_VENDOR_L         45636       41    38633      29       0 │
│    13 U/G_VENDOR_R         45830       72    38589      26       0 │
│    14 U/G_SIG_LEAD         45881       15    38254       4       0 │
│    15 ASP_AUTHORS          42472        3     3040       3       0 │
│    16 U/G_PUBLIC_A         45926      442    38902     161       0 │
│    17 REGIONAL_CON         45923      222    38882      66       0 │
│    23 REGISTERED_U         45927      240    38851      77       0 │
│    24 UNREGISTERED         43319        5    38127       1       0 │
│    25 NEW_USER_(UN         45678        6    38591       3       0 │
│    26 Mail_Box            45893      658    38825       0       0 │
│    27 COMDEX              45918      493    38912      58       0 │
│    28 EXECUTIVE_FO        45498       12    38824       2       0 │
│    29 REACH_AWARDS        42818        1     3040       0       0 │
│    30 APCUG_AFFAIR        45920      641    41681     102       1 │
│                                                                    │
│ Would you like to receive these messages (Y/N)?                   │
│ ALT-Options ALT-Menus ALT-Learn ALT-Run ALT-Files ALT-Help   9:38 │
└──────────────────────────────────────────────────────────────────┘
```

The download will proceed just like any "normal" download, just like you see in figure 11.6; the BBS can preselect a standard name for the file. For instance, the GlobalNet BBS automatically assigns the mail packet a file name of GLOBLNET.QWK; the Phoenix PC User Group's BBS uses PHXPCUG.QWK.

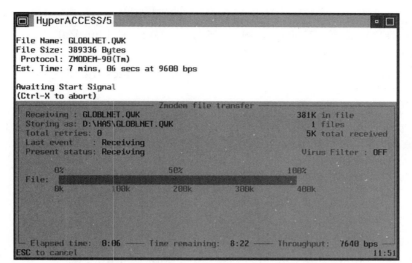

Figure 11.6

Downloading a mail packet is just like downloading any other file.

4. Log off the BBS.

5. Start your offline mail reader. Select the file that you just down-loaded.

6. Using the instructions distributed with your offline mail reader (they're all slightly different), read the messages in the different conferences, reply to messages, and, in short, have a great time. You aren't online, right now, so you aren't being charged in any way for what you do. Figure 11.7 shows a typical offline reader in action.

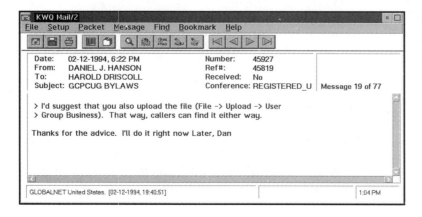

Figure 11.7

Reading a message in an offline message reader.

7. When you're done, close the mail packet and exit the program. The program will probably compress (zip) your files automatically and do other things to "put the packet away."

8. Start your communications program again. Call back the BBS, log in, and enter the mail door.

9. This time, select "upload mail packet." Upload your reply file (which will have a similar name to the original file name—check the specific program carefully). The upload will proceed just like any upload. At the end, the mail door will examine the contents of your mail packet and will distribute the messages where they belong.

Using Navigators

Offline readers require that the BBS have a mail door that will create mail packets. Most offline navigators for the consumer services, such as those for CompuServe, don't have that option. Navigators don't do very much more than you would do—they type in the commands that retrieve messages, search for files, and so on. They just do it much, much faster than you could type the information, and they automatically save the data to your disk. Plus, they provide tools that make it easy to read and respond to messages, download files, and most of the other things that you'd want to do online. In this way, they're very similar to the BBS offline readers.

There are navigators available for nearly every service and nearly every hardware platform. Because the consumer services are on a pay-as-you-go basis, they can quickly get very expensive if you use them interactively. If you have to add long distance charges to that, the cost becomes prohibitive. Navigators address that problem and make it easier to be efficient with your online time.

Using the Online Toolbox

There are an astounding number of tools and utilities intended to improve your online efficiency and to make your online life easier. Although most of them won't save you any money directly, anything that can help you work better is a good idea.

One example is a *thread management* program. Because most of the offline readers and navigators save the messages you've read to disk, you can amass lots of files that contain nothing but message threads. You might want to keep some of those messages (for instance, the really funny jokes), but delete the others. Although you could edit the files with an ordinary text editor or with a word processor, a *thread management tool* enables you to select, move, mark, or delete messages based on section, topic, age, or any of several other options. (See fig. 11.8.)

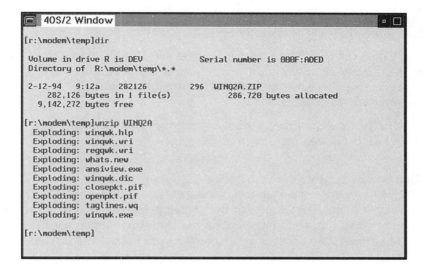

Figure 11.8

Recon is a shareware program that manages messages captured from CompuServe.

Saving Money on the Phone System

There's just so much you can do to save money with your computer system. Scrutinize your telephone usage to see if you can save money there, too.

Packet Networks

Did you ever go past a railroad's "piggyback" freight yard? Packet networks work like that. At the freight yard, trailers from eighteen-wheeler trucks are loaded onto flatbed railcars headed to a distant city. There, each trailer is removed and latched behind new trucks for delivery to a specific location. To save even more money, many of those trucks combine even smaller loads, from a number of shippers, that can be taken apart and redistributed at a central truck terminal.

Packet networks can save you money in a similar way. Earlier, you learned that files can be broken down into individual packets that are sent separately via the phone system. Your phone line is the truck that picks up these packages at your home and business and sends each to the computer you call. You specify which computer to send a packet to by putting its address on each packet. Because you use fewer resources this way, the cost is controlled.

A packet network works like this:

1. First, you call a local phone number.

2. Next, a piece of equipment called a packet switch (which works like the piggyback freight yard) loads your packets onto a data circuit designed to carry lots of data to a major city near the computer you are calling.

3. At the data circuit, another packet switch puts your packets onto another local phone line for delivery.

Some leading packet networks are SprintNet, BT Tymnet, and the CompuServe network. All use a standard for data transmission called X.25. Major online services such as GEnie and CompuServe roll the cost of using packet networks into their regular charges, and provide you with the local number needed to reach a network from your area.

To reach PCs that lack direct packet network connections, including bulletin boards, you might be able to get a direct connection to a packet network by buying a modem that includes an X.25 packet assembler-disassembler, or X.25 PAD, such as the Hayes Ultra series of modems. In this case, you also need to establish a direct account with the packet network of your choice.

Night-Owl Rates

The most expensive time to make a call is during "business hours." The phone rates are always cheapest between 11 p.m. and 8 a.m., though they're also lower during evening hours and on weekends. If you're doing frequent BBSing, look up the phone rates for the locations you call. You'll be surprised.

If, as I did, you discover that you're getting up at 4 a.m. just so you can reach your favorite service at the cheapest possible time...well, acknowledge that you're an online junkie.

Long Distance Calling Plans

If you dial into a lot of BBSs, you might be calling all over the country. Shop for the best deal you can get for long-distance services. To determine which service is best for you, consider whether you expect to call different BBSs around the country, or if you dial one particular, long-distance BBS frequently.

Calling Out-of-State

Comparing the long distance rates in-state versus out-of-state might surprise you. It is usually significantly cheaper to call a BBS or service in another state than it is to call one that is in your home state, but at some distance from you.

For instance, when I lived on a rural island off the coast of Maine, the nearest 2400 bps dial-in node for CompuServe was in Portland—150 miles away. When I compared rates, it was cheaper to call the Boston node, 250 miles away!

If you make frequent long distance calls, it's definitely worth talking to the customer service department of your local phone company.

Using Your Online Time Wisely

Despite my constant exhortations to get involved with the online community, it's easy to go too far. Too easy, in fact—costs aside, you can drown in the sea of information that pours through your modem, and it's tempting to respond to everyone.

The Data Stream of Consciousness

After you understand just how expensive it is to be online, you'll probably spend some time thinking about how you can take part without having to file for Chapter 11 bankruptcy. The following are some basic points to remember:

- Choose carefully the areas in which to participate.

- Learn to limit the forums or BBSs you follow by deciding what information you really need to acquire. Only visit the other places occasionally. For instance, keeping up-to-date on the technical advances in your profession might be important, but debates about professional ethics are a secondary priority.

ℂ   Develop your ability to scan, rather than read. The "cyperpunk" term for this is *data surfing*, and it's an apt one. Scan just enough of a message to find out if you *really* need to read it. There's an amazing amount of information out there that is interesting, but not all of it is important. Learning to scan isn't all that hard. Remember, you don't have to read every message as if you had to pass a test on its contents. If it isn't information you really need to have, skip to the next one.

How To Be Online and Keep a Life

You're asking *me*? A person who starts shaking if she doesn't hear the modem squeal at least once every four hours? Hah!

Well, okay. Not everyone wants to be as addicted. Thankfully, you don't have to be. It's entirely possible to act like a normal person and be active online. It's possible for your family to recognize you, your bills to be paid, and to have friends whose appearance you actually recognize.

I just don't know how that's done. Here are a few tips, though:

ℂ   Avoid flame wars. They're expensive to read, and much more expensive to participate in. They're also completely predictable, so you aren't missing anything if you sit one out.

ℂ   Don't download every file in sight. Discovering a cache of really cool files that sound interesting can be almost a spiritual experience. Resist it. Look carefully at the file description and decide if you *need* this file or you merely *want* it.

ℂ   When you do make friends online, incorporate them into your life rather than keeping them separate, as some sort of guilty secret. When you travel to their city, make a point to get together for lunch. You might be surprised to discover what they really look like. Then again, you might not; the people you meet online are usually just as much "themselves" in person as they are in cyberspace.

Chapter 12

Beyond BBSs
and Online Services

The most well-known uses for modems are to access online services, databases, and BBSs. There are some comparatively unusual uses for modems that are really cool, however. This chapter will give a brief overview of what else you can do.

After you start to pay attention to modems and different online services, you will be amazed at how many there are. You'll find that your church has a BBS, and that your local congressman is available on the Internet (heh, heh, heh). The world keeps expanding, and it's all at the other end of your telephone line!

Using Host Mode

Throughout this book, the emphasis has been on accessing small or large established services. What do you do if you and a friend simply want to exchange a few files?

The user group newsletter editor needs to get articles from the regular contributors every month, for instance. The contributors could use the user group's BBS, but with a small file for which the editor is anxiously awaiting, it's just as easy to send it directly.

Host mode, sometimes called Answer mode, lets remote users access your PC. Depending on the way the host mode is configured, the experience is similar to a BBS, but not exactly. For instance, the person who dials in can examine what's in the directories on your hard disk, upload or download files, or print files on your printer (as well as his own).

You can impose some limitations when you put your computer in the host mode. The person dialing in can't perform disk management (such as delete or rename files) or use your applications. You can limit the capabilities depending on the security level you set for each user, or you can let anyone dial in and mess around. Because you'll usually use host mode in a limited, observed capacity (such as the example above for the user group editor), security isn't quite as much of an issue as it might have seemed at first.

Lord of Hosts

A computer that is dialed into is the *host*; the computer at a remote location, calling-in, is the *remote user*. As the host, you set up passwords and restrictions for the people who are permitted (or disallowed) to dial into your computer.

From HyperACCESS/5's main menu, select **A**nswer. To create a new user password, select **M**anage Password List, then **A**dd. Add the new password and, if you like, an identifying name. Press Esc to leave the menu and select **W**ait for Data Calls. (See fig. 12.1.)

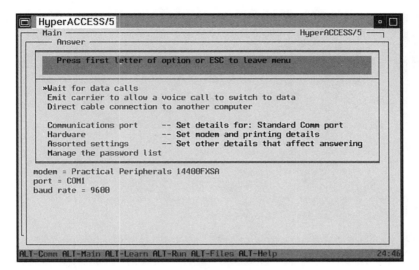

Figure 12.1

Select Wait for data calls to put the modem into auto-answer mode.

HA/5 will prepare the modem and wait for the phone to ring. (See fig. 12.2.)

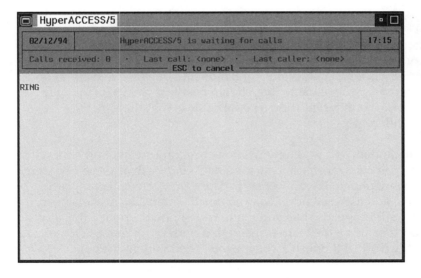

Figure 12.2

Waiting for the phone to ring was never like this before...

When someone does call, HA/5 makes the system available to both the caller and to you. Either of you can type commands, or upload or download a file, as shown in figure 12.3. You can also enter a *chat mode* where the two of you can write back and forth.

Figure 12.3

Sending a file in host mode.

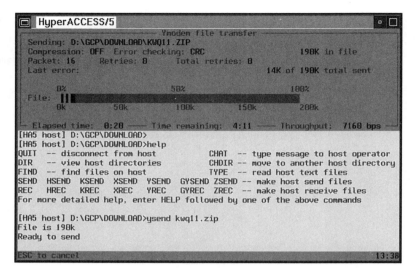

A Null Evening

Sometimes the physical distance between computers is very short —just a few feet—but it may as well be miles. Even when two computers can't easily share the same data (perhaps they use different floppy drive formats, or one is a Macintosh and the other a PC), they can usually be connected with a serial cable and a null modem. A *null modem* is a specially configured piece of cable that should cost less than $10; the only thing that makes it different from a serial cable is that the wires are connected differently.

Using a null modem and a communications program running on both computers, you can transfer information back and forth as if the two were attached over a phone line. However, because they're connected with serial cables, and as serial ports can run much faster than modems, you can use faster line speeds than you could with a phone connection. Try transferring files using the fastest speed that both programs will handle; it will probably work. If it doesn't, reduce the speed until it does.

Playing Online Games

The chapter on BBSs briefly touched on the interactive games that are available. Some of these games are straightforward and simple, such as solitaire card games or poker games. Other games can be played with the other people online. Most of these are text-based adventure or "fantasy role-playing" games, although you will find quite a few variations. As RIP graphics becomes more prevalent, graphics-based BBSs are sure to add more true graphical games.

The consumer online services also offer interactive games. Think twice before you let yourself get involved in these, as few of them are included in the basic services fee. Also, log in at the slowest (and therefore cheapest) speed available. You probably don't type much faster than 300 bps, so there's no reason to pay for high-speed access.

One example of an online game is Black Dragon, available on CompuServe. *Black Dragon* is a fantasy role-playing game set in a multilevel maze. You can use magic in the maze, and you encounter many strange and wondrous creatures (most of them deadly). The object of the game is to accumulate treasure, and, by converting gold into experience points, to gain strength. To win the game, you must be strong enough to conquer the Arch Demon on the final level of the maze. Skill, experience, and some luck are required.

Some games also are available that let you play with someone else over a direct modem connection, such as Microsoft Flight Simulator. (Unfortunately, my self-control did not permit me to do any testing of these games for this book.)

Remote Control Programs

Remote control: it's the next best thing to being there. Sometimes, it's like being there.

Here's a real-life example. At seven o'clock on a Sunday morning, a client called me at home. He suddenly had the urge to create a pile of payroll reports—but he couldn't get his accounting program to do what he wanted.

continues

*The client was a twenty-minute drive away, and I was still in
my robe. Instead of driving to his office, I started up my
computer and, using a remote control program, dialed in to
his PC. I started the accounting program and, peering at
his screen being shown on mine, realized that he had
entered the data backwards. Fixing the data took just a
few keystrokes. Had I driven to the client's office, the
solution would have only taken thirty seconds, but the bill
would have been for an hour.*

A remote control program lets you use the computer at the other end of
the telephone line as if you were sitting at its keyboard. It enables you to
perform tasks remotely that once could only be performed at the local
machine. It's like you have really long arms!

Using a remote control program, you take control of the other user's
workstation to upload or download files, to chat with the remote user at
his PC, and to see re-created problems. It's a wonderful tool for supporting other computer users (or being supported by someone else) and is
ideal if you want to work on your office system when you're at home.

Both keyboards are active. If you're the expert dialing in, for instance, you
can type the commands to start the program, then watch as the user
enters her password. Because in many technical support situations, it's
hard to figure out what the exact problem is, a remote control program is
an ideal solution. You can help someone else with a problem, or simply
use the hardware, software, and data resources on their system.

If you're shopping for a remote control program, look at its features
carefully. Not all applications will work, and some of them will operate so
slowly at slower modem speeds that you might as well drive the twenty
miles. In particular, graphics-based applications may or may not be
supported (depending on the version of the program you own), and they
most definitely perform best with a high-speed modem.

*Are you planning to purchase a modem so that you can
support a user at a remote site or be supported by a
software company? (This is common among many "verti-
cal" or specialized software developers, such as those who
make software for grocery stores, funeral homes, or gas*

*companies, etc.) If so, this is the time to consider buying
the same modem as the one used by your cohort. Modems
generally operate faster when they are connected with
another of their own kind and, on long support calls, any
speed increase will help.*

There are several remote control programs on the market today. The two
most popular are Norton pcANYWHERE by Symantec, and Carbon Copy
Plus by Microcom. Some PC utilities programs, such as PCTools by
Central Point Software, include remote control programs.

The *host* in a remote control program is the computer that the others are
"visiting." (It's just like a party, although with fewer drinks.) The host can
control the names and passwords of the people who are permitted to dial
in (see fig. 12.4).

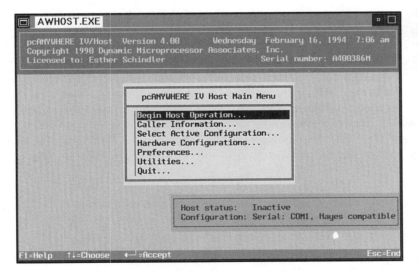

Figure 12.4

*The host for
pcANYWHERE.*

The remote PC dials in to connect with the host PC (see fig. 12.5). After
they connect, the remote PC can use the resources on the host.

Figure 12.5

Setting up a remote connection in pcANYWHERE.

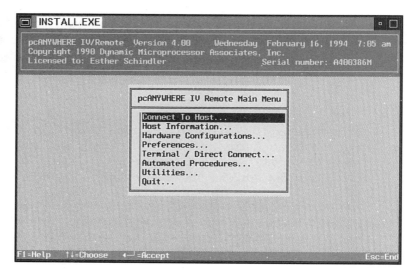

```
┌─[■]─INSTALL.EXE─────────────────────────────────────────□─□─┐
│ pcANYWHERE IV/Remote  Version 4.00    Wednesday February 16, 1994  7:05 am │
│ Copyright 1990 Dynamic Microprocessor Associates, Inc.                     │
│ Licensed to: Esther Schindler              Serial number: A400386M         │
│                                                                            │
│              ┌─ pcANYWHERE IV Remote Main Menu ─┐                          │
│              │ Connect To Host...               │                          │
│              │ Host Information...              │                          │
│              │ Hardware Configurations...       │                          │
│              │ Preferences...                   │                          │
│              │ Terminal / Direct Connect...     │                          │
│              │ Automated Procedures...          │                          │
│              │ Utilities...                     │                          │
│              │ Quit...                          │                          │
│              └──────────────────────────────────┘                          │
│                                                                            │
│ F1=Help   ↑↓=Choose   ←─┘=Accept                             Esc=End       │
└────────────────────────────────────────────────────────────────────────────┘
```

Talking to Mainframes

Standard communications programs, such as HA/5, enable you to reach mainframes and minicomputers in addition to the other services discussed in this book. Ordinarily, you would use in person a *terminal* (mostly a microcomputer without the brains but with hard-wired display capabilities) to access a mainframe. Different terminals use different display standards. The display standard for, say, the DEC VT100, is another standard like the ANSI standard—which is discussed in the BBS chapter.

Mainframe computers are large computers that are designed to meet the needs of a large corporation. By contrast, a minicomputer meets the needs of a department within an organization or corporation. A minicomputer can be defined as a mainframe if a small business uses it as its only computing resource.

When you use a communications program to access a mainframe, you use a *terminal emulation*. Instead of telling your communications program to use the ANSI standard, for example, you tell it to use the VT-100 standard or the IBM 3101 emulation. Figure 12.6 shows the emulations available in HA/5.

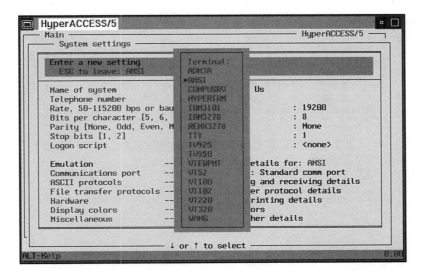

Figure 12.6
Terminal emulations.

There are also other, more specific communications programs available that are designed to work specifically with mainframes.

Video Conferencing

When you need to collaborate with someone else on serious work, there are times that a BBS or electronic mail simply won't do. You really need the personal interaction available from a face-to-face meeting, but you don't want (nor can you afford) to fly people cross-country.

Fortunately, the technology of telecommunications has reached the point where live video conferencing is a reality. With a high-speed modem (or a local area network) and the appropriate video hardware, you can communicate across telephone lines with live video.

One program that makes this happen is IBM's Person to Person/2. Person to Person/2 has separate windows for chatting and file transfer, but it also shares a "chalkboard" on which all the people in the video conference can scribble or make annotations (see fig. 12.7).

Figure 12.7

Using IBM's Person to Person/2.

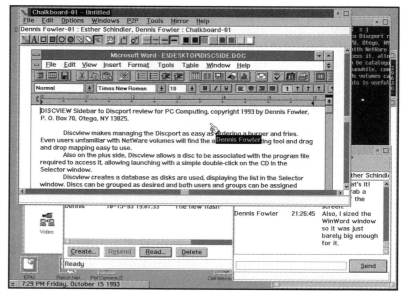

Cool Places to Call

When modern people want to find a means to communicate, computers are bound to get involved. Here are a few more examples of how you can use your modem to reach cool places and do nifty stuff.

Call Your Library's Card Catalog

It's raining, but you want to know if the library has a book about modems, Thai cooking, or folk music of the 1930s. Do you want to drive all the way to the library to discover that someone just checked it out?

Many libraries (and other social services) provide online access. The screen in figure 12.8 looks just like the "card catalog" system at my local library, except I didn't need to go there to look at it.

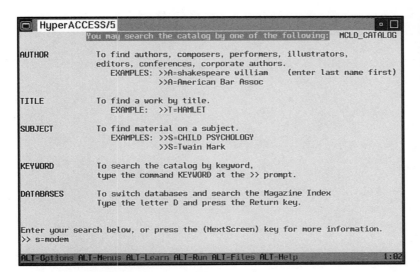

Figure 12.8

Accessing the library card catalog from home.

Do You Have Time for This?

If you're a stickler for getting the exact time, you can use your modem to set your computer time to the atomic clock at NIST in Boulder, Colorado, or USNO in Washington, DC. There are several free and shareware programs that will (automatically!) dial the phone number and correct your PC's time every "n" days that you set.

Calling Mom

If you have a time-management program on your computer, you can use it to dial the telephone for you. If your program supports the feature, tell the program that you have a modem and add your friends' and relatives' phone numbers to your personal database. When you schedule an alarm that says, "Call Mom," the program can automatically dial the phone.

Chapter 13

Journey to the Internet

After you become an experienced modem user, you might want to learn about the most powerful, yet most complex, online network in the world: the Internet. Whether you want files, online conversation, electronic mail, news, or information, you have no richer source at your disposal than the Internet.

Unfortunately, accessing the Internet's wealth of online services is often difficult, especially for the novice. Still, after you understand the basics, you'll be ready to go modem treasure-hunting through the connections and nodes of the Internet. This chapter covers the following topics:

- ☾   Accessing the Internet
- ☾   Choosing an Internet front-end
- ☾   Using Internet e-mail
- ☾   Using Internet e-mail addressing
- ☾   Understanding mailing lists
- ☾   Reading Internet newsgroups
- ☾   Writing to Internet newsgroups

- *C*   Using telnet

- *C*   Using ftp

- *C*   Using archie

- *C*   Using gopher and WAIS

- *C*   Using World Wide Web (also known as WWW)

Getting to the Internet

The *Internet* consists of hundreds of smaller networks and systems bound together by Transport Control Protocol/Internet Protocol (TCP/IP) network connections. Imagine a sophisticated office local area network (LAN) that connects PCs, Macintoshes, and workstations into a harmonious whole. Now imagine a LAN that spans the globe rather than just an office, and you have the Internet.

The Internet isn't a commercial service such as CompuServe or Prodigy, although you can access the Internet from such online services as BIX, the WELL, and DELPHI. Other major online venders, such as America Online, also are planning to bring Internet services to their customers.

Internet Access

You can access the Internet at one of three levels:

- *C*   Mail Only

- *C*   Mail and Usenet News

- *C*   Mail, Usenet News, and Network Services

At the first level, which all major online services and many BBSs support, your one net capability is to receive and send mail on Internet-connected systems. If all you want is to be able to exchange electronic letters with your friends, then Mail access is all you need.

Many people also want to access Usenet newsgroups—the second access level to the internet. Newsgroups are similar to online services' discussion forums, but differ from discussion forums in that there's rarely a sysop or moderator to monitor threads. Systems with access to both newsgroups and mail are part of Usenet—a superset of the Internet.

Threads are messages concerning a single subject within a newsgroup. For example, the newsgroup rec.music.beatles is about the Beatles. Within the newsgroup, there may be threads on Beatles reunion rumors, bootleg live Beatles recordings, and whether Sgt. Pepper or Abbey Road was the best Beatles album.

Thousands of newsgroups exist on almost every imaginable subject, and some on subjects you might never have dreamed of. For example, newsgroups such as comp.sys.ibm.pc.games for PC-based games and comp.sys.unix.admin for UNIX system administrators are what you expect to find in online discussion groups. You probably don't expect to find groups for topics such as bionet.xtallography for students of protein crystallography, alt.monty-python for Monty Python fans, or alt.pets.chia for anyone who's ever gotten emotionally attached to their Chia Pet, but these groups are out there.

The third level of Internet access include systems that actually are part of the Internet and have a TCP/IP, or (rarely) another network protocol connection with the net. These systems enable you to use the full range of network tools. These include the ability to log in to remote computers (called telnet) and to move files from around the world (called file transfer protocol or ftp) almost as easily as copying a file from your hard disk to your floppy.

Networking isn't quite as complicated as it seems. The only real difference between your PC and a network is that a network uses remote resources whereas your PC uses only local resources. Instead of finding a file on your hard disk, the Internet lets you find files in hard drives thousands of miles away. Specialized network programs are required to make this work. As an Internet user, you don't need to worry about how the system works—that's the system administrator's job.

continues

A little knowledge of how the Internet works can be more helpful then dangerous. TCP/IP is the network protocol that binds the Internet together. In essence, when Internet computers from Macs to supercomputers talk to each other, TCP/IP is their common language. Your PC doesn't need to have TCP/IP for you to connect to the Internet. An asynchronous communications program like DataStorm's ProComm is all you'll need. Asynchronous simply means that the computers take turns talking to each other. On the Internet network side, the computers talk to each other synchronously. Which, as you probably know, means that the computers speak to each other at the same time.

Each Internet system is a network node. That simply means that it's connected by TCP/IP with the other computers. There are even ways to make your own computer a network node, but most users don't need the advanced abilities, and headaches, that goes with being an actual network node.

What you will need to learn is how to use a text editor. These editors are like word processors like WordPerfect and WordStar. The difference is that, unlike word processors, these don't use special format codes to make documents. By avoiding format codes, text editors can't give you special effects like bolding or underlining. Instead, you get the ability to send messages that almost any e-mail program, text editor, or word processor can read.

Getting Internet Access

Gaining access to the Internet has not always been easy. Until recently, you had to work for a company or attend a school that had net-connected computers. Now, dozens of businesses sell Internet access. Prices range from fifteen dollars to several hundred dollars a month. The more you pay, the faster you telecommunicate and the more services you receive.

Locating companies that sell Internet access can be difficult. National and regional online services for end users are listed in table 13.1.

Table 13.1
Internet Service Providers

Service	Phone Number
BIX	800-227-2983
Clark Internet Services (ClarkNet)	410-730-9764
Computer Witchcraft (Usenet services only)	502-589-6800
DELPHI	800-544-4005
Express Access	800-969-9090
Netcom Online Communication Services	800-501-8649
The Whole Earth 'Lectronic Link (WELL)	415-332-4335
The World	617-739-0202

If you can't get the deal you want, or if Internet service suppliers do not have local phone numbers, you might still find an information road to the Internet. Peter Kaminski compiles the Public Dialup Internet Access List (PDIAL). This regularly updated list has addresses, costs, phone numbers, areas served, and services supplied by all North American Internet providers. To receive the most recent copy of PDIAL, send a message to the following Internet address: info-deli-server@netcom.com. In a matter of minutes (if not seconds), you will receive the latest PDIAL by return post.

For a complete listing of the PDIAL list, see Riding the Internet Highway, Deluxe Edition, *published by New Riders Publishing. That book gives you a quick introduction to using the features available on the Internet, including file transferring, sending e-mail, and joining newsgroups.*

Comparing Internet Interfaces

Most opening Internet interfaces, and the interfaces throughout a session, leave a lot to be desired aesthetically. You frequently see nothing but a

cryptic "%" or "$" prompt, for instance, when you go online. Such inter-
faces are fine if you are familiar with UNIX. (Most of the Internet runs over
the UNIX operating system.) Although a familiarity with UNIX is helpful,
you don't have to be a UNIX wizard to use the Internet.

Whether you can work magic with UNIX, or you're not sure what "ls"
means (it means to list out a file directory), customer support is vital.
Your Internet provider, the company that's selling you your Internet
access, should always offer both voice and online help. Always ask your
provider how much online help is available, how much it costs, and the
help desk's hours.

If you'd rather deal with a kinder and gentler interface, ask the sales-
people about their service's interface before you hook up with a particular service. Many services now have friendly menu systems. Others, such
as BIX with InterNav and Computer Witchcraft with WinNET, have
Windows-compatible front ends with their services. Also, for users who
pay for their PC to become part of the Internet, some services provide
Windows-compatible TCP/IP programs such as Mosaic.

Using Internet E-Mail

The bread and butter of the Internet is e-mail. Many Internet e-mail
interfaces exist—too many to explain all of them in this chapter. Check
your manual or check with an Internet provider's help desk for information on specific interfaces.

Using mail and elm

You have access to the Spartan mail program through almost all systems.
The mail program is about as friendly as a punch in the face, but after you
learn its commands, you can live with it.

For example, if you want to send a message to Uncle Joe on America
Online, first write your letter with a text editor on the Internet system.
Then, to send it, use a command line that looks like this:

```
%mail -s "Hi Uncle Joe" unclejoe@aol.com < your_message_filename
```

Piece by piece it works like this: *Mail* is the program you'll be using. The *-s* tells mail that the subject line should read *Hi Uncle Joe*. Joe's address follows as *unclejoe@aol.com*, and the < tells the operating system to insert the text in *your_message_filename* into the body of the letter. Once this line is completed, pressing Enter will send your message on its way.

Many systems—even if they don't support anything fancier—will also have elm (elementary mail). *elm* supplies an easy-to-use menu-driven interface (see fig. 13.1). If you have never run elm from your UNIX prompt, give it a try—you might be pleasantly surprised.

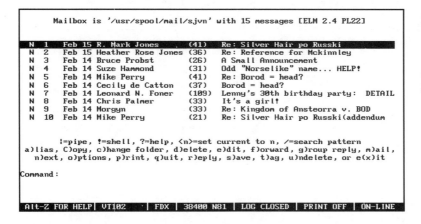

```
        Mailbox is '/usr/spool/mail/sjvn' with 15 messages [ELM 2.4 PL22]

 N   1   Feb 15 R. Mark Jones       (41)    Re: Silver Hair po Russki
 N   2   Feb 15 Heather Rose Jones  (36)    Re: Reference for Mckinnley
 N   3   Feb 14 Bruce Probst        (26)    A Small Announcement
 N   4   Feb 14 Suze Hammond        (31)    Odd "Norselike" name... HELP!
 N   5   Feb 14 Mike Perry          (41)    Re: Borod = head?
 N   6   Feb 14 Cecily de Catton    (37)    Borod = head?
 N   7   Feb 14 Leonard N. Foner    (109)   Lenny's 30th birthday party:  DETAIL
 N   8   Feb 14 Chris Palmer        (33)    It's a girl!
 N   9   Feb 14 Morgyn              (33)    Re: Kingdom of Ansteorra v. BOD
 N  10   Feb 14 Mike Perry          (21)    Re: Silver Hair po Russki(addendum

        !=pipe, !=shell, ?=help, <n>=set current to n, /=search pattern
a)lias, C)opy, c)hange folder, d)elete, e)dit, f)orward, g)roup reply, m)ail,
   n)ext, o)ptions, p)rint, q)uit, r)eply, s)ave, t)ag, u)ndelete, or e(x)it
Command :

 Alt-Z FOR HELP| VT102     | FDX | 38400 N81 | LOG CLOSED | PRINT OFF | ON-LINE
```

Figure 13.1

There are fancier mail interfaces then elm, but none are easier.

To get instructions on how to use mail, elm, or other Internet programs, type the following at the UNIX prompt:

```
man program_name
```

The preceding command string presents you with an online manual. The information in online manuals tends to be highly technical, so be prepared to spend some time online.

Use your communication program's print option to print the pages. It's easier to read long manual pages on paper rather then doing so online where you can't easily back up to check something you saw two pages ago.

Using Common Internet Text Editors

A wide variety of text editors work with the mail interfaces. If you're working with a system that gives you a native UNIX interface to the Internet, your choice in editors will almost certainly include EMACS and vi. If so, read your Internet provider's documentation on those editors. EMACS is very powerful, but it also can be very complicated. vi has a minimum of commands that you must learn, but the learning curve is very steep because vi includes almost no online help while running.

Understanding Internet E-mail Addressing

No matter what the mail interface or editor, net addresses always have the same format, as shown in the following example:

```
user name@domain name.system type.
```

You don't even need that much information if you are sending a message to someone on the same local system; just use their user name. If you're on a machine, for instance, where your friend Esther has an account under the user name *esther*, you can reach her by sending mail to that name.

More commonly, you probably will be writing to someone at another network node and must use the full net address. For example, you could reach Fubar (a made-up name), at either fubar@access.digex.net or fubar@well.sf.ca.us.

The preceding addresses reflect certain style differences. In the first address, for instance, you have a machine name and a system type. In the second address, after the name and the @ sign comes a machine name and a geographical location. Both these addresses are correct for each system. No matter what the exact elements in the format, the part before the @ sign is called the *mailbox name* and the section following the @ sign is known as the *domain*.

Regardless of what you see on screen, the actual address that the network sees is numerical. The numeric format is an Internet Protocol (IP) number that has been uniquely assigned to the system by the Network Information Center (NIC). You can use IP addresses for mail if you want, but let's face it: you more easily can remember a name such as

*x25.bix.com than you can remember the number
192.80.63.6.*

The mnemonic components that make up an address come in two forms, as shown in the two previously cited addresses. In the first, the last three-letter group tells you what kind of system you're talking to. In the first case, "net" tells you that the digex address is a system primarily used for Internet connectivity. Other examples are *.edu* for education, *.com* for commercial, and *.mil* for military. The second format specifies where the network is located, rather than what the computer's owners are using it for. The WELL node is in San Francisco, California, in the good old USA.

In both cases, the technical details of the address format are defined in a document called RFC-822. Thus Internet addresses are also known as RFC-822 addresses.

How do you find out someone's address? You ask them or have them send you a message at your address. Although a network Yellow Pages is available, it's an address book for systems and network connections, not users.

For a directory of Internet resources, newsgroups, and other areas on the Internet, see the New Riders' Official Internet Yellow Pages.

After you get the hang of net addresses, you will find that they're easy to use. You also can use Internet mail to send e-mail to users on other networks or online services. The address formats for several popular online services are listed in table 13.2.

Table 13.2
Online Service Address Formats

Service Name	Address Format
America Online	user_name@aol.com
BIX	user_name@bix.com

continues

Table 13.2, Continued
Online Service Address Formats

Service Name	Address Format
CompuServe	user_number@cis.com*
DELPHI	user_name@delphi.com
GEnie	user_name@genie.geis.com
MCI Mail	user_number@mcimail.com
Prodigy	user_number@prodigy.com

*To send mail to CIS users, use a period instead of a comma in the user number.

One final note: in an RFC-822 address, case is important. For example, networkXXIII.com is not the same thing as NetworkXXIII.com. Although most mailers, programs that actually do the grunt work of forwarding mail from one system to another, can cope with mixed-case addresses, older ones still throw up at the very thought. You can make the mailers' job easier—and ensure that your message arrives where you want it to—by making sure that your addresses are in the correct case.

Understanding Mailing Lists

Besides ordinary one-to-one mail, some users and businesses have set up mailing lists that automatically forward mail to many users. These mailing lists are used for everything from keeping college friends in touch, to boat builders comparing notes, to Macintosh fans writing about their favorite computer.

If a list's subject matter sounds interesting to you, you can ask to be added to the list by sending a message to the RFC-822 address, such as the following:

```
listname-request@domain_name.system_type
```

For example, if you want to join the mailing list devoted to Traveller (a science-fiction role playing game), you would send a message to the following address:

```
traveller-request@engrg.uwo.ca
```

Not all mailing list use this join-up format. If the one you're trying to get into doesn't use this, try sending a message to the address:

```
listserv@the_system_where_the_list_is_located
```

Don't give the letter any subject. In the letter's body put

```
SUBSCRIBE listname your_first_name your_last-name
```

and nothing else.

For example, if I wanted to send join the space mailing list, which is about space exploration, my request to join the list would be sent to the following address:

```
listserv@ubvm.cc.buffalo.edu
```

In the message I would put

```
SUBSCRIBE SPACE Steven Vaughan-Nichols
```

and nothing else.

After you're on a list, you automatically get all mail sent to the list, including your own. Some systems also will let you set up your own lists. Check with your Internet provider to see if it's possible. Lists are easy to maintain, and can be invaluable for keeping in contact with people with common interests.

Using Usenet Newsgroups

When many people think of the Internet, they're thinking of Usenet newsgroups. *Usenet newsgroups* are free-form discussion groups on every subject imaginable. If you have an interest in something, chances are there's a newsgroup for you.

Using the trn News Reader

The secret to managing even that many groups is using a good news reader program such as trn. *trn*, one of the most popular news readers around, is available on most systems. *News readers* are programs that give newsgroups and threads a user-friendly interface. Without one, trying to read news is a lot like trying to catch a cup of water from Niagara Falls: almost impossible. Even with trn, getting the most from the news can be challenging.

Such groups are message collections that are passed from system to system over the network. Tens of megabytes of information flow through the groups every day. No one, unless they have no life away from their computer, can keep up with all of them.

With hundreds of newsgroups, thousands of networked computers, and hundreds of thousands of readers, it doesn't take much to turn Usenet reading into drudgery rather than joy. There's invaluable information hidden away in net news; the problem is finding it.

Advanced news readers such as trn make it possible to wade through the net news swamp and get only the information you want, instead of spending hours online becoming an Internet zombie.

When you run trn, the first thing that happens is that trn searches for your ".newsrc" file. This hidden file (in most UNIX/Internet sites, hidden files have names that start with a period) contains a list of all available news groups and your current subscription status. If trn doesn't find a .newsrc, it makes one for you. trn then makes sure your listing is up to date; if not, trn automatically fixes the .newsrc. You don't need to worry about the process damaging your .newsrc—trn automatically backs up the file when it starts working.

Due to the sheer volume of news (we're talking megabytes a day), many sites don't receive all available newsgroups. Even so, on most systems you'll find that you have subscribed to every available newsgroup. This discovery can be more than a little daunting when you realize just how many newsgroups are around. In such a situation, the first command to use is the "u" for unsubcribe command—a lot.

Try your best not to fall prey to the temptation of subscribing to interesting but nonessential newsgroups. You could spend your life reading newsgroups, but only if you give up the rest of your life.

If all goes well (and 99 percent of the time it will), you'll be at the top command level (see fig. 13.2). Many users get confused by trn's use of three different command levels; which set you're using depends on where you are in reading the news. At the top is the newsgroup selection layer, followed by the article selection layer, and then the paging level.

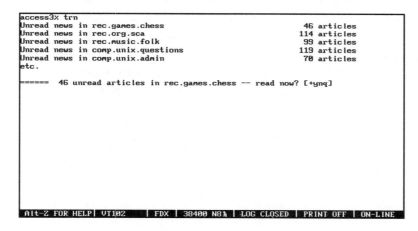

```
access3% trn
Unread news in rec.games.chess                        46 articles
Unread news in rec.org.sca                           114 articles
Unread news in rec.music.folk                         99 articles
Unread news in comp.unix.questions                   119 articles
Unread news in comp.unix.admin                        70 articles
etc.

======  46 unread articles in rec.games.chess -- read now? [+ynq]




 Alt-Z FOR HELP  VT102       | FDX | 38400 N81 | LOG CLOSED | PRINT OFF | ON-LINE
```

Figure 13.2

The number of new articles in your subscribed newsgroups.

The commands look about the same on each level, and they have about the same effect. The difference is in the scope of these commands. If you search, for instance, with the command /trek, and press the Enter key on the newsgroup level, you're looking for newsgroup names with the word "trek" in them. On the other hand, the same command at the article selection level finds articles or messages, not newsgroups, with "trek" in the header.

*No matter what newsgroup level you're on, the one com-
mand you'll always need to know is h (for help.) Besides
working for trn, you can solve many of your online problems
with online help.*

If you just want to dive in and start reading, just type **y** (or press the
spacebar) and you're on your way. trn normally starts with the earliest
messages and works its way forward in time through message threads.
This sounds trivial, and it is for messages on centralized systems such as
Ziffnet. On the net, however, messages are maintained on thousands of
computers around the world. Keeping messages straight is a big job, but
it's one that you as a user don't have to worry about.

*It's one thing, however, to catch up with the latest mes-
sages in a low-traffic group such as comp.compression,
about data compression, and another thing entirely to try
to read the hundreds of messages that pour through the
comp.unix.questions newsgroup daily.*

*The right way to handle this situation is to type the letter
for any subjects that look interesting. Then, you simply
press the spacebar to see the subjects for the next batch
of messages. When you reach the end of the messages,
simply press the spacebar, or press Enter, and you'll be
looking at the first message in the first thread you
marked. At this article level, your screen will look like figure 13.3.*

Figure 13.3

*To select article
threads, you press
the thread's corre-
sponding letter.*

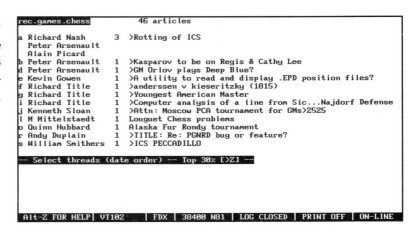

If, after reading a few messages in a thread, you find that you're not interested in any of the messages, you can leave the thread. You do this by marking all the rest of the messages in that thread as being read and move on to the next thread by simply typing **k**.

No matter what level you're on, if you don't want to read a group or select an article or read the rest of an article, you can always move on with the n command. The newsgroups or messages you leave unread remain marked as unread. This means that the next time you use trn, the unread messages will still be easily accessible.

No system anywhere has room to store an unlimited number of newsgroups online, so messages (articles) end up going to "data heaven" at a time determined by the system.

This time varies depending on how many newsgroups an Internet node carries and its maximum storage capacity. Even systems stuffed to the gills with newsgroup articles keep them for two to three days. Other systems might hold on to articles for two to three weeks.

Even if an article is dead and buried, you still may be able to recover it. Many newsgroups have archive sites. At an archive site, the newsgroup's messages are stored permanently. To find out if a newsgroup you're interested in has an archive site, ask in the newsgroup. Someone will tell you in a matter of minutes.

If you want to mark every article in a group as read, without the trouble of reading messages, use the c command at any level to mark all messages in the current newsgroup as read. For more drastic situations, you can use the ^K command. ^K opens a text editor that enables you to edit a file that contains one-line records. The exact editor depends on the value of the system variable EDITOR. If the EDITOR value isn't set, chances are the vi editor is the default. You would be editing the KILL file, normally located in your News directory. Each record in this file consists of a pattern search in the format:

```
/whatever offends you/j
```

Trn takes this to mean that you want it to search the currently subscribed newsgroups and mark every message with the pattern: "whatever offends you" in the header as read. This makes it unnecessary for you to deal with messages that do not interest you.

Suppose you subscribe to comp.unix.pc-clone.32bit, the font of information about PC UNIX, but SCO UNIX does not interest you. The solution is to make an entry in the form given above in the KILL file, and unless the subject sneaks in through what's called topic drift (the tendency for any online conversation to ramble away from its subject heading), you won't have to read about SCO UNIX again.

Another way to handle this in the article selection level is to use the K command. This automatically enters the current article's subject in the terminate with extreme prejudice file without any manual editing.

Most newsgroups have frequently asked questions (FAQ) lists. These are articles, usually posted monthly, that lay out the newsgroup's rules. For instance, the newsgroup alt.internet.resources is not the place to ask about getting Internet access. The proper group for that is alt.internet.access.wanted.

The other purpose of FAQs is just what the name says: it answers frequently asked questions. Before bursting in with questions in a newsgroup, you should read the newsgroup's FAQ first. Chances are good you'll find the answers you need there.

You might notice that pressing Enter hasn't been mentioned. That's because trn operates in cbreak mode. The important thing to remember about cbreak is that, except for commands that take an argument, such as g some_newsgroup, you don't press Enter after a command. If you press Enter, trn will run the command and then do whatever an unadorned Enter does at that level. Normally, pressing Enter moves you down a level, or if you are already at the page level, pressing Enter displays the current message's next line. That's not harmful, but it can be confusing.

There are other ways of moving through news. For instance, if you want to get to the last newsgroup, you read in a hurry. The quick way is to type $, which takes you to the bottom of your subscription list. Conversely, to get to the top of the list, you can type **1**.

The same commands also work at the article selection level, except you'll be moving to the last and first unread articles. Besides these commands, you can move about in trn at either level with the additional commands in table 13.3.

Table 13.3
trn Movement Commands

Command	Newsgroup Level	Article Level
p	Go to previous newsgroup with unread mail.	Go to previous unread article.
P	Go to previous newsgroup.	Go to previous article.
n	Go to next newsgroup with unread mail.	Go to next unread article.
N	Go to next newsgroup.	Go to next article.
$	Go to last newsgroup.	Go to last article.
1	Go to top newsgroup.	Go to top article.

The g command on the newsgroup level uses the full name of a newsgroup to move that newsgroup instantly. The l command finds newsgroups in the system's master .newsrc file. For example, l pc would find all newsgroups with "pc" in their title. Armed with this information, you can then subscribe to a newsgroup by typing the g command. This would look like: g alt.internet.services. This example group, by the way, is an information sorting house for questions about Internet services. If you have access to TCP/IP services, such as ftp and telnet, but aren't sure what to use them for, alt.internet.services can help.

Posting Articles to a Newsgroup

You're all set: you've subscribed to the newsgroups that you want and you've been reading them for a while. You now are ready to ask (or respond to) a question on Usenet or other newsgroup. To post a brand-new message to a newsgroup, you must use a *news writer*, such as Pnews or PostNews, to post original messages. Check your documentation for exact details.

If you want to post a message to a newsgroup, trn is not the program to use. Trn, which stands for "threaded read news," enables you to read and post a reply to someone's else message, but you can't use it to post new messages.

Replying to newsgroup messages can be done with two sets of commands from within trn. R and r reply to an article over net mail services. The distinction between them is that R includes the text of the message you're replying to.

Before writing any articles for a newsgroup, read the articles in the newsgroup thoroughly. Posting a message to the wrong newsgroup wastes not only your time, but the time of every system connected to the network and your fellow users.

The other set of commands, F and f, work similarly, but your message will be posted to the newsgroup. Remember, anything you write can, and will be, read by perhaps millions of net news readers. Scary thought, isn't it?

Saving Newsgroup Messages

You can save these or other important articles for future reference by using the s command at the bottom article read level. S, at this same level, takes a file or pipe name as an argument. For example, S MacFAQ will save the message to the file MacFAQ.

If the information you want to save is broken down into several articles, you can append it to a single file by simply saving again to the same file name. Unless set otherwise, the resulting file will be located in your current directory.

Using telnet

telnet provides direct communications with other computer systems through TCP/IP networking. In essence, telnet enables you to log in to other computers on the network.

As an example, if you're running a complex query on a monster Unify database—but must work on something else as well—you can simply telnet to an idle system and start anew there.

This is easy enough when you're working with your own in-house systems, but telnet knows no distance barriers. If two systems are on the Internet (one in San Diego and you're logged in to one in Washington D.C.), you can telnet your way to the California computer as easily as you can switch to the workstation in the next cubicle. Some interfaces such as BIX's InterNav make telneting about as easy as pointing and clicking (see fig. 13.4).

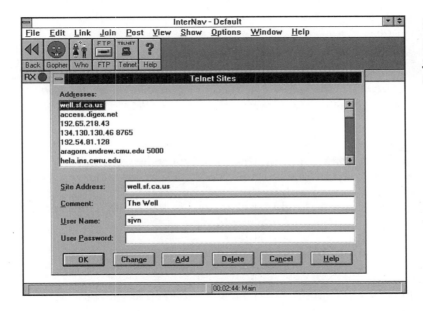

Figure 13.4

BIX's InterNav lets you pick your destination.

Working with telnet is almost mindlessly easy. To connect to another system, you just type the following and you're on your way:

```
telnet remote_host_name port
```

On most systems, the port is optional because the telnet daemon, the always-running program that handles telnet, automatically uses a default port.

For the name of the system you're trying to contact, you usually use the system's host name; for example, access.digex.net, princeton.edu, or well.sf.ca.us. If that doesn't work, you may need to specify the host's IP address; 192.132.20.3, for instance, is the IP address of well.sf.ca.us.

The main reason you sometimes must spell out the IP address is that your system's hosts file does not have that particular site listed. Another reason, however, might be that your system doesn't have permission to use that stretch of virtual highway. The most common case of this is systems that are attached to the commercialized parts of the Internet road trying to reach systems that are on NSFnet. NSFnet is one of the Internet's main backbone networks, and it can be used only for research and education.

Some systems also restrict their users' ability to use telnet. If you're having trouble, check with your system administrator before you assume something is wrong. You simply may not have permission to use telnet or ftp.

After you log in to another system, you proceed just as if you were logged in to the computer next door. Everything you type in feeds directly into the remote system. If you need to issue a command to the telnet program, you precede the command with the "escape character." This is usually set to "^]"—control key and right-bracket key. For instance, to quit telnet and return to your local system you would type

```
^] quit
```

Besides telling telnet to attempt to open a session across the network with a command line, you also can run telnet interactively. To do this, you type **telnet**. This will bring up the telnet prompt:

```
telnet>
```

From here, you can start a session by typing:

```
open host_name
```

There are other possibilities, but these vary with the interface you're using and the telnet implementation. Some versions of telnet, for instance, allow you to connect to multiple systems at once.

Even if you don't have another account to log in to, telnet can still be useful. You can telnet your way to many libraries' online public access catalogs (OPAC). Want to find if your local library has Stephen King's latest thriller? If your library has an OPAC, you can find out if the book's in with a few keystrokes.

Using ftp

ftp stands for file transfer protocol and the name says it all. *ftp* enables you to download files from remote systems to your local system over the network. As with telnet, you can do this as easily across the country as across the room.

Many systems around the world keep file archives, usually in directories named pub for ftp access. ftp is the tool you need to get copies of these files. The range of files available for anonymous ftp runs from the complete C code for X Windows, to collections of bawdy songs, to the source code for the EMACS editor.

Unlike telnet, which is really useful only when you have full-fledged accounts on remote systems, ftp comes in handy even if you have only a single account. That's because many sites allow what's called anonymous ftp. In anonymous ftp, you gain access to remote files by logging in with the name "anonymous." Common network etiquette is then to use your full mail address as your password.

Here are the basics of using ftp. The simplest way to use ftp is to type the following at the command line:

```
ftp remote_host_name
```

You'll be prompted for a login name and password; use the process described earlier to log in. After you are in the system, you're in the pub, or the local directory. From here, you use the ls command to list available files. Some systems will use the dir command for the same purpose. Still others may have a file named ls -lR, which contains complete file listings; use the cat command to screen or ftp to home to examine later. You can use the cd command to investigate additional subdirectories.

One command that you'll get to know quite well is the help command. In ftp and telnet, typing a question mark normally gets you the Reader's Digest condensed version of command syntax.

The ftp command you'll get to know best is get. get works a lot like MS-DOS's copy command. get copies a file from the remote system to your local Internet system. From there, you'll need to use an asynchronous file-transfer protocol such as Zmodem to bring the file home to your PC.

In many ways, ftp's get is similar to the asynchronous file-transfer protocols of dial-up connections such as Xmodem, Zmodem and Kermit. The critical difference is that ftp only works across network connections. Although it's possible to use ftp over an ordinary modem connection using Serial Line Internet Protocol (SLIP) or Point to Point Protocol (PPP), these are examples of networking across phone lines. Some Internet providers will let you hook straight into the Internet through their service, but this usually is an expensive option. Prices range from twice the cost of the cheapest kind of Internet connection to ten times that or more.

To get down to cases, you copy a file using ftp with a command that might look like:

```
ftp> get nifty.file
```

For binary files, such as programs or compressed files, you should first enter the binary command at the ftp prompt. The following command, for example, successfully downloads the compressed file that you want:

```
ftp> binary
ftp> get nifty.neat.file.Z
```

If you don't do this, your file will be a garbled mess. ftp's default is to send ASCII files, not binary. More time has been wasted and more tears have been shed over that simple mistake than any other in the ftp command collection.

Some services, such as BIX's InterNav, offer an easier interface to ftp (see fig. 13.5).

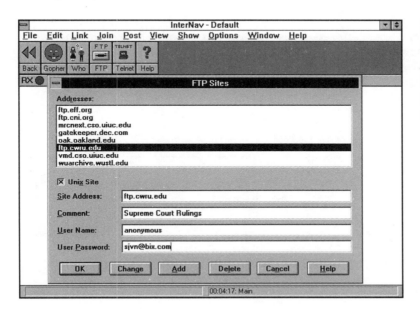

Figure 13.5

If you're happier with a mouse than a keyboard, then you'll like InterNav's ftp interface.

Using archie

Is there anyone alive who isn't thrilled by exploration? Although you might not be Indiana Jones, you *can* search for temples of software treasure in the Internet. To computer fans, a new program or an interesting data file can be as exciting as any golden idol. And, besides, you never ever have to run into snakes!

Thanks to sites that allow anonymous ftp logins, it's possible for anyone with net access to download files—if you know where to find them. Although ftp enables you to search for files, if the files you're looking for aren't there, hunting for them won't do any good. Worse still, looking for a specific file can be like looking for a needle in a haystack. The virtual universe of cyberpunk science-fiction is already with us in one way; the Internet really can be a confusing and confounding maze.

Fortunately, for all would-be Internet explorers, there's a faithful guide to lead you through the deepest, darkest network nodes: archie. *archie* is a database program that does the hard work of finding and indexing files throughout the Internet. Instead of tracking down elusive files on your own, you can contact an archie site and use archie to find your elusive quarry.

Archie sites are scattered across the world (see table 13.4). Although you can use any archie server, it's fair play to use the one for your geographical area. Not only should this take up less online time, but by spreading out the load, the service is more likely to avoid being overburdened.

Table 13.4
Worldwide archie Servers

Internet Name	Area Served
archie.au	Australia and Oceania
archie.doc.ic.ac.uk	United Kingdom
archie.funet.fi	Europe
archie.mcgill.ca	Canada
archie.rutgers.edu	Northeastern USA
archie.sura.net	Southeastern USA
archie.unl.edu	Western USA

How To Use archie

To use archie, you have three choices: you can use a local copy of archie, you can use archie by mail, or you can telnet your way to the closest archie site. The most popular way is the latter. To perform an archie search with telnet, type the following:

```
telnet archie.sura.net
```

When you have a connection, login as "archie." You are not asked for a password. You see the prompt:

```
archie>
```

From here on out, you talk to the archie program rather than the operating system—the way you normally do with telnet.

The first command you should enter is:

```
archie> show
```

This displays all of archie's settings. For the most part, you can ignore these settings, but you might need the pager and search settings.

Pager tells archie whether you want it to dump its results to screen or whether you want it to wait for either a carriage return or press of the spacebar after filling the screen. If you're unable to scroll back your screen to catch something that just disappeared off the top, set the pager on with the following command:

```
archie> set pager
```

Search defines how archie goes about looking for your entry. Different archies have different search defaults. For example, some default to case-sensitive searches, while others could give a hoot as to whether your search string is in all caps or all lowercase.

If archie comes back with a search value of "exact", then you'll know that's it currently set to find only exact case matches. For example, a search for DOg would not find Dog. File names being what they are—without rhyme or reason with respect to capitalization—you probably don't want to search using exact cases.

You can set this parameter to your liking by using the following command:

```
archie> set search X
```

X can have one of four values. One is exact, as you've already seen; your other choices are regex, sub, and subcase. When you use regex, the search string works like a regular expression. In short, wild cards such as * and ? are allowed. You can search for Do* and get all references to Dog and Doggie. Unfortunately, you'd still miss DOG.

If you search using sub, your expedition will find any file names that contain your search phrase regardless of case. For instance, a search with

"Dog" would now uncover DOg and DOG. It's also going to dig up files with words such as dogma in the title. Sub is very powerful but it can deluge you with false hits—files that contain your search string but have nothing to do with what you're actually looking for.

Subcase works like sub but is case-sensitive. Regardless of which method or methods you use, the most important thing you can do before beginning an archie hunt is to decide how you want archie to look for a file. You'll not only save your own time, you'll save everyone's time.

Searching with archie

Now, you're ready to start a search. Searching is done by simply entering:

```
archie> prog search_string
```

Archie then proceeds to give you a running score on how many hits it has found and the percentage of the database that has been searched. After that, archie reports on the files that meet your specifications.

You will then see a list describing the files' locations. This list comes in a multiline format. At the top of each record is the site name for the system with the file. You also will see the file's directory, name, and some size and date information.

Using archie without telnet

Without telnet access, you may still be able to use archie with a local archie client. In this case, you'd just run archie from your system's command line. This is the best way to use archie because it saves wear and tear on the network.

You're not out of the hunt even without telnet or a local archie. You can also use archie by mail. To do this, send a message addressed to archie to an archie site. For example:

```
archie@archie.rutgers.edu
```

In the text of the message enter archie commands. A sample search message might look like

```
path you@your.mail.address
prog what_ever_it_is_you're_looking_for
quit
```

The first line tells archie where to send its findings. While archie can read your return address, you don't want to trust archie to get your address right. Mail systems vary widely with where they put return addresses, and archie can't always tell if it's gotten the right address. Therefore, it's much safer to explicitly tell archie where to send its results then to trust archie to get it right.

The prog line gives archie its search orders. The default for mail searches is regex, but you can reset the default by using the set search command. Quit does what it sounds like. If there was nothing else in your message, you wouldn't need to write quit. Sometimes, information ends up in your message that doesn't belong there. So, it's safer to end your search request with quit to avoid confusing archie.

Combining archie, E-mail, and ftp

After you have the file name and the location, you can use anonymous ftp to retrieve the file. Suppose, however, you don't have ftp access? Sometimes, you can use mail to obtain files even without full Internet access.

There are three ways of doing this. Some servers are set up to respond specifically to mail requests for files. Others, especially on BITnet, have "listserv" servers that use a different method for file requests, but like direct mail requesters, you can get files from these systems.

In a mail request, you get a file by sending a message to the site with your request in the subject line. Such a request might look like:

```
To: mail-server@some_machine.somewhere.edu
Subject: send /directory/file_name
```

And, that's all there is to it. You put absolutely nothing in the text part of the message.

For a BITnet system, your message would run:

```
To: listserv@an_ibm_mainframe.somewhere.com
```

In the message's body, write

```
get file_name file_type
```

Because BITnet runs on IBM VM mainframe systems, file type is mandatory. Don't panic about getting information from a hulking IBM mainframe. The preceding commands are all you'll need.

More generally useful are ftpmail application gateways. The most popular one is ftpmail@decwrl.dec.com. Just to make things annoying, it uses ftp syntax rather than anything that looks like the first two methods. A sample of this:

```
To: ftpmail@decwrl.dec.com
subject: The Best File Ever
```

Then in the message itself, you type the following:

```
connect system.somewhere.com
chdir pub/file_location
get file
quit
```

You don't need to type a subject, but doing so can help you remember what that large, mysterious-looking letter in your electronic mailbox is. The important thing is that you enter ftp commands (be careful of typos!) one command per line in the text.

Presuming that everything went right, you can expect to see your file in anywhere from a few hours to a few days. Speaking of getting it right, you can always send the single command "help" to any of the mail servers or archie to get more help.

Using gopher and WAIS

Getting the most out of the Internet isn't easy. Even archie only helps with one specific area of net use: finding and ftping files. Probably more than a few of you have been saying, "The net is cool but why does it have to be so hard to use?"

These days, with the right software, the Internet doesn't have to be so hard to figure out. There are two user-friendly programs that make using the Internet's resources easier than ever before: gopher and Wide Area Information Server (WAIS).

Before those two resources became available, some of the net's most valuable resources were only available to a lucky few. The most important of these resources are the online databases. These systems provide public access to everything from library catalogs to technical documentation collections. Unfortunately few people knew how to access these databases. Now, with gopher at your side, you can liberate this information for your own uses.

Using gopher

gopher and WAIS may sound like Ren and Stimpy, but they're anything but cartoons. Unlike ftp and archie, gopher is a general purpose information tool. gopher builds on the foundation of ftp, archie, and other information sources to erect an easy-to-use, menu-driven interface to the net's file and informational resources. gopher was 'born' at the University of Minnesota, the Golden Gophers.

Unlike archie, which relies on a centralized archie database of ftpable files, gopher doesn't rely on any particular data collection. To use the analogy of a library, archie is like a card catalog dedicated to publicly available files. gopher, on the other hand, is like a librarian. gopher doesn't know where a particular item is but it knows how to find it.

The best thing about gopher is that you don't have to have a clue about where some file or bit of information is located. IP addresses, file formats, domain names—forget 'em. With gopher, you don't need to know UNIX esoteria. gopher does the dirty work; all you have to do is pose the questions.

To get gopher started, you should have a gopher client on your system. If you don't, you can telnet your way to a site with a publicly accessible gopher client the same way you can access archie.

You shouldn't have to do this, however. gopher client programs are free and come in makes and models for almost every architecture and operating system under the sun. Although the UNIX character-based interface is the most common gopher front end, you also can get a HyperCard-style gopher for the Macintosh and a DOS-character interface-based subspecies for PCs.

Some systems, like BIX, with InterNav, have their own gopher front end (see fig. 13.6). You can get the right one for your system by using archie to find a nearby site with ftpable gopher files. If all else fails, you can always find the gopher clients at the site: boom-box.micro.umn.edu in the pub/gopher directory. Always look for a closer site first. Everyone who's a net expert knows about boom-box, and that site can be very busy.

Figure 13.6

Internav's gopher may be prettier than a character gopher interface, but the two function exactly the same.

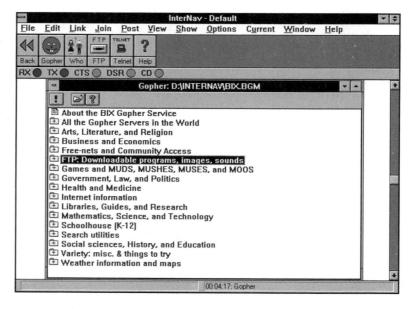

After you've installed the program, usually a simple task, type **gopher** at your command prompt. You're then presented with a set of menus; select the choice that looks like the best path to your informational destination. You might, for example, decide that you want to find a library with a copy of the newest Tom Clancy thriller.

In the pre-gopher days, you'd do this by telneting to every computerized library catalog. Right, like everyone knows IP addresses or domain names for automated card catalogs. Even after you found your library and its access point, you then faced the problem of how to log into the system. Some just let you right in, some require a user id of "guest," others, "anonymous" and so on. If you made it that far, you'd have to figure out that system's particular idiosyncrasies. It's no wonder that until recently Internet information access has been a black art practiced only by net gurus.

With gopher, however, the gopher server takes care of all this. Your client gopher starts looking for the information. It does this by first checking for local resources, usually a gopher server or telnets to a preset gopher service.

gopher clients come with a preset gopher server they look to for information, but this can, and should be, changed to access the closest available gopher server. The server, presented with your request, then tries to find the information. In a few seconds, gopher presents menu choices that take you closer to your destination.

These choices come in two forms: resources and directories. A directory, marked with a slash (/) at the end of its menu item, indicates that choosing this item will lead you to a submenu. Resources are, like the name indicates, actual sources of information.

From the menus, you proceed to narrow down your choices until reach an appropriate resource. In our search for our Clancy high-tech shoot 'em up, for example, we can probably live without looking into card catalogs for libraries thousands of miles away.

Eventually, you end up with what you and gopher agree is probably a system or program that can supply you with the information or file you need. At this point, you and gopher gofer it.

When you access a resource, gopher takes over the job of logging in to the computer and service. gopher also shields you from the local system. No matter what you're logged into, you use your gopher's search interface, not the remote system's.

This has one great advantage: you never have to learn the ins and outs of a database you might only use once. There are two mirror image problems to gopher's approach. The first is that while gopher can perform fairly complicated searches, you may not know if the server gopher is talking to can handle it.

archie, for example, can only search for a single word. Or, you could try searching for, say, "386DX and UNIX." Some systems take that to mean you want to know about books or articles that contain both the words "386DX" and "UNIX." Others assume you really want the phrase "386DX and UNIX." With gopher, in the way, you'll only know that your searches are going wrong.

The flip side to this is that gopher defaults to the lowest common denominator searching. The resource you're accessing may be capable of very precise searches, but you'll be limited to your local gopher's search capacities. gopher, for instance, can't tell the difference between lowercase and uppercase. This may not be a big deal if you're only occasionally on a data hunt, but big-time information hunters will sometimes want to throw gopher out of camp. At least they'll feel that way until they recall how much work hunting for information is without gopher.

Another thing you should keep in mind with gopher is that sometimes gopher may dig up an information resource that you can't access. The most common example of this is a news service. The UPI news feed is available as Clarinet, but it's inaccessible from many sites no matter what the gopher menu says. That's because Clarinet services are only available to systems that pay for the news access.

Still, another interesting point is that not all gopher servers are the same. Some servers may be much stronger in certain areas than they are in others. That's because gopher servers tend to be connected to local resources. The original gopher server at the University of Minnesota, to no surprise, is filled with information resources from that school. One of the neater things about gopher, however, is that you're not limited to a single server. You can use gopher to hunt for other gopher servers that might give you access to information you need.

Flaws, and all, you'll never mistake gopher for such powerful single-purpose online information retrieval engines as Ziffnet's Computer Library, but gopher does have its good points. Because gopher brings the almost limitless information resources to your reach, gopher is an invaluable tool for any Internet explorer.

Using WAIS

gopher is not the only one making the Internet a better place for information hunters. WAIS (pronounced wayz) works like gopher in that it's a tool for finding information and resources on the Internet. With gopher, though, you need to point it through its menus in a certain direction. gopher's very easy to use, but it helps if you have an idea where to look before you go looking for it.

WAIS, on the other hand, does the legwork for you. Of course, WAIS can't do everything. It's not capable of searching willy-nilly through public directories throughout the Internet universe. (Good thing it can't or it would eat up network bandwidth like peanuts.) Instead, WAIS relies on indexed data collections or, as they're called, libraries.

These libraries are file collections consisting mostly of informational material. For instance, one WAIS library can tell you which organizations in the former Soviet Union have or are planning to have e-mail links with the West. On the lighter side, you also can access a WAIS library containing "Not Just Cows." In case you're wondering, the Cows library is devoted to agricultural Internet resources.

Every WAIS client, which may be on your local system or accessible through telnet from a remote site, knows where to find the WAIS libraries. Presently, there are more than 200 free libraries. Volunteers at academic sites maintain and index most of these data collections. Commercial WAIS libraries, such as the Dow Jones Information Service, also are available.

Most of the libraries are free. WAIS library coverage can be very spotty. For instance, computer science subjects tend to be well covered. If you want to know about car stereos, however, you're out of luck... for now. WAIS libraries keep springing up at a surprising rate, and there's no telling what may be available by the time you read this.

WAIS itself is mindlessly simple to use. WAIS clients are available for everything from Macintoshes to PCs to supercomputers. In every case, you simply key in words for WAIS to search on and then let her rip. WAIS will respond with a listing of libraries where it thinks the information that you're looking for is hiding out.

You could instruct WAIS to search everywhere, but that's a waste of time and Internet resources. For instance, searching for information about antique clocks in the WAIS library devoted to the Simpsons won't do any good.

Armed with a library's listing, you select the most likely targets and WAIS narrows down its search. If all goes well, you'll be looking at the documents concerning your subject in a matter of seconds.

Then again, maybe you won't. WAIS searching doesn't recognize any of the Boolean search terms. In other words, although you can search for references to "Modem and V.32" you won't get just documents that contain both terms. Instead WAIS uses an internal weighing system that measures each term's value for the search, including the "and." It's possible that an article containing many "ands" and "V.32's" will be tagged by WAIS as more important than a short document containing "Modem" in the title, but makes more references to v.32bis then V.32. It can make researchers' blood boil just thinking about it.

Why use WAIS then? Because WAIS does just fine at simple, one-term searches. WAIS also has the unique ability to perform "relevance feedback" searches. Say you find an article on V.32 modems that exactly hits the spot. You then can pull terms from that document and use them to start a new search. WAIS gives you the ability, after you're on the right trail, to travel down that path to other relevant articles. For this ability alone, WAIS, even in its current teething stage, is an excellent information gathering tool.

Using World Wide Web

World Wide Web (WWW) is still in development, but some Web sites are publicly accessible and Web points to the future of Internet data hunts. Web brings hypertext to the Internet. *Hypertext* is a way at looking at documents that, although not unique to computers, makes full use of a computer's ability to interconnect data. In a hypertext document, certain words are links to other documents or files. For instance, in a biography of Bill Clinton, you could jump from a description of his presidential campaign to an article on his years as a governor. Then, from a reference in it, jump to Hillary Clinton, and from there to a story on how Socks became part of the family.

Web takes the hypertext idea and applies it to information available on the Internet. The result is potentially the most powerful automated information gathering tool in existence.

Alas, for now, Web remains mostly potential. Web servers are available, by telneting, only in a few sites. Its full, hypertext informational resources are limited at this time, but they are growing. Web is the informational wave of the future.

Like gopher and WAIS, Web boasts several easy-to-use interfaces. Of course, the read-only version of Web really only has two commands, so it's not hard to make it easy to use. These commands are: start a search and follow a link. That's it. Web takes care of the rest of the details. This leads to a quite different way of looking at information. For example, you can use Web to wander about WAIS libraries and leap from term to term regardless of a document's format or location.

Unfortunately, because much of the data that Web deals with isn't in hypertext format, Web usually comes across as a slower version of WAIS with a more consistent interface. This is true now, but as more true hypertext documents become available, Web's uniquely strong searching capacities will stand out more and more.

Part 4:

The Online Toolbox

Virus Protection

Using Fax/Modems

Chapter 14

Virus Protection

A common fear that prevents many people from going online is that their computer will become infected with a computer virus. What are viruses, and what can you do to prevent getting one in the first place or to cure one if you do?

Despite its name, a computer virus isn't something that your computer can catch very easily. In fact, I should stress that your chances of running across one are very slim indeed. But for the same reasons that you need to know about sexually transmitted diseases, even if you're blissfully monogamous, you should know about what computer viruses are—and aren't.

Understanding Computer Viruses

A computer virus is a specific kind of program with two key attributes:

- 🌀   A computer virus stores a copy of itself in another part of a computer system (usually on a hard drive or a floppy disk).

- 🌀   A virus has the capability to replicate.

When a virus replicates, it makes a copy of itself and distributes the copy in the nooks and crannies of your computer system. When your computer has a virus, it is said to be *infected*, just as biological viruses can infect you with a physical illness.

Viruses attempt to self-replicate without letting you know that they are even present. They spread either from an infected floppy disk or by direct access to other computers. Direct access can be through a local area network (LAN) or by connection to a modem.

The Two Main Viruses

There are two main types of computer viruses: *boot infectors* and *file infectors*.

When you turn on (or *boot up*) your computer, DOS looks in an area of the hard disk or floppy disk that is called the *boot sector*. Boot infector viruses infect this part of the disk. When you start your computer from an infected disk, the boot infector virus will load itself into memory.

After the virus is in memory, the virus will pay attention to your actions while you work at the computer. If you access another disk, for example, the virus will attach itself to that disk, too. Some boot sector viruses only infect floppy disks; others infect hard drives; still others are less picky and will munch on whichever drive comes along.

File infector viruses infect files by attaching a copy of themselves to a file already on the disk. The files infected can be part of any kind of program—a word processing application or a communications program. Viruses usually infect only executable files, which are the files that can be "run," such as applications. In DOS, these files have file extensions that end in .EXE or .COM. Usually, data files (such as word processing documents or spreadsheets that you have saved) are perfectly safe.

The virus usually adds itself to the very end or the very beginning of the infected file. A few viruses overwrite part of the file, but these types of viruses are rare. When you run the infected file, the virus will load itself into memory and/or infect other files.

One advantage to using OS/2 as your operating system is the protection it provides. Almost no DOS-based viruses have an effect on an OS/2 system, because OS/2 prevents any program from having access to the boot sector or from messing around in memory. Some clever but malevolent programmer is sure to find a way around this someday, but, at the moment, OS/2 systems are reasonably secure.

What Does a Virus Do to a Computer?

Different viruses do different things. It all depends on the intention of the virus' programmer. Some viruses do nothing except make copies of themselves. Although this sounds fairly benign, the virus eats up more and more of your hard disk memory. And, as the virus replicates, it slows down the operation of your computer.

In general, the viruses that just make copies of themselves are the dorky nephews of the virus world; they just hang around, consuming whatever you have in the refrigerator, but they don't do anything useful either. In addition, some of these viruses can attach themselves to a file in a way that damages part of the file. So, even though these viruses aren't that serious, you'll want to get rid of them in any case.

On the other hand, the Dark Avenger waits until it has infected sixteen files. Then it randomly writes over a sector on your computer's hard drive. The Michelangelo virus, which gained quite a bit of attention a few years back, waits until March 6th of any year before overwriting your entire hard drive. Pretty friendly, huh?

Many viruses wait for a particular condition before they spring their trap. This is usually to allow time for the virus to replicate and spread, and so that you don't discover it "too soon." After a virus begins to replicate and spread, it usually becomes easy to detect. The two most common activation conditions are reaching a certain number of infections or reaching a particular date.

The seriousness of a virus' action can vary. Some actions are annoying, but not harmful. There are some viruses that might display text messages, such as "Legalize Marijuana!" Other viruses might bounce a ball across your screen. Destructive viruses, on the other hand, can wreak havoc on your computer system.

Where Do Computer Viruses Come From?

Viruses, like any other kind of program, are written by computer programmers. It's hard to generalize about the kind of person who would bother to write a virus, because few virus authors rush to brag about the activity. Some seem to write one because it was technically interesting, and it got away.

For instance, a programmer might write a virus just to understand how one works, but inadvertantly pass the virus to another computer system. Others write viruses as a prank or a practical joke. But clearly, there are programmers out there who are malicious; how else could someone justify the writing of The Dark Avenger?

How Viruses Spread

As mentioned earlier, viruses spread from disk to disk (usually via floppy disk) or when transferred to your system by some other means. One of the ways to get an infected file onto your hard disk is to download it—which is why we've devoted this chapter to the topic.

Because BBSs are accessed by so many people, it is possible that a virus-infected file could be uploaded to the system. Responsible BBS Sysops screen all files before making them visible to ensure that nothing on the bulletin board is infected.

Many BBS programs will automatically check files for viruses before the software even lets the Sysop see it. On CompuServe, every file is screened for viruses before it becomes visible to the membership.

However, there is always a chance that one file will slip by. The degree to which you can trust that files are virus-free is completely dependent on how much you trust your BBS Sysop. If you dial into many BBSs, you take a greater risk. It's just like dating: if you're monogamous and reasonably cautious, you don't have very much to worry about.

Some companies are so afraid of contracting a computer virus from a BBS that they prohibit their employees from using BBSs or from purchasing shareware. In fact, BBSs are among the safest places to visit and the least likely locations from which to contract an infection. You're much more likely to get a computer virus from a college computer lab.

Preventing Computer Viruses

Okay, that's what a virus is. What can you do to make sure you never see one? What can you do if your computer does become infected?

Virus Scanning Software

There are at least twenty computer applications that directly address the virus problem. They use a combination of techniques to do so.

Virus Scanners

Virus scanners search for known viruses in your computer's memory and in files that you specify. Each virus has a unique "string" of program code, which the scanning program is trained to recognize.

Virus scanning is the most common technique used for virus detection. However, new viruses come along frequently (hopefully not *too* frequently), and your scanning program has to know about the new virus' string "signature" to be able to detect and get rid of that virus. That means that you have to update your software quite often. (Plus, you have to remember to *use* the virus scanner.)

Memory Resident Virus Detectors

Memory Resident Virus Detectors are terminate-and-stay-ready programs (TSR) that are usually loaded automatically when you boot your computer. These programs stay in your computer memory all the time, checking every single program before you run it. To some degree, these programs work in the background.

A memory-resident virus detector will find a virus as soon as you attempt to run the infected file. However, because it takes up memory in your computer, you won't have that memory available for other applications—all of which are greedy for every byte they can get. Memory-resident virus detectors also slow down your system, somewhat, because it takes time to check every file you run. Like the regular scanning programs, this type of scanner needs to be updated often.

Change Detection Programs

Change Detection Programs look for files that have been altered. First, the program determines a baseline size for each executable file on your hard disk. Some time later, you run the change detection program to look at the files again. If the size of the program has changed, something is definitely fishy. Change detection programs don't have to be updated frequently, because all they're looking for is an alteration, not a specific string of characters.

If they do find something amiss, however, there's no way for them to tell you exactly what's wrong. There are several good reasons why a file size might change, and these programs don't know the difference. In a few cases, there might be an advanced virus that manages to infect your system without changing the file size; you'd never know.

Virus Removal Programs

Virus Removal Programs get rid of a virus after a scanning tool detects one. Some remove one particular kind of virus. For instance, there were several free Michelangelo-removal programs available during that scare. Most removal programs do their best to restore an infected file back to its original state, but some programs just can't be fixed. Re-installing is your only real option.

An Ounce of Prevention...

As in any other disaster, the best thing you can do is work to prevent it from occurring. There are several actions you can take to minimize your risk of computer virus infection.

Back Up to Your Backups

The best thing to do is to back up your computer often. It's a good idea to back up (copy) the information on your hard disk to disk or tape. When you have reliable backups, viruses are among the least likely things to cause problems for you. Having a reliable backup program and using it can save you from hard disk failures, from oh-no-I-just-deleted-the-accounting-system, and from unintentionally misbehaving software (software bugs). They are also the ultimate in virus protection—after removing a virus, you can restore your original programs and data from backup.

Scan for Viruses

Use a virus scanner program regularly. How often you should do so depends on how often your system comes in contact with other computer systems. If you log into several BBSs every day, it would make sense to check your files daily. For most people, running one of these programs once per week or month is fine.

How can you tell if you're at a high risk for viruses? Here are a few examples.

- ✆   You dial into lots and lots of BBSs, without any certainty of how that BBS is managed.

- ✆   You work with a lot of data from disks that come from unknown and unknowable sources. (For instance, you're an accountant and most of your clients supply their financial data to you on disk. Who knows where those disks have been?)

- ✆   You suspect someone with malicious intent, who might have access to your computer.

Use Memory Resident Virus Detectors

You can use a memory resident virus detector to check every program that is loaded into memory. These kinds of virus detectors can be impractical because memory resident programs, as their name implies, take up the memory that you would use to run other programs.

I personally find this level of caution to be overkill, except in situations where the chance of infection is very high. It can make sense to load one of these programs temporarily, however. For instance, load a memory-resident virus detector before you install new software.

Write-Protect your Floppies

Use the write-protection tabs that are available on your floppy disks. You can place a piece of tape over the square notch on the edge of a 5.25-inch disk or move the notch on the tabs on a 3.5-inch disk.

Be Consumer Aware at the Service Desk

If you bring your computer in for service, you should make sure that the service personnel scan their diagnostic tools for viruses.

Keep Floppies Out when Booting Up

Do not turn on your computer with a floppy disk in drive A if you aren't completely positive of the disk's contents. Boot sector viruses might be lying in wait on that floppy disk, hoping to munch on your hard disk space.

Update Your Protection Programs

Make sure that you update your anti-virus software often. New viruses seem to appear in waves (much like relatives at Christmas-time). Older versions of virus-detection software will not be able to spot the newest viruses.

Using a Virus Detection Program

The interface between you and your virus detection program varies by the application you use. Some shareware applications, such as McAfee's SCAN (shown in fig. 14.1) are command-line based. Others, like the Norton Antivirus, have a full-screen, interactive interface.

```
SCAN 9.19 V108 Copyright 1989-93 by McAfee Associates. (408) 988-3832
Usage:      SCAN d1: ... d26: /A /ADx /AF filename /AG filename /AV filename
            /BELL /BMP /CERTIFY /CF filename /CHKHI /CG /CV /D
            /DATE /E .xxx .yyy /EXT d:filename
            /HISTORY filename /MAINT /MANY /NLZ /NOBREAK
            /NOEXPIRE /NOMEM /NOPAUSE /REPORT filename
            /RF filename /RG /RV /SAVE /SHOWDATE
            /SUB @filename

Examples:   SCAN C:
            SCAN A: B:
            SCAN C:\TEST\*.* D:\ E:\
            SCAN A:TESTFILE.EXE /BELL /MANY

Options are:
    \                    - Scan root directory and boot area only
    /A                   - Scan all files, including data, for viruses
    /ADx                 - Scan all drives ('L'=local,'N'=network,' '=both)
    /AF filename         - Store recovery data/validation codes to file
    /AG filename         - Add recovery data/validation codes to specified
                           files EXCEPT those listed in filename
    /AV filename         - Add validation codes to specified files EXCEPT
                           those listed in filename
    /BELL                - Ring alarm if virus found
More? ( H = Help )
```

Figure 14.1

Some of the command-line switches that enable you to run McAfee's SCAN program.

Being Pragmatic about Viruses

Now that you understand how viruses work—and you know how to use a virus detection program—how much does it matter? How much do you really need to worry?

Not much.

In ten years of online life, I have never personally encountered a virus. Oh, viruses are real, all right–but they aren't nearly as prevalent as you might be afraid they are.

As a novice, it's easy to get paranoid. Some computer users are certain that if they run into any problem, it must be a virus. That's almost never the case. In 99 percent of cases, the problem is caused by the user, software, or hardware.

In other words, you probably screwed up and shouldn't blame someone else. Only after every other possibility has been eliminated should you consider that you might have a computer virus.

Chapter 15

Using Fax/Modems

Instead of sending a fax the traditional way—with paper and a dedicated fax machine—you can send, receive, and manage faxed information on your computer. There's no wasted time standing in line, no rekeying, and little chance of "lost" faxes. Much more convenient than traditional faxing, computer faxing gives you the option to print only the pages you need and eliminates wasteful printing of junk faxes. Computer faxes are much clearer and crisper looking than even the plain-paper, stand-alone fax output.

To send a fax with a computer, you need a modem with fax capabilities, and fax software that enables you to send, receive, and manage faxes.

Just the Fax, Ma'am

There are several advantages to using your computer for faxing:

- ✆   When you send a fax, you know that it will come across "clean." The fax won't have ugly smears on it. It won't be sent at a weird angle.

- ✆   In general, the quality of a fax sent by computer will be better than one from a stand-alone fax machine. It's far better than the quality provided by a cheap fax machine, plus the fax/modem is a lot cheaper than the cheapest fax machine.

- ✆   You can automate sending faxes so that it's cheaper and more convenient for you. If you have a fax to send to 40 clients around the world, you can send them all at midnight and save a bundle on telephone charges.

- ✆   When you receive a fax, you can view it before you print it. If the fax is junk or irrelevant, you can trash it without printing it, saving trees and expensive fax paper.

- ✆   When you do print a fax, you print it on your own printer—for the price of a cheap fax/modem, you also get a plain-paper fax machine.

- ✆   You probably got the hardware free when you purchased your modem, so you may as well use it.

Naturally, there are disadvantages as well:

- ✆   The fax software can tie up your computer. The computer has to be left on, all the time, or it can't answer the phone to receive faxes.

- ✆   The fax software can use up your computer's resources. If you're using DOS, you have to give up some of the computer's memory to the terminate-and-stay-resident (TSR) application that manages the fax in the background. Even with Windows or OS/2, you have to give up some system resources.

- Because the faxes you send or receive are stored on your hard disk, you'll use up hard disk space.

- Unless you own a scanner, you can only fax documents that you create on your computer or receive via computer from someone else. For instance: you write a contract in your word processor and fax it to your client. If she says, "Okay, I've signed it and faxed it to you. If you sign it and fax it back, we've got a deal," you'll be out of luck unless you have a scanned-in copy of your signature. Sure, you could print out the fax, and sign it, but how are you going to get the signed or marked-up document back into the computer? It won't take long before you'll want to buy a scanner.

- Faxes are sent and received as graphics images. When you print a fax, you'll tie up your printer with a document that could take quite a while to print.

Despite this long list, the advantages are stronger than the disadvantages. A fax/modem is a very handy thing to own!

Understanding Fax Hardware

As described way back in Chapter 2, fax hardware uses separate circuitry from the modem. Most new modems include fax capabilities, however, with the logical justification that both of them use the telephone line.

Using a fax/modem, you can fax to any phone number. The fax on the receiving end can be a stand-alone fax or it can be another fax modem. Neither the sending nor the receiving fax equipment cares.

Fax Speeds

Like modems, fax/modems are available in more than one speed. You might find an older 4800 bps fax/modem, especially if you buy a used model, but the usual speeds are 9600 bps and 14400 bps send-and-receive fax. As with modems, get the fastest one that you can afford.

Have Some Class

When you look at fax specifications, you'll see reference to a fax's "class." This has nothing to do with its behavior at parties. Instead, fax class relates to the features included with the equipment.

Class 1 fax/modems use a series of Hayes-type AT software commands to control fax boards. Class 1 modems do not have the capability to automatically detect whether an incoming call is data or fax. The modem has to be set for one or the other.

Class 2 fax/modems have hardware that provide the capability to detect whether the incoming call is a data or fax call. The work of sending or receiving a fax is divided between the modem processor and the computer processor.

Previously, with Class 1, the computer processor did all the real work, and it used the fax/modem like a data modem, passing data through it. With a Class 2 fax/modem, much of the work is offloaded to the modem processor, primarily the part that communicates with the other fax machine. A Class 2 fax/modem dials the phone, and does all the "talking" to the other fax machine. This then allows an "independent" processor (the modem) to worry with the timing dependent protocol, instead of the computer processor that is busy and distracted doing other things locally.

Using a Class 2 fax/modem is no faster than Class 1. However, Class 2 is more dependable, and should reduce the load on your computer. Don't get too excited; the computer fax software still does the intensive work of preparing and printing files. The processor spends a lot of time reading and writing data to disk. The advantage to Class 2 is that, when the remote fax machine wants a reply in 20 milliseconds, the fax/modem responds, and the processor doesn't have to be Johnny-on-the-spot.

Intel sells fax/modems that use the Communicating Applications Specification (CAS). Like most stand-alone fax machines, the CAS modems support MR (Modified Read) encoding for fax compression. According to Intel, this feature reduces connect times and phone line costs an average of 25 percent. Although this sounds good, most PC fax/modems do not support MR encoding.

Group Therapy

The "Group" designation refers to the speed at which a fax is transmitted.

Group 1 is for fax/modems and fax machines that transmit a standard 8.5 × 11-inch page in approximately six minutes.

Group 2 indicates that the fax/modem or fax machine will transmit a standard 8.5 × 11-inch sheet of paper in three minutes or so.

Group 3 and Group 4 modems are not yet standard. Group 3 will be a digital machine or 9600 bps machine or modem. Fax/modems in this group will send an 8.5× 11-inch page in as few as 20 seconds! Group 4 includes those state-of-the-art machines and modems that operate at 64,000 bps. That's fast!

Most fax/modems are Class 1 or Class 2 and at least Group 2. The only time that you need to worry about this is when you install your fax software. Because there aren't that many choices, it's hard to make a wrong guess.

About Fax Software

When you buy a fax/modem, a simple fax application is usually included. The program may be adequate for your needs, but, as with the basic communications software included with your modem, they are usually limited or "lite" versions. There are several stand-alone and add-on fax programs that you may want to explore.

Basic Fax Software Features

Even the most basic of the bundled fax software provides the following features:

- *C* You can send or receive faxes in the background while you operate from DOS or Windows.

- *C* You can preview faxes sent or received.

- *C* You can print faxes sent or received.

- *C* You can add a cover sheet to your fax (see fig. 15.1).

    ✆   You can schedule your fax so that it will automatically be delivered at a later time and/or date.

    ✆   You can maintain a telephone book of fax numbers.

Figure 15.1

Fax programs let you include custom cover sheets.

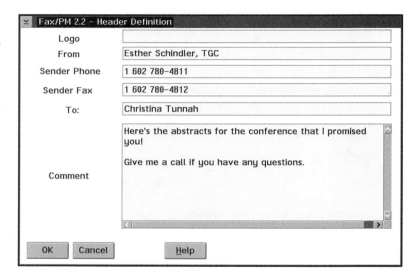

Scheduling capabilities offer you maximum efficiency and convenience, facilitating easy communication with other time zones and taking advantage of lower telephone rates.

When you use fax software, the faxes you create or receive are stored on your hard disk as a graphics file. The benefit of storing faxes this way is that you can reuse or refer to the fax, just as you refer to other documents. The disadvantage is that those faxes take up hard disk space. A fax of a simple, one-page letter can be 20K; a longer, more complex document can consume 300K of your hard disk space.

...And Other Stuff

One common feature is support of fax groups. For instance, you might have one group of people to whom you send the quarterly business reports, another list of regional managers, and, because this is real life, a list of people to whom you generally fax your favorite cartoons. Just about any fax program will let you annotate the phone book so that you can include a listing in a group; how extensive that feature is will depend on the specific package.

Some fax programs support scanners directly. With these programs, you can tell the fax program to use the scanned image as the outgoing fax; the scanned file will be automatically discarded after the fax is sent.

If you want to fax your boss a package of information that is generated by several applications—for example, a spreadsheet, a report from the company database, and a cover letter—only a few packages will let you do so. Most of them (especially the less expensive programs) cannot combine pages from multiple pages and files.

Most fax programs permit you to modify the cover sheet, at least in simple terms. Other programs get fancy, including libraries of business-like and "fun" cover sheets, and letting you create new ones.

While every fax program has a telephone book of the fax numbers you dial, not every one supports multiple telephone books. Some of the high-end Windows fax programs will link the telephone book to other applications, especially time managers and personal information managers such as Lotus Organizer. This eliminates the need to enter data twice.

Some companies produce add-on tools for managing faxes. These can be very useful if your business uses a lot of faxes that need to be filed or indexed. For instance, SofNet's FaxTracker for Windows is a management tool for retrieving and storing faxes. It lets you:

- Store faxes with a search index
- Attach notes to stored faxes
- Compress fax images for storage
- Search for faxes for date/time, index, or sender
- Edit, draw, and annotate faxes

Another product, Fax and Find, keeps the full text of the documents in a Personal PageKeeper document. Its database is automatically indexed, without any keyword entry on your part.

How Fax Software Works

There are two kinds of fax software:

- Stand-alone applications

- Integrated fax software

Many older fax programs are stand-alone. They don't work with any of your applications directly. Instead, you create your document and print it to a file. This may sound complex, but the idea is simple: you tell WordPerfect or Word or 1-2-3 that you're using an IBM Proprinter, but instead of sending the data out the printer port, you instruct the program to save the data on a disk file.

Unfortunately, learning how to tell each program to save information to a file can be complex. Because it's also certain to be a different process for each DOS application (and possibly for Windows and OS/2 applications as well), this procedure is, well, less than ideal.

Also, the stand-alone fax software only support a few printer formats. These are often the older, less snazzy formats, such as the dot-matrix Epson and IBM Proprinter formats; in may cases, you will not have all of your printer fonts available.

In any case, once you save your document to a file, you start the fax application, and instruct it to send the file you created. The fax program converts the printer file to its own format (see fig. 15.2), and sends the document over the fax/modem.

It's more than a bit awkward, but the process works. It may also be your only option if you're using older DOS applications.

Under both Windows and OS/2, integrated fax programs are more common. When you install these programs, they create a new "virtual printer." You don't get a real printer, of course, but the fax software tells Windows or OS/2 that you have another printer and, as you can see in figure 15.3, that's how the operating system treats it. That's why it's called "virtual"—it isn't really there, but you can act as though it were. When you set up the fax printer, you provide basic information just as you would for a "real" printer, such as choosing portrait or landscape. You also choose information specific to a fax virtual printer, such as a fax's "fine" versus "standard" resolution.

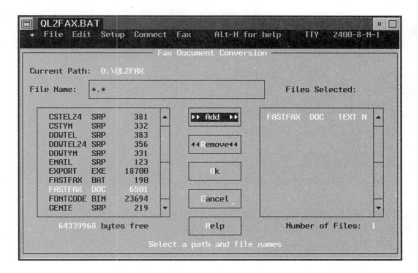

Figure 15.2

Converting a text file into a fax format with a stand-alone program.

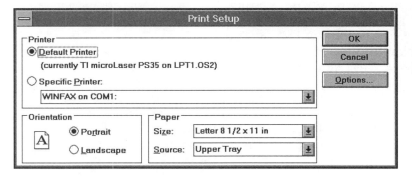

Figure 15.3

To use an integrated fax program, you select the fax as the printer.

When you want to send a fax from one of the integrated fax programs, you just *print*. Your information is sent to the fax "printer" and, because it "knows" that it isn't really a printer, a little more is added to the printing process. For example, you will be prompted to specify to whom the fax should be sent, asked to provide information for the cover sheet, and so on. (See fig. 15.4 for an example.) In most cases, the fax is sent just as it appears on-screen. The fax program sends the file in the background, while you continue working.

Obviously, the integrated software is much more convenient to use!

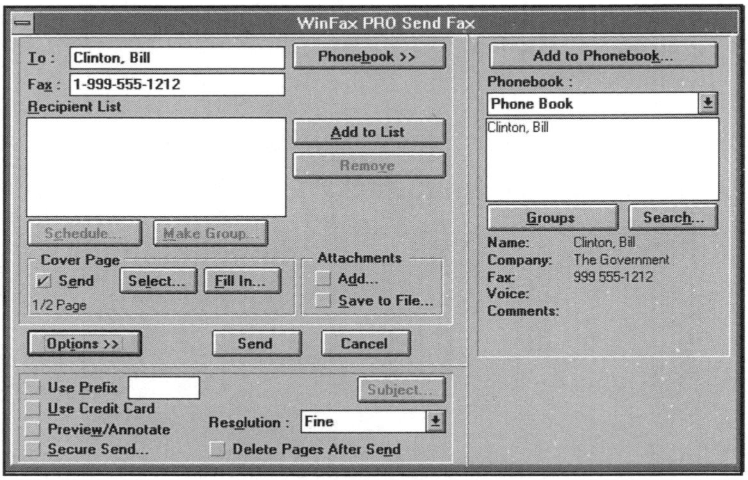

Figure 15.4

When you print to the fax, you are prompted to choose the fax's recipients.

One of the great advantages of sending and receiving faxes with a computer is that you can continue to work while a fax is sent or received in the background. To accomplish this under DOS, the fax application needs to load a program called a terminate-and-stay-resident (TSR) program. Because of the "...and stay resident" part of the TSR, these programs use memory that would otherwise be available to your applications. For instance, one DOS-based fax program uses 10K RAM for its TSR interface, and 71K of conventional or EMS memory when the full program is loaded. If you're short on memory resources, this might present a serious problem. It often seems that DOS fax software is destined to be a hassle.

Some DOS applications include a fax program that is designed to work with them. One example is the DOS version of WordPerfect 6.0. This makes it relatively easy to fax directly from WordPerfect (see fig. 15.5), but you certainly need more than the minimum memory requirements to make it work well.

The situation under Windows is somewhat better, as Windows can manage the available memory so that you can still run most of your applications. However, receiving a fax in the background under Windows can slow down the performance of the other applications to a crawl unless you're using a very fast computer.

Under OS/2, the memory problem is almost nil because the fax program will be "swapped out" to disk if it isn't being used. Because of its better

capability to multitask, OS/2 is better suited to any telecommunications—
modem-based *or* fax-based.

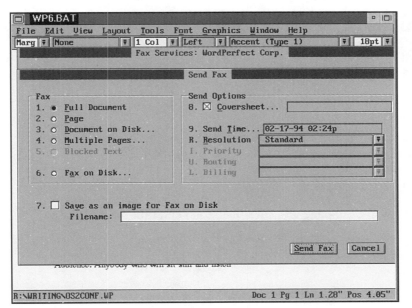

Figure 15.5

Faxing from within WordPerfect.

Receiving and Printing Faxes

You don't have to receive faxes with your fax card; turning on the "auto answer" is up to you (see fig. 15.6). In some low-memory situations, you may want to turn it on only when you're actively waiting for a fax. Under ordinarily circumstances, however, you will want to run the fax program in the background whenever the computer is turned on. (The fax software may load its TSR whether or not you explicitly start the fax program, in any case.)

Figure 15.6

You can adjust many settings for receiving faxes.

When the phone rings and the fax software is set to "wait for a call," the fax/modem will pick up the telephone. Your fax/modem and the other fax will make the familiar warbling tones that sound like a troubled cat in heat. When they connect, the fax software will manage the call and save the received fax to disk. During this time, you can usually continue your regular work. You might notice a performance degradation; how much of one you'll see depends on your computer hardware, application, and operating system.

After the transmission is complete, you can view or print the fax.

Printing a fax is usually a piece of cake. After you view the fax and determine that you want to have it on paper in your hot little hands, you tell it to print, and it prints on your printer.

Any of the fax programs will print the faxes that you receive. However, because they are full-page graphics files, they can take a long time to print.

OCR

When you receive a fax using fax software, the image of each page is stored on your hard disk. As far as your computer is concerned, the files are graphics, not text; you have a snapshot picture of a page, not a document. If you want to work with the text on the page, you will need to use a program that supports *optical character recognition*, OCR.

An OCR program translates graphics images (which include faxes) into editable text or characters. In other words, the OCR software examines a small section of the page and looks at a particular blob. It matches one blob up with an item in its database that looks awfully like the letter "e" until it decides that it's an "e." One by one, OCR software recognizes each character, and turns the graphics page into a document that you can edit in your favorite word processor. At least, it does its best to do so.

Some fax programs include OCR, or have an option for the feature. OCR is still a developing technology and is not completely reliable. You should proofread anything you pass through an OCR program. To get the best quality from an OCR program, consider these factors:

- ✆   The fax hardware that sent the document
- ✆   The quality of the original document

C   Skewing

C   Transmission mode (Fine versus Standard)

You get the best results when you receive a fax from a fax board. In general, older fax machines will deliver poorer quality than newer fax machines.

OCR achieves the best results when the sender faxes an original document. After several generations of photocopying, a document suffers a significant loss of quality. That makes it harder for the OCR software to do a good job at recognizing the text; it might decide that the blob that once looked like an "e" looks just like a blob—or maybe it's an "o."

When a document is fed into a fax machine, it is often fed at an angle (skewed). OCR can tolerate a small amount of skewing and still accurately recognize the text. However, too much skewing makes the text unrecognizable to OCR, though you may be able to read it very easily. (One reason why you're still smarter than a computer.) A fax from a fax board will have virtually no skewing, whereas the amount of skewing on a fax from a fax machine depends on how the operator inserts the page and how the fax machine feeds it through.

OCR achieves the highest degree of recognition on faxes sent to you in Fine mode (200×200 dpi). The capability for the software to recognize the text is decreased when documents are sent to you in Standard mode (200×100 dpi).

Part 5:

When Things Go Wrong

Troubleshooting Telecommunications

Chapter 16

Troubleshooting Telecommunications

Sometimes, the darn thing just won't work.

This chapter discusses the kinds of problems you may encounter with modems and with telecommunications software. You receive advice about how to solve those problems. Finally, you learn some suggestions about where to turn if the advice fails.

Finding the Source of the Problem

Your first task is to figure out the true source of the problem. Is it the hardware? The software? The phone line? The wetware (a human error)?

Try to eliminate all the variables. Simplify the problem. Try to use the modem with a different communications package. If the modem works with one communications program but not with another, you have determined that it isn't a hardware problem.

If the modem still doesn't work, you have eliminated the software as the problem source. If you suspect a hardware conflict, remove all of the hardware that isn't strictly necessary (you won't be able to diagnose the problem very well if you remove the video card and monitor) and add back each component—one at a time. As soon as the problem reappears, you know which one to blame.

Wetware Problems

Most problems are caused by our own ignorance. Thankfully, ignorance is curable.

Check the obvious. Make sure that the equipment is really turned on and plugged in. I once embarrassed myself by calling technical support for help with a printer, not realizing that I had never attached the printer cable. Gee, no wonder it wouldn't work!

Are you sure that the phone number you're telling the modem to dial is actually another modem? Are you *really* sure? Would you bet your job on it?

Several years ago, a co-worker told me a story about checking the modem connections that the mainframe computer reported were inoperative. He was in a lull between projects, so he sat and listened as the mainframe instructed the modem to dial each phone number in its list of other mainframe computers. In one case, the modem dialed, the phone rang, and the modem tried to connect. A man's voice said, "Hello?" A moment later, my co-worker heard the man shout, "Hey, Martha! It's the guy with the whistle again!"

Phone Line Troubles

Throughout this book, I have focused on the hardware that makes it possible for you to communicate and on the software that lets that hardware actually do something. I've given very little attention to the telephone cable and the telephone service that makes it all possible.

Turning off Call-Waiting

If you have call waiting on the phone line you use for the modem, consider turning off that service. If you're online when another call comes in, the "click-click" that indicates a call waiting is almost certain to cause you to lose the modem connection.

Alternatively, you can disable the call-waiting feature temporarily. Include the keys in the initialization string in your communications program. If you aren't sure what the disable code is, try *70. If that doesn't work, call your phone company.

Coping with Bad Phone Lines

When things don't work, you probably will be tempted to blame the telephone company. In some cases, the phone company may be at fault. But do remember that the telephone line connection starts at your modem. You might have a bad phone cable connection (or a good dog chew-toy) or a problem with the internal phone wiring in your house. Before you call the telephone company to complain, try the phone connection from a different phone jack in your home.

Overall, however, phone service is pretty good. Don't be afraid to call the phone company if you suspect that there is a problem, but don't automatically blame them, either. Here's an example that demonstrates an effective methodology for solving a modem problem.

Trust Ma Bell! She has been around longer than your modem/computer manufacturer.

A friend, Brian Nelson, purchased a full-tower 486/33 system with great expectations of sailing the cybersea. Because he was a bit strapped for a modem purchase, he whipped out a Courier 2400 that was blazingly fast in his

continues

CP/M BBSing days. Brian plugged into COM2, set up his Crosstalk software, and dialed. He was fervently upset by the enormous line noise and intermittent garbage showing on his screen. Brian lives in a semi-rural area of Sacramento, California, and the power glitches, browns, and blacks out on many occasions. So, he automatically assumed Pacific Bell had left the lines in this area to rot as well. Tech call, no problem on the line. Okay, must be line noise from downstream of the modem Brian figured; put it first and put the voice extensions downstream. Then he got even more noise.

This called for serious construction. Brian hauled out the electrician and carpenter tools, fished for pulling wire, and got some telephone wire. Crawled through the attic (insulation, cobwebs, 100 years of dust) to run 100 feet of non-interrupted wire to the block. TAPCIS still bombed and gave him trash, as did the local BBS.

Then his roommate suggested plugging into my COM1. Unplugged mouse, plugged in 2400 baud modem. Finally, everything ran flawlessly.

Calling Out Indirectly

In some cases, you will need to use a modem in situations where the phone company's involvement is minimal, such as fax/modem connections through local area networks or minicomputers. Many software programs, especially the less expensive ones, aren't equipped to handle these complications. In these cases, your company should provide a network expert to help you solve the problem. You might need a network-aware version of the program.

Do note that several office phone systems will not work directly with a modem; you have to find a way to get a direct phone connection. This will probably make you scowl. (Don't do it—your face might freeze that way.)

Calling From a Hotel Room

Using a modem from a hotel room brings a whole host of problems. Fortunately or unfortunately, most of those problems are wetware-based.

If you're lucky enough to find a hotel that has regular modular RJ-11 telephone plugs, by all means become a regular customer. A few of the better hotels have a data jack directly on the side of the telephone. In those cases, the only concession you will need to make to hotel life is to dial a 9 or, more likely, a 9,. The comma gives their phone system two seconds to provide the outside line.

You'll have to move the bed around to find the phone outlet; for some reason, hotels like to hide the access plates. You might also consider bringing along a basic power strip, less for the power protection than for the extension cord. Most hotels have an outlet that is suited for any two of a modem, a laptop computer, or a lamp—but not all three. In fact, take an extra-long phone cable—you rarely will find the phone outlet close to the electric outlet.

In other cases, you will be faced with a telephone that is bolted into the wall. If you really want to use the modem (you do, don't you?), you will need to do some surgery on the system. You may be able to find a "phone kit" for sale in a store that caters to travelers, but be prepared to put one together by yourself. Or you can do as I do—change hotels.

Phone Surgery for Modem Junkies

Most hotels are less than thrilled with the thought of you taking apart their equipment. Before you do so, ask the management for a room with proper modem access. Be aware that most desk clerks have never heard the word "modem" before and aren't interested in learning about it. (If they are, recommend this book.) If you have to use a phone kit, keep in mind that you will need to leave the original equipment in the condition it was when you arrived.

If there are no obvious modular outlets, look at the point where the phone wire disappears into the wall. If you see a cover plate with a hole in it, with the phone wire going into that, you are almost certain to find a modular outlet hanging loose just behind that cover plate. Just unscrew the plate for access.

If there is no modular adapter at all, you will need to use an in-line adapter and a second phone cord. The phone cord will need a modular plug on one end, and small alligator clips soldered, crimped, or screwed onto the red and green wires on the other end. You can buy these or construct your own.

The phone line usually is screwed onto the baseboard. Unscrew the cover and clip onto the terminals where you see the red and green wires.

If you can't get at the wires on that end, unscrew the screws on the bottom of the phone itself. That will allow the guts of the phone to fall out into your hand in one piece; with the cover off, you'll have to depress the phone hook with your fingers, a book, or a rubber band. Clip on where you see red/green wires inside the phone set. You usually can connect the wires so that you can put the phone back together.

If you can't reach the connections in any other manner, you can use the mouthpiece. This is a little more clumsy, however. Pick up the handset and, if you can, unscrew the mouthpiece. A microphone will usually fall free. Inside the mouthpiece, under the mike, there will be two spring clips. Clip right onto these with your alligator clips, and you have the same connection as if you used any of the above techniques, with the only additional requirement being that you'll have to raise the hook to make a call.

Sooner or later, though, you'll get a real phone call while set up this way. Have the microphone inside the mouthpiece, all ready to be put back on. As soon as the phone rings, smoothly pull the 'gator clips off, pop the mike and mouthpiece back into place, screw it down tight, and *then* pick up the phone to answer. With a little practice and mental preparation, you should be able to answer on the third or fourth ring. Without preparation, you'll instinctively pick up the phone and say "Hello?" and the party on the other end won't hear a thing, except for the click of the phone being picked up.

Personally, I'd rather change hotels.

Hardware Woes

There are several hardware components that can fail:

- *C*   Your modem

- *C*   Your serial cable

ⓒ   Your serial port

ⓒ   Your PC setup

Looking for Modem Problems

It's possible that something can go wrong with the modem itself. As with other pieces of equipment, suspect a hardware failure if the modem is old, if it's brand-new (that is, untested), or if it was a no-name, bargain-basement purchase.

If you think the fault lies with the modem, call the modem manufacturer. The manufacturer may have diagnostic tools that will test the modem, and can help you discover the source of the problem. In most cases, they will let you send the modem back to the factory for repair.

Suspecting the Serial Cable

Serial cable connections can extend quite far. You shouldn't run into any difficulty if the modem connection is under 50 feet. If your connection is over that limit, test the equipment with a shorter cable.

When PCs were new, serial cables cost $50. They now cost $5. The cost of manufacturing has gone down, but in many instances so has the quality. I'd suspect the cable before I'd look askance at the modem. Swap serial cables and see if that solves the problem. One client paid me $200 to debug a problem that was the fault of a $5 cable; I would have preferred to earn that money in pursuits more joyous to us both.

Grooving on Serial Ports

Every serial port uses a communications chip called a UART (Universal Asynchronous Receiver-Transmitter) to send and receive data. Part of the UART's job is to convert data to a serial format so that your port can read it.

Older machines still use an 8520 or a 16450 UART chip. Newer ones use the 16550AFN UART chip; there was a 16550 (without the "A") at one time, so check for the A or AFN. The 16550AFN uses a first in/first out (FIFO) buffering scheme, which can dramatically improve performance for modem transfer speeds of 9600 baud or higher. If you usually set your modem to 2400 or 1200 baud, you probably don't need the 16550AFN UART.

If you are using a slower computer and/or a fast modem, and you find that you are losing characters, check for the existence of a 16550A in your computer. You can do this with the mode command at a DOS prompt:

```
MODE COM1: BUFFER=ON
```

If the computer responds Asynchronous Communication mode has been set, then you already have a 16550A. If the message returned says something to the effect of *Say what?* (such as The MODE parameter BUFFER= is not supported by this COM port), then you don't have one.

Checking Your PC Setup

Verify that you don't have an IRQ conflict, a topic we discussed in Chapter 4, "Installing An Internal Modem." Many serial communications problems result from two devices attempting to use the same IRQ. For example, if you install a serial mouse on COM1 and a modem on COM3, both devices could attempt to use IRQ4 (the default setting) at the same time. Unless your PC supports *IRQ sharing* (the ability to have multiple ports using the same IRQ), this could cause your mouse or modem to lose functionality.

Several programs can help you figure out which COM ports are active. Some of them, such as CheckIt, go into explicit detail about what devices you have installed in your computer and report on system performance. Another good one to check out is the free diagnostic utility included with Windows 3.1 and OS/2, called *MSD*. (It will automatically be installed in your Windows subdirectory or your OS2\MDOS\WinOS2 directory.) MSD gives you a very good diagnostic report about your system, including a status report about your COM ports.

In practice, don't install a modem on COM3 if you have a mouse on COM1, or a modem on COM4 if you have a mouse on COM2. The only exception to this is when your machine or serial I/O card explicitly supports IRQ sharing, but even then I would play it safe. Microsoft Windows, in particular, can be very ill-behaved when it runs into this problem.

Software Problems

In most cases, you'll find that the source of the problem is in your interaction with the communications software. Using the instructions in its manual, make sure that you have correctly set the line settings, speed, and so on. Don't be afraid to call the Technical Support line for the company—that's what they're there for. You don't want those Technical Support people to get bored and resort to watching afternoon TV.

Also, check the initialization strings in the communications program. Changing one setting can make a lot of difference.

Troubleshooting in Multitasking Environments

There are two types of multitasking in the Intel-based microcomputer world:

1. Cooperative multitasking

2. Preemptive multitasking.

Cooperative Multitasking

In *cooperative multitasking*, the applications share the attention of the processor (80386 or what-have-you) by time-slicing. A *time slice* is the amount of time allocated to an application, usually measured in milliseconds. The smaller the time slice, the more efficiently the environment can multitask. The most common of the time-slicers are Microsoft Windows 3.1 and Quarterdeck's DESQview.

Communications programs can be problematical in cooperative multitasking environments because, especially during file uploads and downloads, they demand a lot of processor attention. If you are downloading a file in the background in Windows, for instance, you don't want Windows to suddenly give its attention to the word processor, causing you to drop characters in the download. Getting these programs to work as a background task can take quite a bit of tweaking; you may learn more about the settings functions in Windows or DESQview than you ever had planned to.

In these cases, a 16550A UART becomes that much more necessary, in part because of the buffer (or holding area) that is included on that chip. If the buffer can hold onto those extra characters, it won't matter as much if the operating system or desktop environment is distracted for a few milliseconds.

You can also get a so-called "smart" serial card such as the Hayes ESP card. This card handles more buffering and takes the serial communications load off the processor. Most fast processors with a 16550 AFN can handle high-speed modems well, but the newer, faster modems might cause problems. At 28 Kbps plus compression, even a 16550AFN UART in a Windows environment may cause problems.

Preemptive Multitasking

OS/2, Windows NT, and UNIX use preemptive multitasking. The operating system changes the priority of the applications so that each program gets the response that it needs. You won't have as many communications problems in these environments, because they were designed with multitasking in mind. In these situations, you may want the 16550AFN UART simply because you will be able to run so many applications at once!

Troubleshooting Windows Communications

If you are using Windows, consider getting a Windows-based communications program. It will work better than will a DOS application running under Windows.

DOS Communications Programs under Windows

To run a DOS-based application under Windows, create a PIF file that specifies how Windows should schedule that application's processor time. Microsoft doesn't recommend running DOS-based communications applications in standard-mode Windows, as doing so "may cause data loss or other problems." That's a polite way of saying, "Don't do that."

If your computer is a 486 machine running at 25 MHz or faster, you can change the DOS communications program's PIF file to set the background setting high. Some people say that background communications works fine that way. Your mileage may vary.

For better performance, run your DOS-based communications program in full-screen mode rather than in a window. If you run a DOS-based communications application in the background during a data transfer, run it minimized as an icon rather than in a window.

Creating a PIF File for DOS Communications Programs

In the main PIF Editor dialog box, be sure to select the Background check box. Otherwise, your DOS-based communications program will stop running when you switch away from it.

If you have a permanent swap file and 32-bit disk access is enabled: In the PIF Editor Advanced Options dialog box, select the Lock Application Memory check box, or you might receive an error message.

If you encounter errors during data transfers, specify a larger Background Priority or Foreground Priority setting (in the Multitasking Options area of the Advanced Options dialog box).

Hardware Conflicts and Windows

For serial communications to be successful, three settings must match:

- The port addresses in the BIOS data area

- The COM port entries in the SYSTEM.INI file

- The switches on your serial hardware

In Windows, two applications sometimes simultaneously request the use of a device (such as a COM port). This is called *device contention*. To run a DOS-based communications program in Windows Enhanced mode, you need to set device contention options in the Control Panel. Doing so specifies how Windows should handle device requests from your MS-DOS-based applications. If you don't change these, you may be unable to access a COM port.

Sometimes, a communications program will run correctly before you start Windows but will not run or initialize after Windows Enhanced mode has been run and exited. The most likely culprit is that the serial ports have not been fully reset upon exiting Windows. Microsoft supplies only two solutions to this, neither of which is precisely heartwarming nor encouraging:

- Reboot the computer. This fully resets the serial ports.

- Run a program specifically written to reset serial ports.

16550A UART Support for MS-DOS-Based Applications

Windows provides support for the 16550AFN UART. However, some DOS-based applications may not recognize the 16550AFN UART, treating it instead like the earlier 8250 version. This may result in data loss. Whether you experience these problems also depends, to a certain extent, on your hardware manufacturer and the speed of your computer.

IRQs and Windows

If you change the IRQ on your COM port to anything other than the default, make sure that you direct Windows to the alternate IRQ by using the Control Panel to place an entry in your SYSTEM.INI file. Your serial device setting must match the COMxIRQ setting in your SYSTEM.INI file. If the settings don't match, the COM port will not work properly.

To reassign the IRQ from the Control Panel, follow these steps:

1. From the Main group, select the Control Panel icon.

2. In the Control Panel window, click on the Ports icon.

3. In the Ports dialog box, select the COM port for the device whose IRQ you want to change. Then click on the Settings button.

4. In the Settings dialog box, click on the Advanced button.

5. Open the Interrupt Request Line (IRQ) list box and select a number that matches your hardware setting.

6. Choose the OK button twice to exit the settings dialog boxes. Then choose the Close button to exit the Ports dialog box.

If you use an IRQ-sharing I/O card on a machine that does not have MCA or EISA architecture, you need to add the following line to the [386Enh] section of the SYSTEM.INI file:

```
COMIrqSharing=TRUE
```

Another sign of IRQ conflicts can occur when you have an internal modem and a serial I/O card with any of these symptoms:

✆   The modem dials and rings but does not connect.

(✆)   The system reboots when the modem attempts to dial out.

(✆)   The system reboots when the modem should have connected.

(✆)   The cursor does not work in Windows Terminal.

To correct this problem, disable the COM port setting on the serial I/O card. For example, if your internal modem is set to use COM2 and you have a serial I/O card that recognizes COM2, you may need to disable COM2 on the serial I/O card for the modem to work correctly.

Windows may not be able to access a serial device whose address refers to a COM port that is located to the right of an absent COM port in the BIOS data address table (BDA). This can often occur if a modem is installed on COM4, and COM3 is not physically present on the computer.

This behavior is normal for many BIOS versions and can be compensated for by adding a COMxIrq=-1 line to the SYSTEM.INI in the [386Enh] section. Using the COM4 example, the following lines should be added to the SYSTEM.INI file:

```
COM3IRQ=-1     ; disables the false COM3 appearing BIOS data area
COM4Base=02E8  ; sets correct COM4 address
COM4IRQ=3       ; sets correct COM4 IRQ
```

This tells Windows that COM3 does not exist on the computer and that the BDA value in the third slot is actually for COM4. This approach may be easier than writing a DEBUG script to pack zero values into the BDA. However, you may need a DEBUG script to compensate for BIOS and other non-COM4 problems. If things get that serious, find a local Windows guru to help you out. Ways to find expert help are discussed in the last section of this chapter, "Finding Help."

Troubleshooting in the OS/2 Environment

OS/2 is an ideal environment for telecommunications applications because its multitasking supports background execution so well. Figure 16.1 shows you an example of the OS/2 environment. However, there are a few items to keep in mind.

Figure 16.1

OS/2 makes it easy to multitask tele-communications as well as other applications.

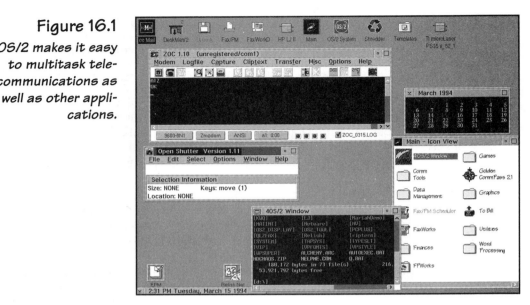

IRQs and OS/2

DOS is much more forgiving of problems with IRQ settings than is OS/2. That's because OS/2 likely will need to use several devices at once. If two adapters are sharing the same physical IRQ, then the processor does not know which adapter (and therefore which OS/2 session) should get the interrupt request (IRQ). If some adapters were previously set up using shared interrupts, then the stage is set for mysterious things to happen— things that probably didn't happen under DOS.

OS/2 can detect that an interrupt line is shared and will not permit simultaneous use. If you try to use both COM1 and COM3, sharing IRQ4, OS/2 will refuse to allow the second one to start. A well-written OS/2 communications program will see and report the error from OS/2 that the port could not be opened. A DOS application, however, is probably not prepared for this situation, and it may simply hang—waiting for a port that will never open.

To avoid these problems, make sure that all of your hardware adapters have their own unique I/O addresses and IRQ assignments. Even though there is some flexibility for printer and COM port assignments, try to stick to the standard assignment as shown in the IRQ table in Chapter 4, "Installing an Internal Modem."

OS/2 Settings for DOS Communications Programs

Each OS/2 program object can have its own settings. You can change these from the Settings notebook attached to each object. You can change the settings for DOS and Windows communications programs so that each runs optimally. (The ability to customize each program to run the way it "wants" to is on the long list of nifty OS/2 features.)

Under DOS and Windows, a lot of applications (especially Windows applications) seem to want your computer to be set up a particular way—a way that is optimized for that application. Unfortunately, the settings and configuration that works well for one application can mess up another, sometimes to the point where the second one no longer works at all. Because OS/2 enables you to create completely different settings for each program object, that gives you the utmost in flexibility; all of your programs can run just the way their designers intended, but they won't bump into one another. For instance, one program can use FILES=85 if it insists, while the others toddle along with FILES=40. Another can load a weird device driver, but only that application will load it and it won't take memory away from the other applications (which don't even realize that the driver is there, much less care).

When COM_DIRECT_ACCESS is set *on*, a DOS application can access the communication ports directly. This DOS property makes LapLink III, FastLynx, AS/400 Asynch Router, and Microsoft Word work in a *virtual DOS machine* (VDM) session. However, because the buffers in COM.SYS cannot be used, characters may be lost and some applications may suffer from the lack of buffering. With most DOS applications, COM_DIRECT_ACCESS should be set to *off* as the default setting.

COM_SELECT allows the DOS session to select only one communication port to be used by the session. The communication ports that are not selected will be hidden from the DOS session. Some DOS applications rudely take over every available communication port (even if they don't use it), and this setting effectively dissuades them from doing so. An example of a DOS application that attempts to control all the communication ports is LapLink Pro. If LapLink Pro and another application that accesses a communication port are executed at the same time, it is necessary to set COM_SELECT. The default setting is *All*.

This setting also keeps other communications programs from accessing that COM port while the specified program is active. It's a good way to protect you from yourself; you don't inadvertently want to send a fax while your modem is busy with a download, for instance.

Table 16.1 shows the recommended settings for most DOS communications programs.

Table 16.1
DOS Communications Programs:
Recommended Settings under OS/2

Attribute	Setting
COM_HOLD	ON
COM_DIRECT_ACCESS	ON or OFF
COM_SELECT	Specific COMx
HW_ROM_TO_RAM	ON
HW_TIMER	ON
IDLE_SECONDS	60
IDLE_SENSITIVITY	100

The Idle_Seconds and Idle_Sensitivity settings are especially important if you'll be doing file transfers. They tell OS/2 to raise the priority for the communications program.

If you have a DOS application that uses QBasic or Basic CTTY, such as Dow Jones Link, make sure the DOS setting has DOS_DEVICE: x:\os2\mdos\commdd.sys.

The following are some other specific examples for DOS and Windows communications under OS/2:

- ☎   CrossTalk for Windows needs BUFFER=OFF

- ☎   For LapLink III, remark out VCOM.SYS or use COM_DIRECT_ACCESS

The Port Isn't Recognized or Won't Work

If your port is not recognized or just won't work, check the IRQs. That's the most likely problem. You might get a message when you turn on the computer that says something like: COMx not installed because interrupt already in use. It means it. You will have to solve the IRQ problem before you go further.

Obtain the latest OS/2 communication drivers from IBM. There's also a shareware communications driver called SIO, from Ray Gwinn. Find that on a local BBS or obtain it from your local computer users group.

If the system boots without error but a COM port is still not working at all, issue a MODE command from an OS/2 command prompt to the problem COM port. For example:

```
MODE COM2:
```

If you get a message that says the COMx port is not installed, check for IRQ conflicts.

The Application Hangs

If the application is an OS/2 application, ensure your COM port works in stand-alone DOS. Use the MODE command to turn off IDSR, ODSR, and OCTS. This also will help to ensure that the hardware connected to the COM port is not preventing the port from transmitting or receiving. The following command line sets COM3 to 9600, no parity, 8 data bits, 1 stop bit, and OCTS, ODSR, and IDSR to OFF.

```
MODE COM3:9600,N,8,1,OCTS=OFF,ODSR=OFF,IDSR=OFF
```

Instead of typing the previous command at a command prompt every time you want to use your modem (which could become tedious), add it to the STARTUP.CMD file in your root directory.

If OCTS and/or ODSR are set to ON, the COM port will not transmit data unless CTS and/or DSR signal lines are enabled. If set to OFF, the COM port will transmit regardless of the state of signal lines CTS and/or DSR. If IDSR is set to ON, the COM port will discard the incoming data unless the DSR signal line is enabled. If set to OFF, the port will receive data regardless of the state of DSR.

Losing Data

If you're losing data, lower the baud rate. Make sure you're using the latest communications drivers. Get a 16550A UART if you don't already have one. Get a native OS/2 communications program.

Poor Performance or Reliability

Experiment with increasing or decreasing the CACHE statement in your CONFIG.SYS to reduce disk activity. Decreasing disk caching may reduce swapping on low RAM systems.

Also, in the CONFIG.SYS file, set as indicated:

```
PRIORITY_DISK_IO    NO
MAXWAIT             1
```

Don't expect too much. Slower microprocessors, such as a 386SX at 16MHz, will not have enough power to support communications above 9600 bps. Even on faster machines, there may be problems with supporting high-speed communications. Some internal modems have been known to induce spurious interrupts that take away from the total number of interrupts that can be processed. Much depends on the quality of the hardware and the ability of the software to work with advanced communication processors such as the 16550AFN.

Finding Help

In this chapter, I have tried to provide solutions for common problems. But it's entirely possible that you tried to implement my recommendations and things still don't work right. Or, perhaps you became overwhelmed by all the techie-talk, and just don't want to mess with this stuff.

That's fine. There are other ways to solve your problems.

You can either find a computer users group near you—an activity I recommend whether or not you need help—or find a computer consultant who is willing to help you debug your problem.

Finding a Computer Users Group

Computer users groups are "users helping users." They are all-volunteer organizations of people who get together to help each other learn more about computers. People who are involved in users groups share an enthusiasm for computers and generally believe that learning about them is *fun*. For a small membership fee (between $15–$45 annually), you get a variety of services, often including meetings, a newsletter, a BBS, product discounts, and training courses. Perhaps most importantly, you can interact with a community of computer users from all walks of life. If you attend a users group meeting, you almost certainly will find someone who can help you solve your telecommunications problems.

The easiest way to find a computer users group near you is to call the User Group Locator Service at (914) 876-6678. There also are listings of user groups in *Computer Shopper* magazine, as well as in your local newspaper's calendar section.

Finding a Computer Consultant

A computer consultant will charge anywhere from $15 to $75 per hour to solve your computer problem. That might sound like a lot, but if you're trying to run your own business, you have to take into account how much money and time you're wasting while trying to solve the modem difficulty by yourself.

In the U.S., the easiest way to find a consultant near you is to call the Independent Computer Consultant's Association that maintains a list of members and their specialties. The toll-free number for the ICCA is 1-800-774-ICCA (or 314-997-4633). You can also find computer consultants by asking other people for recommendations. Some other guidelines are as follows:

🄒 Word-of-mouth is the best way to find someone, but make sure that they know something about modems and telecommunications before you let them fuss with your machine.

🄒 Ask the consultant a few simple questions that are at your own level. Don't try to ask a super-techie question, because you probably don't know enough to know if the answer is right. Ask something you want to understand better. If the consultant can explain things so that you understand them, that's a good sign.

🄒 Don't be afraid to ask for references. Call them, and ask why the reference liked the consultant. Determine if those reasons matter to you. ("She tells good jokes" may or may not be important.)

Part 6:

Appendixes

BBS Listings and Online Services

Contact Information for Companies Mentioned

Important AT Commands

Appendix A

BBS Listings
and Online Services

What good is a modem if you don't know where to call? This appendix can help you get started accessing various BBSs.

Recommended BBSs

A great big hug goes to Dennis Fowler for helping with this section. Dennis writes a monthly column for **Computer Shopper** called "Treading The Boards," and knows more about BBSs than I know about chocolate. This list just barely scratches the surface; there are about 50,000 BBSs available.

Exec PC

Elm Grove, WI; (414) 789-4210

Probably the largest in the world with 280 lines, a half million files or so, and megabytes of new uploads each day. Dan Linton, Sysop.

Canada Remote Systems

Etobicoke, Ontario, Can; (416) 213-6002

Largest in Canada, one of the three largest in the world at 200 lines. Neil Fleming, Sysop.

Channel One

Boston, MA; (617) 354-8873

A very friendly board with great Sysops, lots of files, UseNET newsgroups, conferences, games, etc. Brian Miller and Tess Heder, Sysops.

Software Creations

Clinton, MA; (508) 368-7139

Probably the single best source of shareware games, Software Creations is the home board for Apogee (Commander Keen, Castle Wolfenstein) and others. Eighty-three lines—but it still can sometimes be hard to access because of its popularity. Dan Linton, Sysop.

Invention Factory

New York, NY; (212) 274-8810

One of the largest in New York City, 250,000 files, newsgroups, large adult section. Mike and Kathy Sussell, Sysops.

Westside

Los Angeles, CA; (213) 933-4050

A very large adult chat board with access numbers all over Southern California. Also has a fair number of files, but mainly a chat board. Dave Harrison, Sysop.

Fun University Network

San Francisco, CA; (415) 327-4591

A BBS for families and children, which is a bit of a rarity. Online games and chat are great, and the use of RIP graphics is superb. Wendy Lash, Sysop.

Computers and Dreams

New York, NY; (212) 888-6565

Another New York City board, very well run, not as large as Invention Factory but still has plenty of files (and NO adult files). William P. Stewart, Sysop.

ProStar

Auburn, WA; (206) 941-0317

A large, well run board for the Pacific Northwest area. Robert Michnick, Sysop.

Wizard's Gate BBS

Columbus, OH; (614) 224-1635

This board is free, gives immediate access, 90 minutes on the first call, no registration, no hassles. It has lots of good stuff on it. Joe Balshone, Sysop.

PC OHIO

Cleveland, OH; (216) 381-3320

Another large, general board. Lots of message areas, files and doors (usually games). Norm Henke, Sysop.

Albuquerque ROS

Albuquerque, NM; (505) 299-5974

60,000+ files, very active on social and community issues. Steven Fox, Sysop.

Garbage Dump BBS

Albuquerque, NM; (505) 294-5675

Adult chat board with access numbers in New Mexico and Colorado, and packet network access all over the country. Dating registry, ASP shareware.

Windows Online

Danville, CA; (510) 736-8343

An excellent source of Windows shareware, information, Truetype Fonts, etc. Frank Mahaney, Sysop.

America's Suggestion Box

New York, NY; (516) 471-8625

NYC area board specializing in consumer feedback. Joe Jerszynski, Sysop.

User Group BBSs

Call one of these BBSs to find out about the user group activity near you. An advantage to a user group BBS is that the cost is usually free when you belong to the group.

If you don't find a BBS near you in this list, call the User Group Locator (voice) at (914) 876-6678. The Locator will help you to find a group near you. If the user group doesn't have a BBS of its own, someone there is sure to be able to recommend a few.

APCOMBBS

San Antonio, TX; (210) 496-2270

Largest organization in South Texas; over 1,200 members. Robert Schoenert, Sysop.

Phoenix PC User Group BBS

Phoenix, AZ; (602) 222-5491

Largest PC user group in Arizona with 1,000 members. Ray Moore, Sysop.

Alumax Online

(501) 234-3361

South Arkansas PC User Group Support Board.

Healthcare BBS

Vancouver, BC; (604) 432-7626

The BBS of the HealthCare Computer Users Group and other health professionals in British Columbia, Canada.

Vancouver PC Users Society (VPCUS)

Vancouver BC; (604) 736-6001

The VPCUS BBS has its own access number, but is set up as a SIG of the multi-line Dial-A-File (DAF) system in Vancouver. Steve & Greta Fairbairn, Sysops.

GLOBALNET

Scotts Valley, CA; (408) 439-9367

Operated by the Association of PC User Groups and sponsored by Borland International, Dell Computer Corp, BT North America and Intel PCED, with contributions from IBM, eSoft, MICOM, Lotus, Digiboard and many others.

The Spirit

Ben Lomond, CA; (408) 336-5532

Devoted to Supporting San Lorenzo User Group (SLUG) FidoNet and Slugnet Hub, Supporting Remote Access BBS software and FrontDoor Mailer Software.

Desert Data

Edwards AFB, CA; (805) 277-6227

Sponsored by the Edwards Air Force Base Microcomputer Users Group.

Sacramento PC Users Group BBS

Citrus Heights, CA; (916) 722-0660

Open to all; must be a member for full access.

MICROwire

Denver, CO; (303) 752-2943

BBS of the Mile High Computer Resource Organization (MICRO). James Kochman, Sysop.

The PC Users Group of CT BBS

Trumbull, CT; (203) 332-1594

BBS for The PC Users Group of Connecticut. Free for Group members; $5.00 for non-members.

Frogpond By The Sea

(904) 241-9537

BBS of the PC Users' Group of Jacksonville, FL.

Atlanta PC Users Group BBS

(404) 879-5985

Open to public. Downloads okay on first call.

FOG-Line

Ankeny, IA; (515) 964-7937

BBS of Central Iowa Computer User Group—SysOp: Dan Buda. Central Iowa's Original FidoNet BBS—FidoNet Node 290/627. Also Region 14 Echo Hub—125+ Message Areas—Silver Express Offline Reader—5000+ files online.

Chicago Computer Society

(312) 879-9021

Chicago, IL user group BBS.

Indianapolis Computer Society

Indianapolis, IN; (317) 251-2067

Members get 75 minutes a day. 1.5 GB Storage Online. Connected to Indynet, the statewide echo.

The BGAMUG BBS

Bowling Green, KY; (502) 781-4875

The BGAMUG BBS is run by The Bowling Green Area MS-DOS Users Group. The BBS is open to all. Non-members of BGAMUG have a 3:1 file ratio but no other restrictions. Over 2100 files and growing. All file types except adult.

Cajun Clickers BBS

Baton Rouge, LA; (504) 756-9658

Sponsored by the Cajun Clickers Computer Club of Baton Rouge.

The Simple Board

Denham Springs, LA; (504) 664-2524

OS/2 User Group Support, Binkley, Maximus, Fernwood, IBM/Net files online.

Winnipeg PC User Group BBS

Winnipeg, MB; (204) 338-0272

CD-ROM online, 1 gigabyte and growing. NANET, INET, and WINECHO. Robert Snyder, Sysop.

Columbia-Baltimore Users Group (CBUG)

Columbia, MD; (410) 750-1253

Non-members are afforded 20 minutes per day and download privileges in the ASP-approved shareware area.

Mid-Coast Computer Society of Maine BBS

Camden, ME; (207) 236-8537

The Bulletin Board System of The Mid-Coast Computer Society of Maine. MS-DOS SIG, MAC SIG, Game SIG.

Wolverine BBS

(517) 631-3471

The "Official" BBS of the Midland Computer Club. Carries the most up-to-date versions of the BEST shareware. Rick Rosinski, Sysop.

UPCO BBS

Lansing, MI; (517) 487-6452

Sponsored by The Users' PC Organization, serving PC users since 1982. New users have full access on first call. Mark Blum, Sysop; Dick Luer, CoSysop.

St Louis Users Group

St Louis, MO; (314) 878-7614

Recently upgraded hardware to 500M/9600 with Wildcat software. Fido node.

Seacoast IBM Users Group

Dover, NH; (603) 743-3385

User group meets the third Friday of every month at Dover High School.

Las Vegas Center

Las Vegas, NV; (702) 597-1932

Official Board of the Las Vegas PC Users Group. 2400 baud line available at (702) 597-1931.

CPU:bbs

Monticello, NY; (914) 434-3550

Catskill Power Users (CPU) maintains this BBS at the Sullivan County Community College.

Buffalo IBM-PC User Group BBS Service

Buffalo, NY; (716) 695-0583

The Buffalo IBM-PC User Group BBS Service is open to all callers on the public node listed above, with full download privileges (albeit with reduced time online vis-a-vis member callers) granted upon answering a short online questionnaire.

NYPC BBS

New York, NY; (212) 679-6972

FidoNet node 1:278/722. Relay net NYPC (5082)

LICA LIMBS

Valley Stream, NY; (516) 561-6590

BBS of the Long Island Computer Association, Inc. Dave Minott, Sysop.

MegaBaud

Wellington, New Zealand; (644) 389-5371

The BBS of the New Zealand Personal Computer Association, Inc.

Oklahoma City PC User's Group BBS

Oklahoma City, OK; (405) 348-9810

Online CD-ROM with over 9,000 files. Tony Valuikas, Sysop.

ET Scribe/PPCUG

Portland, OR; (503) 624-7752

BBS for the Portland PC Users Group. 100M of public domain/shareware files. 100+ Message areas.

Adelaide PC Users Group BBS

Adelaide, South Africa; (618) 396-3539

David Read, Sysop.

deBUG

Columbia, SC; (803) 776-2076

Palmetto PC Club BBS. Conferences for members, newsletter, administration and evaluations of shareware. Also 2 local FIDO echoes: COLANET and COLAPNT.

Memphis PC Users Group BBS

Memphis, TN; (901) 368-1764

Rick VanHooser, Sysop. RIME Address: MPCUG.

The SWIPCC Clubhouse

El Paso, TX; (915) 594-0144

Southwest International PC Club—non-member access limited. FidoNet Node 1:381/66.

Pacific NorthWest PC Users Group

Seattle, WA; (206) 728-7085

766M of bulletin board, lots of Windows applications and support. Two non-member lines and two member lines currently running at 14,400 baud.

Online Services

If you are interested in signing up with and using some online services, the following list might help you.

America Online

(703) 448-8700 or (800) 827-5938

AT&T Mail

(201) 331-4132 or (800) MAIL672

BIX

(800) 227-2983

BRS/After Dark

(703) 442-0900 or (800) 289-4277

CompuServe

(614) 457-0802 or (800) 848-8199

DASnet

(408) 559-7434

DataTimes

(405) 751-6400 or (800) 642-2525

DELPHI

(617) 491-3393 or (800) 695-4005

DIALCOM

(800) 872-7654

Dialog Information Services

(415) 858-3785 or (800) 334-2564

Dow Jones News/Retrieval
(609) 452-1511 or (800) 552-3567

EasyNet
(215) 293-4700 or (800) 220-9553

GEnie
(800) 638-9636

IQuest
(215) 293-4700 or (800) 220-9553

Knowledge Index
(415) 858-3785 or (800) 334-2564

LEXIS and NEXIS
(800) 227-4908

MCI Mail
(202) 416-5600

NewsNet
(215) 527-8020 or (800) 345-1301

PC-Link
(703) 448-8700 or (800) 827-8532

Prodigy
(914) 962-0310 or (800) PRODIGY

Promenade
(703) 448-8700 or (800) 525-5938

SprintMail
(800) 736-1130

USA Today Sports Center
(800) 826-9688

The WELL
(415) 332-4335

Appendix B

Contact Information for Companies Mentioned

Golden CommPass

Golden CommPass
Creative Systems Programming
P.O. Box 961
Mt. Laurel, NJ 08054-0961
(609) 234-1500
(609) 234-1920 (fax)
CompuServe: 71511,151
GO GCPSUPPORT on CompuServe

HyperACCESS

HyperACCESS
Hilgraeve
Genesis Centre
111 Conant Avenue, Suite A
Monroe, MI 48161
(313) 243-0576
(313) 243-0645 fax
GO PCVENF on CompuServe

KWQ Mail/2

KWQ Mail/2
Kurt Westerfeld
7935 Tyson Oaks Circle
Vienna, VA 22182
GO OS2SHARE on CompuServe

RECON

RECON
Orest W. Skrypuch
Amdox Co. Ltd.
217 Terrace Hill Street
Brantford, Ontario, Canada
N3R 1G8
(519) 752-5453
GO TAPCIS on Compuserve

TAPCIS

TAPCIS
Support Group, Inc.
Lake Technology Park
McHenry, MD 21541
800-USA-GROUP
301-387-4500
GO TAPCIS on CompuServe

WinFax Pro

WinFax Pro
Delrina Technology
6830 Via Del Oro, Suite 240
San Jose, CA 95119-1353
800-268-6082
408-363-2340 (fax)

Zap-O-Com (ZOC)

Zap-O-Com (ZOC)
Markus Schmidt
Waagstr. 4
90762 Fuerth
GERMANY
GO OS2SHARE on CompuServe

Appendix C

Important AT Commands

Data communications, like many things in the computing world, has its own set of rules and standards.

When you join the growing group of modem users and learn to follow rules and standards in data communications, you quickly learn that your modem must be Hayes compatible. When a modem abides by Hayes standards, that means it acknowledges and acts on certain commands and command strings known as *AT commands*. You need to make sure that the modem you buy follows the basic Hayes command set. The modem can have additional commands added to the set, but it should contain the basic set of commands. This ensures that the modem will function and take commands from most any communications software package that you buy to use with your modem.

The AT Command Format

When you think of the role of an AT command, think of it as if someone were getting your attention to give you an instruction. These commands are set up so that when you enter a command, you precede it with AT. These two letters tell the modem to pay attention to the following command.

You can type the command names in uppercase or lowercase letters, with the exception of a few commands including +++, ^C, ^K, ^Q, ^S, and A/. You also can include these commands in script files to automate particular modem functions. You'll find that you need to know and use these commands very rarely because many communications software packages provide you with a reasonable configuration setup for your modem.

The following is a list of standard AT commands that you may find helpful:

Command:	Description:
AT	Attention; precedes all other commands.
<CR>	Carriage return character; terminates the command line.
A	Go off-hook; remain in command mode, waiting to answer incoming calls.
A/	Re-execute previous command. You do not have to precede this command with an AT or follow it by a <CR>.
Anykey	Will terminate current dialing operation resulting from an issued Dial command.
B*n*	U.S./CCITT answer sequence.
B0	CCITT answer sequence.
B1	U.S./Canada answer tone, default.
&c0	Assume presence of carrier detect signal.
&c1	Track status of carrier detect signal.
&c2	Assume presence of carrier detect signal until online, then track status of signal.
D*n*	Dial the number (*n*) that follows and go to originate mode. Any of the following options will follow the letter D: 0-9, A, B, C, D, #, *, telephone numbers, access codes.

Command:	Description:
P	Pulse dial; default.
T	Touch tone dial.
,	Delay; pause for 2 seconds.
;	Return to command state after dialing.
!	Flash switch-hook to transfer call.
W	Wait for second dial tone (if X3 or higher is set).
@	Wait for an answer (if X3 or higher is set).
R	Reverse frequencies or reverse mode if dialing originate-only modem.
DS=*n*	Dials one of the four telephone numbers stored in non-volatile memory (NRAM), for example: n=0,1,2,3.
E*n*	Command mode local echo: display copy of modem commands entered at the keyboard.
E0	Echo off.
E1	Echo on.
&f	Recall factory configuration as active configuration.
hO	Hang up and place modem in command state.
h1	Go off-hook and operate auxiliary relay.
H1	Off-hook.
I*n*	Inquiry. For example: **I0** Show product code **I1** How checksum on firmware ROM **I2** Compare checksum on firmware ROM; provides OK or Error message

continues

Command:	Description:
L	(preceded) Controls speaker volume, by 0, 1, 2, 3. Higher numbers indicate higher volumes.
M0	Speaker off.
M1	Speaker on until carrier detected.
M2	Speaker always on.
M3	Speaker on until carrier detected, except during dialing.
O0	Go to online state.
O1	Go to online state and initiate equalizer.
Qn	Quiet Mode; result codes are displayed/suppressed.
Q0	Result Code displayed.
Q1	Result Code suppressed.
Sr=n	Set register commands; r is any S-register; n must be a decimal number between 0 and 255.
Sr?	Query S-register r.
Vn	Displays response codes in numeric or verbose form.
Xn	Result Code options.
Z	Reset modem to defaults.
z0	Reset and recall stored user profile 0.
z1	Reset and recall stored user profile 1.
+++	Escape code sequence.

Glossary

Glossary of Telecommunications Terms

A

Analog loopback. A way to test a modem without the use of a phone line. Type the command AT&T1 so that all the data sent to your modem is then "looped back" to the screen rather than going out through the phone line.

Analog signal. An electronic signal that is measured by a physical variable-pressure, voltage, or length, for example. Analog signals usually are measured by their wavelength.

ANSI. The American National Standards Institute is an organization that sets standards. ANSI graphics is a set of cursor control codes to help improve sending characters to communications programs. ANSI graphics allow movement of the cursor on the screen, a change of color, and more.

ASCII. American Standard Code for Information Interchange. ASCII data consists of a standard seven-bit code with one parity bit. ASCII data can be transferred to and from most types of computers.

Asynchronous. A form of data transmission also known as serial. An asynchronous transmission allows the data to be sent at irregular intervals. A data unit is preceded with a start bit and followed by a stop bit.

Auto answer (AA). A mode that enables a modem to answer an incoming call automatically, without interaction by the user.

Auto dial. Some communications software programs provide this feature for storing phone numbers. You later can retrieve the numbers and dial them by executing one command.

B

Baud. A unit of measurement that denotes the number of transitions in the modem signal per second. Each transition can carry multiple bits of information.

BBS. Bulletin board system. A computer software application designed to answer calls and provide a message base for modem users.

Bit. A unit of measurement that represents one figure or character of data. The word is derived from **b**inary dig**it**. A bit is the smallest unit of storage in a computer. Because computers actually read 0s and 1s, each of these is measured as one bit. The letter A consists of eight bits, which equals one byte. (See *Byte*)

Block. A group of data bytes. For example, when you download a program, data is often sent in blocks of 128 or 1024 characters.

Block size. Block size refers to the number of characters to be sent at one time. Typical block sizes are 64, 128, 192, or 256 characters. When line quality is bad, choose smaller block sizes.

Bps. Bits per second. Another way of measuring the speed of data transmission. (See *Baud*)

Buffer. A storage location in a modem's internal RAM where the modem can temporarily store data it receives until it can process the data.

Byte. A group of consecutive bits of data. A byte consists of eight bits.

C

Capture. "Catch" text that is being sent to your computer from a BBS and put it in a buffer or a file.

Carrier. Used to identify a signal of continuous frequency. Carrier is achieved when one modem recognizes the signal of another modem. If modem A attempts to connect with modem B and receives no response, then modem A finds no carrier.

Carrier detect (CD). When your modem has detected the carrier of another modem. The wire in an RS-232C cable that holds the information about whether or not the modem senses a carrier (and therefore is connected to another computer). On an external modem, the CD LED will light up.

CCITT. An international standard committee that issues standards for telecommunications issues. CCITT stands for ***Comite Consulate Internationale Telegraphique et Telephonic***. The committee is responsible for standards such as V.32, V.32bis, V.42, and V.42bis. ***bis*** means the second version of a particular standard.

CCITT V.1. Defines binary 0/1 bits as space/mark line conditions.

CCITT V.2. Limits power levels of modems used on phone lines.

CCITT V.4. Sequence of bits within a character as transmitted.

CCITT V.5. Standard synchronous signaling rates—dialup lines.

CCITT V.6. Standard synchronous signaling rates—leased lines.

CCITT V.7. List of modem terms in English, Spanish, French.

CCITT V.10. Unbalanced high-speed electrical interface characteristics (RS-423).

CCITT V.11. Balanced high-speed electrical characteristics (RS-422).

CCITT V.13. Simulated carrier control (full-duplex modem used as half duplex).

CCITT V.14. Asynchronous to synchronous conversion.

CCITT V.15. Acoustic couplers.

CCITT V.16. Electrocardiogram transmission on phone lines.

CCITT V.17. Application-specific modulation scheme for Group 3 fax (provides 2-wire half-duplex trellis-coded transmission at 7200, 9600, 12000, and 14400 bps).

CCITT V.19. DTMF modems (low-speed parallel transmission).

CCITT V.20. Parallel data transmission modems.

CCITT V.21. 300 bps modems.

CCITT V.22. 1200/600 bps FDX modems.

CCITT V.22bis. 2400 bps modems.

CCITT V.23. 1200/75 bps (host tx 1200, rx 75, terminal tx 75, rx 1200); also supports 600bps in the high channel speed.

CCITT V.24. Known as EIA RS-232 in the USA. V.24 defines only the functions of the circuits. EIA-232-E, which is how the current version of the standard is designated, also defines electrical characteristics and connectors. The 232-equivalent electrical characteristics and connectors are defined in ISO 2110.

CCITT V.25. Automatic answering equipment and parallel automatic dialing (defines the 2100Hz "answer tone" that modems send).

CCITT V.25bis. Serial automatic calling and answering—CCITT equivalent of AT commands. (This is the current CCITT standard for modem control by computers via serial interface. The Hayes AT command set is used primarily in the USA.)

CCITT V.26. 2400 bps 4W modems.

CCITT V.26bis. 2400/1200 bps HDX modems.

CCITT V.26ter. 2400/1200 bps FDX modems.

CCITT V.27. 4800 bps 4W modems.

CCITT V.27bis. 4800/2400 bps 4W modems.

CCITT V.27ter. 4800/2400 bps FDX modems (also used in half-duplex 2-wire mode to implement the 2400 and 4800 bps transmission schemes in Group 3 fax).

CCITT V.28. Electrical characteristics for V.24.

CCITT V.29. 9600 bps 4W modems (also used in half-duplex 2-wire mode to implement the 7200 and 9600 bps transmission schemes in Group 3 fax).

CCITT V.31. Older electrical characteristics (rarely used).

CCITT V.31bis. V.31 using optocouplers.

CCITT V.32. 9600/4800 bps FDX modems.

CCITT V.32bis. 4800, 7200, 9600, 12000, and 14400 bps modems and rapid rate renegotiation.

CCITT V.33. 14400 bps (and 12000 bps for 4-wire leased lines).

CCITT V.35. 48 kbps 4W modems. (The CCITT no longer recommends the use of this standard. It was made obsolete by V.36).

CCITT V.36. 48 kbps 4W modems.

CCITT V.37. 72 kbps 4W (V.36 and V.37 are not really "4-w modems." They are group band modems, which means they combine several telephone channels).

CCITT V.40. How teletypes indicate parity errors.

CCITT V.41. An older, obsolete error control scheme.

CCITT V.42. Error-correcting procedures for modems using asynch-to-synch conversion (V.22, V.22bis, V.26ter, V.32, V.32bis); defines LAPM protocol and provides fallback to MNP4.

CCITT V.42bis. Lempel-Ziv-based data compression scheme for use with V.42 LAPM.

CCITT V.50. Standard limits for transmission quality for modems.

CCITT V.51. Maintenance of international data circuits.

CCITT V.52. Apparatus for measuring distortion and error rates for data transmission.

CCITT V.53. Impairment limits for data circuits.

CCITT V.54. Loop test devices for modems.

CCITT V.55. Impulse noise measuring equipment.

CCITT V.56. Comparative testing of modems.

CCITT V.57. Comprehensive test set for high-speed data transmission.

CCITT V.100. Interconnection between PDNs and PSTNs (Public Data Networks, Public Switched Telephone Networks).

CCITT V.110. ISDN terminal adaption.

CCITT V.120. ISDN terminal adaption with statistical multiplexing.

CCITT V.230. General data communications interface, layer 1.

Chat. Two or more people (almost always a Sysop and a user on a BBS) can chat, or communicate directly with each other using the modem. Each participant can see what the others are typing at all times, and can interrupt them. (You can make a beeping sound with a CTRL+G).

COM. In DOS, a code that refers to a serial port. Most serial ports and internal modems can be configured to either COM1 or COM2. The DOS MODE command is used to change the output direction to serial devices, such as modems.

CPS. Characters per second. A measurement of data output speed, much like baud or bits per second. This form of measurement is commonly used to judge the speed of printers.

CTS. Clear to Send (CTS) is an RS-232C signal that tells the computer it can start sending information.

D

Data compression. A method that decreases file size. The sending modem looks for repetition in the data and removes it according to a predefined algorithm. The receiving modem reverses the algorithm to decompress the data. The most common types of data compression are MNP5 and V.42bis.

Data Set Ready. Data Set Ready (DSR) is an RS-232C signal that tells the computer (or terminal) that the modem is connected to the telephone line.

Data Terminal Ready. Data Terminal Ready (DTR) is an RS-232C signal that tells the modem the local computer (or terminal) is ready for data transmission. Some communications programs hang up by "dropping DTR," or changing the signal on the serial line, rather than issuing a "hang up" (ATH) command to the modem.

DIP switch. Dual In-line Package switches enable you to change the configuration of a circuit board to suit your particular computer. These are a group of small switches placed together on electronic equipment which can be changed to alter various settings. For example, one DIP switch on a modem may change the status of the DTR.

Direct connection. Using a null modem cable, you can directly connect one computer to another via their serial ports. By using communication software, these two computers can communicate as if they were using modems. (See ***Null Modem***)

Duplex. An asynchronous communications protocol. Full duplex is when the communications channel can send and receive signals at the same time. Half duplex is when the communications channel can handle only one signal at a time. The two stations alternate their transmissions.

E

Echo (local, remote). Local echo causes all transmitted data to be sent to the screen of the sending computer. Remote echo means that everything the remote computer transmits is duplicated on your computer's screen.

Error correction. If both modems have error correction and line noise causes errors in the transmission, the modems catch and correct the problem. Error correction is almost standard with fast modems and optional for many 2400 bps modems. The most common types of error correction are MNP1-5 and V.42.

Escape Sequence. A sequence of three characters (normally +++) that switches the modem from the online mode to the command mode without breaking the telephone connection.

F

File Transfer Protocol. An error-checking protocol for file transfers (such as KERMIT, XMODEM, or YMODEM). File transfer protocols monitor information sent with each block of data. If the received data doesn't match the information used to check the quality of data, the system notifies the sender that an error has occurred and asks for a retransmission.

Flow Control. The mechanism that regulates the flow of data between two devices. Modems typically have two methods of flow control: software flow control (XON/XOFF) and hardware flow control (CTS/RTS).

Freeware. Computer programs that are copyrighted, but may be legally copied if no payment is involved. Freeware programs are almost the same as public domain programs, except that public domain programs are not copyrighted and may be sold for payment. Freeware programs often can not be changed when they are distributed.

Full duplex. An asynchronous communications protocol. Data flows in both directions at the same time. When remote echo is on, communication is occurring in full duplex.

H

Half duplex. An asynchronous communications protocol. Data flows only one way at a time. When local echo is on, for example, communication is occurring in half duplex.

Handshaking. The process of establishing an electronic link between two modems. Handshaking lets both modems exchange information, such as the speed they will be using and whether or not the modems share the same kind of error correction capability.

Hayes compatible. A modem is considered Hayes compatible if it supports the Hayes command set, a language used to communicate with and control a modem.

High-speed (HS) light. External modems with the capability of supporting more than one baud rate illuminate the HS light when set on the fastest mode.

I

Initialize. To set up hardware or software to work correctly with your system. Many modems have to be initialized each time they are used so they "know" how to act with the communications program. When the software initializes your modem, it may instruct the modem to expect 2400 baud and no parity and that you do not want any information to echo on your screen.

Initialization string. When the program is started the initialization string is the command sent to your modem by the communications software. Most of the time, it's similar to any AT command that you would type in.

J

Jumper. A small block used to connect two terminal posts. Jumpers complete a circuit when attached to two poles. They leave an open circuit when unattached.

L

Line Noise. Random signal disturbances that sometimes occur over telephone lines. Noise can disrupt communications and corrupt the transmitted data. Line noise is the background sounds you hear when, on a voice call, it seems that your friend is talking inside of a bucket. Modems can be more sensitive to line noise than you are, since every bit transmitted matters.

Logoff. To leave a BBS. When you choose to logoff, the BBS will usually ask if that's what you really want to do; then it will hang up the phone. The BBS may also ask you if you want to leave a note to the Sysop first. Other terms that mean the same thing are exit, quit, goodbye.

Logon. The process of connecting to a BBS, after you have called the computer and the phone starts to ring, but before you actually start using the BBS. "Logon" can also include the process of entering your name and password (also called sign-on).

M

MNP. Microcom Networking Protocol. Provides error control and data compression when your modem is communicating with another modem that supports MNP. (MNP classes 1 through 4 are specified by CCITT V.42 as a backup error control scheme for LAPM.) Your modem supports five MNP classes. Each MNP class has all the features of the previous class, plus its own.

MNP class 1 (also called block mode). Sends data in one direction at a time. About 70 percent as fast as data transmissions using no error correction.

MNP class 2 (also called stream mode). Sends data in both directions at the same time. About 84 percent as fast as data transmissions using no error correction.

MNP class 3. Sending modem strips start and stop bits from data block before sending it. Receiving modem adds start and stop bits before passing the data to the receiving computer. About 8 percent faster than data transmissions using no error correction.

MNP class 4. Monitors the quality of the connection and streamlines the information in the headers of data blocks. If the telephone line is relatively noise-free, the modem sends larger blocks of data to increase throughput. If the telephone line is noisy, the modem sends smaller blocks of data so that less data will have to be resent. This means more successful transmissions on the first try. About 20 percent faster than data transmissions using no error correction.

MNP class 5. Provides data compression. Sending modem detects redundant data and recodes it to fewer bits to increase the effective throughput. Receiving modem decompresses the data before passing it to the receiving computer. Up to 100 percent faster than data transmissions using no data compression or error correction, depending on the kind of data transmitted. (Files that are already compressed will seem to contain less redundant data and may therefore take longer to transmit using MNP class 5 than they would if you were using no data compression.)

Modem ready (MR) light. External modems have this light, which lights up when the power is turned on. The MR light indicates that the modem is ready to receive commands or calls.

N

Null modem. A null modem is a cable used to directly connect two computers via their serial ports. A null modem cable differs from a regular modem cable in that the transmitting and receiving pins are swapped.

O

Online. Describes the status of a connection between two computers with modems. Online means there is a connection. An online system is another name for a BBS.

On/off hook (OH) light. A modem is on hook when it is sitting idle, neither sending nor receiving. When you pick up a phone to dial a number, the phone is off hook. All external modems have a light to indicate this status.

P

Packet. A group of bytes sent by a file transfer protocol.

Packet radio. Packet radio is like a a BBS, but uses radio connections instead of telephone connections. It requires an amateur (ham) radio setup instead of a modem. With the right setup, you can read/send messages, and even files using radio waves.

Packet switching network. A telecommunications service that transmits data from one computer to another using packets of data. Packet switching networks have telephone numbers in most areas of the country, so that you can connect to online services without toll charges.

Parity bit. A check bit added to a data word. A unit of data that is eight bits long would have no parity, and a unit of data seven bits long would have an even parity bit to make an eight-bit word. Parity is used to check a unit of data for errors during transmission through phone lines or null modem cables.

Protocol. Settings and standards that govern the communication of information between computers. Different protocols have been developed to come up with better and faster ways to transfer data between two or more computers.

Public domain. A program in the public domain usually has no copyright and can be copied legally by anybody. BBSs often have public domain software available for people to download.

R

Receive data (RS) light. External modems have an RS light that lights when data is being received from another computer.

Request to Send. The Request to Send (RTS) signal is an RS-232C signal that requests the modem to send data. It initiates any data transmission between the computer (or terminal) and the modem. It is answered by a Clear to send (CTS) signal.

Result codes. When you enter most modem commands, the modem displays a message on your screen, called a result code, that tells you the results of the command. Most modems' factory settings are for result codes to be returned as English words that describe the conditions. You can set the modem to display numbers instead of words.

RS-232C. A standardized connection system for connecting a device to the serial port of a computer or terminal. You will usually hear RS-232C used interchangeably with "serial port."

S

Send data (SD) light. External modems have an SD light that lights when data is being sent through the modem over the phone line.

Serial cable. A cable used to connect peripheral devices through a computer's serial port. It usually has a 25-pin connector on each end. Some serial cables have a 25-pin connector and a 9-pin connector.

Serial port. A port that transmits and receives asynchronous data. Serial ports are used for devices such as printers, mice, light pens, and modems. A serial port can either be plugged into an expansion slot on the motherboard of your computer or built into the motherboard itself.

S-Registers. RAM in your modem that is used to store the current configuration profile (operating characteristics) of your modem.

Shareware. Shareware programs can be distributed freely, but you must pay for these programs if you use them. Most shareware programs allow you to try them for a specified period of time; then you must either pay for the program or get rid of it. Many BBSs have shareware programs that you can download without paying the BBS, but you must remember that if you use a shareware program you are supposed to pay for it.

Start/stop bits. A start bit signals the start of a unit of data in asynchronous communications. A stop bit signals the end of a unit of data. The unit of data can vary in length depending on the protocol.

T

Terminal mode. Using a communication program to enable your personal computer to mimic a computer terminal, which is a keyboard and CRT display or printer. A common terminal mode emulation is VT. 100.

Terminal ready (TR) light. This light comes on when your computer has turned on the RS-232 (serial) interface. At times, this light does not shine until you have loaded your communications software into memory.

X

Xmodem. Xmodem was the first file transfer protocol for PCs. With Xmodem, data is packaged into blocks of 128 bytes along with the calculation of their value, called a checksum. If the figures match on the other end, the receiving modem sends an acknowledgement.

Y

Ymodem. Ymodem was the first batch protocol, meaning that you can send more than once with it. Ymodem first transmits each file's name and length and the date it was last updated. Then it sends the actual file by using Xmodem.

Z

Zmodem. Zmodem is a popular file transfer protocol program because it's faster than Xmodem, uses larger blocks, and it can resume an interrupted transfer.

Index

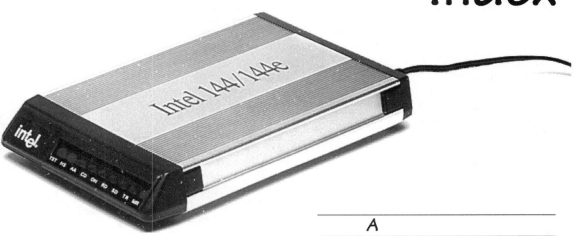

If you're interested in Windows communications software, you'll really like HyperACCESS for Windows.

The software that you've received with this book demonstrates most of the fundamental features that you'd expect from a general-purpose DOS communications program. The retail version of HyperACCESS for Windows does much more.

Here is what some of the press have said about HyperACCESS for Windows.

"Best Buy." **PC World**

"If you're in the market for a great communications program, check out this one right away ... Recommended." **Windows Magazine**

"HyperACCESS may be the best Windows communications package available ... Recommended Product 9.4 (out of 10)." **Infoworld**

"The most exciting product in our roundup is Hilgraeve's HyperACCESS for Windows ... a winner." **Windows Sources**

The best way to find out what HyperACCESS for Windows can do for you is to try it yourself. So we're making this special offer exclusively for owners of this book. For a limited time, you can buy the current retail release of HyperACCESS for Windows for only

$49.⁹⁵

and it's ... **RISK-FREE!** If you don't like HyperACCESS for Windows, simply return it within 60 days for a free refund.

Here are some of the features you'll enjoy with HyperACCESS for Windows.

Full manual and support privileges—user's manual, API guide, and phone support.

Faster terminal emulations—including TVI, ADDS, DEC, LSI, IBM, and Wang.

Fully exploits Windows—a goldmine of exciting new graphical features.

Blazing speed and real multitasking—performance other programs only dream of.

Network support—using INT14.

Virus filtering—scans files while they are downloading for known viruses.

Automation—learns logins rather than just repeating keystrokes.

Host-mode—built-in mini-BBS to let others call your machine.

Call Hilgraeve Inc. (313) 243-0676 (voice); (313) 243-0645 (fax).

New Riders' Guide to Modems
REGISTRATION CARD

Fill out this card to receive information about future modem books and other New Riders titles!

Name _____ **Title** _____.

Company _____

Address _____

City/State/ZIP _____

I bought this book because: _____
_____

I purchased this book from:

☐ A bookstore (Name _____)

☐ A software or electronics store (Name _____)

☐ A mail order (Name of Catalog _____)

I purchase this many computer books each year:

☐ 1–5   ☐ 6 or more

I currently use these applications: _____
_____
_____
_____

I found these chapters to be the most informative: _____
_____

I found these chapters to be the least informative: _____
_____

Additional comments: _____
_____

☐ I would like to see my name in print! You may use my name and quote me in future New Riders products and promotions. My daytime phone number is:_____

New Riders Publishing 201 West 103rd Street • Indianapolis, Indiana 46290 USA

Fold Here

‑ ‑

PLACE
STAMP
HERE

New Riders Publishing
201 West 103rd Street
Indianapolis, Indiana 46290
USA

WANT MORE INFORMATION?

CHECK OUT THESE RELATED TITLES:

	QTY	PRICE	TOTAL

The Graphics Coach. PCX, TIF, BMP—confused by the different graphics file formats? This book helps you figure out the file types that are compatible with your software and the file format that works best with your application. View, edit, and translate your graphics files with the DOS, Windows, and Macintosh shareware included with *The Graphics Coach.* ISBN: 1-56205-129-6. _____ $24.95 _____

The Fonts Coach. From the Personal Trainer Series, this book gives clear, concise explanation of how fonts work on different platforms. Includes a disk containing approximately 25 TrueType fonts and explains how to install these fonts. Provides font style guides to help you produce professional-looking documents. ISBN: 1-56205-130-x. _____ $24.95 _____

Inside Windows 3.1/Maximizing MS-DOS 5 Value Pack. *Inside Windows 3.1* earned a "Highly Recommended" rating in *Byte's* Essential Guide to Windows. CompuServe said *Maximizing MS-DOS 5* "…will guide you from the ranks of the confused to the expert." ISBN: 1-56205-140-7. _____ $44.95 _____

A Guide to Field Computing. The essential guide for linking managers, sales personnel, and other mobile workers with the office computer system. Examines the technologies available for networking mobile computers. Compares the types of computers best suited for field use. ISBN: 1-56205-091-5. _____ $29.95 _____

Name _____

Company _____

Address _____

City _____ State ____ ZIP _____

Phone _____ Fax _____

☐ Check Enclosed   ☐ VISA   ☐ MasterCard

Card #_____Exp. Date _____

Signature _____

Prices are subject to change. Call for availability and pricing information on latest editions.

Subtotal _____

Shipping _____

$4.00 for the first book and $1.75 for each additional book.

Total _____
Indiana residents add 5% sales tax.

New Riders Publishing   201 West 103rd Street • Indianapolis, Indiana 46290 USA

**Orders/Customer Service: 1-800-428-5331
Fax: 1-800-448-3804**

Fold Here

- -

PLACE
STAMP
HERE

New Riders Publishing
201 West 103rd Street
Indianapolis, Indiana 46290
USA

GO AHEAD. PLUG YOURSELF INTO
PRENTICE HALL COMPUTER PUBLISHING.

Introducing the PHCP Forum on CompuServe®

Yes, it's true. Now, you can have CompuServe access to the same professional, friendly folks who have made computers easier for years. On the PHCP Forum, you'll find additional information on the topics covered by every PHCP imprint—including Que, Sams Publishing, New Riders Publishing, Alpha Books, Brady Books, Hayden Books, and Adobe Press. In addition, you'll be able to receive technical support and disk updates for the software produced by Que Software and Paramount Interactive, a division of the Paramount Technology Group. It's a great way to supplement the best information in the business.

WHAT CAN YOU DO ON THE PHCP FORUM?

Play an important role in the publishing process—and make our books better while you make your work easier:

- Leave messages and ask questions about PHCP books and software—you're guaranteed a response within 24 hours
- Download helpful tips and software to help you get the most out of your computer
- Contact authors of your favorite PHCP books through electronic mail
- Present your own book ideas
- Keep up to date on all the latest books available from each of PHCP's exciting imprints

JOIN NOW AND GET A FREE COMPUSERVE STARTER KIT!

To receive your free CompuServe Introductory Membership, call toll-free, **1-800-848-8199** and ask for representative **#597**. The Starter Kit Includes:

- Personal ID number and password
- $15 credit on the system
- Subscription to CompuServe Magazine

HERE'S HOW TO PLUG INTO PHCP:

Once on the CompuServe System, type any of these phrases to access the PHCP Forum:

GO PHCP   **GO BRADY**
GO QUEBOOKS   **GO HAYDEN**
GO SAMS   **GO QUESOFT**
GO NEWRIDERS   **GO PARAMOUNTINTER**
GO ALPHA

Once you're on the CompuServe Information Service, be sure to take advantage of all of CompuServe's resources. CompuServe is home to more than 1,700 products and services—plus it has over 1.5 million members worldwide. You'll find valuable online reference materials, travel and investor services, electronic mail, weather updates, leisure-time games and hassle-free shopping (no jam-packed parking lots or crowded stores).

Seek out the hundreds of other forums that populate CompuServe. Covering diverse topics such as pet care, rock music, cooking, and political issues, you're sure to find others with the sames concerns as you—and expand your knowledge at the same time.

GRAPHICS TITLES

INSIDE CORELDRAW! 4.0, SPECIAL EDITION

DANIEL GRAY

An updated version of the #1 best-selling tutorial on CorelDRAW!

CorelDRAW! 4.0
ISBN: 1-56205-164-4
$34.95 USA

CORELDRAW! SPECIAL EFFECTS

NEW RIDERS PUBLISHING

An inside look at award-winning techniques from professional CorelDRAW! designers!

CorelDRAW! 4.0
ISBN: 1-56205-123-7
$39.95 USA

CORELDRAW! NOW!

RICHARD FELDMAN

The hands-on tutorial for users who want practical information now!

CorelDRAW! 4.0
ISBN: 1-56205-131-8
$21.95 USA

INSIDE CORELDRAW! FOURTH EDITION

DANIEL GRAY

The popular tutorial approach to learning CorelDRAW!...with complete coverage of version 3.0!

CorelDRAW! 3.0
ISBN: 1-56205-106-7
$24.95 USA

To Order, Call 1-800-428-5331

Installing the *New Riders' Guide* *to Modems* Bonus Disk

This book includes a disk that contains a Test Drive version of Hilgraeve's HyperACCESS for Windows, a popular communications program. See Chapter 6 for more information on its features and more instructions on installing and using the program.

To install HyperACCESS for Windows, follow these steps:

1. Start Windows. If you don't have Windows, you will not be able to use the HyperACCESS for Windows Test Drive.

2. Put the *New Riders' Guide to Modems* bonus disk in the appropriate floppy disk drive. These instructions assume that you put the disk in drive A.

3. Start Windows File Manager.

4. Create a new directory (use the Create Directory command on the **F**ile menu) on your system to store the HyperACCESS files in, such as HYPER.

5. Copy the HAWTD1.EXE file from the bonus disk into the new directory on your hard drive.

6. Expand the HAWTD1.EXE file by double-clicking on the file in File Manager.

You now can start HyperACCESS Test Drive by making a program item (icon) in Program Manager and double-clicking on its icon. The HyperACCESS information screen appears on-screen. This screen repeats the limitations and usage requirements for the Test Drive. Click on O**K** to remove this screen and to start HyperACCESS.

See Chapter 6 for information on setting up and using HyperACCESS for Windows.